Uncertainty and Operations Research

Decision analysis based on uncertain data is natural in many real-world applications, and sometimes such an analysis is inevitable. In the past years, researchers have proposed many efficient operations research models and methods, which have been widely applied to real-life problems, such as finance, management, manufacturing, supply chain, transportation, among others. This book series aims to provide a global forum for advancing the analysis, understanding, development, and practice of uncertainty theory and operations research for solving economic, engineering, management, and social problems.

More information about this series at http://www.springer.com/series/11709

Chenyang Song · Zeshui Xu

Techniques of Decision Making, Uncertain Reasoning and Regression Analysis Under the Hesitant Fuzzy Environment and Their Applications

Springer

Chenyang Song
Simulation Lab
Army Aviation Institute
Beijing, China

Zeshui Xu
Business School
Sichuan University
Chengdu, Sichuan, China

ISSN 2195-996X ISSN 2195-9978 (electronic)
Uncertainty and Operations Research
ISBN 978-981-16-5799-3 ISBN 978-981-16-5800-6 (eBook)
https://doi.org/10.1007/978-981-16-5800-6

This Springer imprint is published by the registered company Springer Nature Singapore Pte Ltd.
The registered company address is: 152 Beach Road, #21-01/04 Gateway East, Singapore 189721, Singapore

Preface

With the increasing complexity of decision environment and the limitations of decision-makers' knowledge, how to manage and make full use of different kinds of uncertain information widely existing in practical decision-making problems becomes more and more important. As one of the latest extension forms of fuzzy sets, the hesitant fuzzy sets can depict uncertain information more comprehensively and carefully. Scholars have proposed various theories and decision-making methods concerning hesitant fuzzy sets, which have been widely applied to solve practical uncertain decision-making problems.

Based on the existing research results of hesitant fuzzy theory and applications, we extract the shortcomings and the unsolved problems in the existing methods, further introduce some techniques of decision-making, uncertain reasoning and regression analysis under the hesitant fuzzy environment and expand the applications of hesitant fuzzy sets in solving practical problems. The main work of this book can be summarized as follows:

(1) The TODIM decision-making method based on the psychological distance measure under the hesitant fuzzy environment is introduced. Considering the background information of different alternatives, this book presents the normalized hesitant fuzzy psychological distance measure. Besides, a similarity measure based on the exponential function and the normalized hesitant fuzzy psychological distance measure is also introduced, which is more sensitive to the subtle changes of the distance measure. Furthermore, we consider the risk attitude of decision-maker, and an improved TODIM decision-making method is presented and applied to solve the temporary rescue airport decision-making problem of the Arctic Northwest Passage.

(2) The process-oriented dynamic decision-making method under the hesitant fuzzy environment is shown in this book. We introduce the hesitant fuzzy valence vector and momentary preference function and present a process-oriented hesitant fuzzy decision field theory model. Based on this, we introduce a dynamic group decision-making method and then apply it to the route selection of the Arctic Northwest Passage.

(3) The uncertain reasoning algorithm under the hesitant fuzzy environment is presented. We first introduce the concept of hesitant fuzzy Bayesian network and consider the change of hesitant fuzzy variables with time, and a dynamic hesitant fuzzy Bayesian network is further presented to better depict the evolution process of hesitant fuzzy variables in time series. To depict the causal relationship between two sequences of hesitant fuzzy variables, we provide the concept of hesitant fuzzy information flow. Based on this, this section presents the improved structure learning method with particle swarm optimization algorithm, and the parameter learning and inference prediction methods under the hesitant fuzzy environment are also introduced. Furthermore, the uncertain reasoning algorithm under the hesitant fuzzy environment is provided, and then it is further applied to the optimal port investment decision-making of "Twenty-First-Century Maritime Silk Road".
(4) The regression analysis models under the hesitant fuzzy environment are presented. We introduce the generalized regression neural network model. To determine the most appropriate smooth factor of the generalized regression neural network, an improved fruit fly optimization algorithm with fast decreasing step based on a dynamic step size function is also given. Besides, we also present a new optimized method based on the maximum entropy estimation, and based on which, the optimized logistic regression model under the hesitant fuzzy environment is constructed. At last but not least, the two proposed models are applied to the prediction of air quality index in Beijing and the prediction problem of emergency extreme air pollution event, respectively.
(5) The decision-making method under the environment involving both cognitive uncertainty and probability information is introduced. This chapter presents a probabilistic hesitant fuzzy correlation coefficient formula and a corresponding cluster algorithm. It further improves the theory of probabilistic hesitant fuzzy sets. Then we introduce the concept of interval-valued probabilistic hesitant fuzzy set, which solves the problem that the probability information is in the form of interval values. After that, the properties, comparison methods, basic operations and aggregation operators of the interval-valued probabilistic hesitant fuzzy sets are presented in detail, and based on which, the group decision-making method is also provided. Finally, the presented methods are applied to the human environment risk assessment of the "Twenty-First-Century Maritime Silk Road" and geopolitical risk evaluation for the Arctic area, respectively.

This book reflects some latest techniques of decision-making, uncertain reasoning and regression analysis under the hesitant fuzzy environment, aiming at practitioners and researchers working in the areas of risk analysis and decision-making under uncertainty. We want to offer the readers a new way to study the hesitant fuzzy theory. With this vision in mind, we hope the readers will find this book inspiring. We appreciate the financial support of this book: The Natural Science Foundation of China [No. 72071135].

Nanjing, China
June 2021

Chenyang Song
Zeshui Xu

Contents

Chapter 1
Introduction

In this chapter, we mainly introduce the background and importance of our research about decision making, uncertain reasoning and regression analysis under the hesitant fuzzy environment. The preliminaries used in our book are also presented.

1.1 Background

The classical research of multi-attribute decision-making (MADM) methods and applications mainly depends on the accurate information and knowledge. However, it is never easy to obtain accurate and reliable optimal decision-making results. One of the main reasons is the widespread uncertainty in real problems, which makes the decision-making process more difficult. The rapid development of economy and society is accompanied by a large amount of uncertain information, which also brings more opportunities and challenges to the decision-making discipline, and leads to the upsurge of the research and application of uncertain multi-attribute decision-making. How to deal with uncertain information and improve the reliability of decision-making results is also a focus of this book.

To make full use of uncertain information and measure it effectively and accurately is the key to deal with uncertain multi-attribute decision making problems. There are many reasons for uncertainty, such as various intangible standards, decision-makers' cognitive fuzziness, uncertain consequences of alternatives and so on. From the perspective of decision makers, it is difficult to understand the problems comprehensively and deeply, and furthermore provide accurate evaluation information. Therefore, how to depict and manage the uncertainty of decision-makers' cognitive and thinking has attracted extensive attention of scholars. The theory of fuzzy set (FS) proposed by Professor Zadeh (1965), the father of fuzzy mathematics, breaks through the limitations of classical set theory and provides an effective tool to depict the cognitive and thinking uncertainty of decision makers. On the basis of fuzzy set theory,

C. Song and Z. Xu, *Techniques of Decision Making, Uncertain Reasoning and Regression Analysis Under the Hesitant Fuzzy Environment and Their Applications*,
Uncertainty and Operations Research, https://doi.org/10.1007/978-981-16-5800-6_1

according to different scenarios and needs, scholars expand it to more types from different perspectives for different types of fuzzy preferences and uncertain information in practical problems, which greatly broaden its application scope. For example, intuitionistic fuzzy set (Atanassov, 1986) is composed of membership degrees, non-membership degrees and hesitant degrees. And the type-2 fuzzy set (Zadeh, 1975), whose membership degree is a set. These expanded sets of fuzzy sets constantly improve the description and expression of people's cognitive uncertainty.

With the widespread uncertainty and ever-increasing complexity in actual decision-making problems, there will be more difficulties in depicting the experts' preferences and cognition accurately. Actually, when evaluating alternatives, it is not easy for experts in a group to reach a certain consensus or provide a common measure of the membership degree with sound reliability. In many situations, they are hesitant between several possible membership degrees. Besides, group decision-making method is also an important tool to solve complex decision-making problems. In fact, when it is difficult for decision-makers to reach a complete agreement, it is also an urgent problem to remain and make full use of the original decision preference information of all decision-makers. In order to deal with the situations that there are multiple possible preference values and experts can not reach a consensus in group decision-making problems, Torra and Narukawa (2009) proposed the concept of hesitant fuzzy set (HFS) with the membership degree consisting of several possible values, which can depict the hesitant preferences and uncertain knowledge more comprehensively (Torra, 2010). As a latest extension of fuzzy set, Xia and Xu (2011) defined the mathematical expression of HFS and introduced the concept of hesitant fuzzy element (HFE). They provided the mathematical expressions of HFS and HFE, which greatly promoted the research and application of HFS theory. In addition, Xia and Xu (2011) defined the basic operation laws of HFEs, discussed the relation between HFEs and intuitionistic fuzzy numbers, and further established the relationship between HFE operations. As the basic component of HFS, the HFE is a concise means to convey and depict the evaluation values of each attribute clearly. Since the excellent properties of HFSs in quantitative decision-making problems, many scholars have studied HFS theory and obtained a series of research achievements, including basic operation laws (Liao & Xu, 2014; Xia & Xu, 2011), aggregation operators (Xia & Xu, 2011), information measures (Li et al., 2015; Meng & Chen, 2015; Xu & Xia, 2011a, 2011b) and consistency measures (Feng et al., 2018; Zhu, 2013; Zhu et al., 2017). Furthermore, Yu et al. (2011) defined a hesitant fuzzy Choquet integral operator and applied it to solve MAGDM problems with unknown weights. A priority integration operator for hesitant fuzzy information (Wei, 2012), and a generalized hesitant fuzzy Bonferroni method (Yu et al., 2012) were also defined to solve the MAGDM problems. Besides, a hesitant fuzzy ELECTRE I method was also proposed (Chen & Xu, 2015) and applied to deal with the MAGDM problems under the hesitant fuzzy environment. The method was developed based on the concepts of hesitant fuzzy concordance and hesitant fuzzy discordance, which were provided based on score function and deviation degree.

The HFS, as one of the latest extensions of fuzzy set, aims to depict the situations when there are several possible values of membership in practical problems. Each

HFE is a set of several possible values. Therefore, compared with other extended forms of fuzzy sets, HFS can depict the hesitant preferences and uncertain information more comprehensively, and have been extended to the fields of management science, computer science and economic sociology. However, by analyzing the research results about HFS theory, it is not difficult to find that most of the existing decision-making methods rely on different types of information fusion operators, which can not make full use of hesitant fuzzy information. How to depict the psychology and risk attitudes of experts in the process of decision-making under different backgrounds is a difficult problem. In addition, with the advent of information age, how to explore the causal relationship between different variables under the hesitant fuzzy environment, and how to conduct decision making, uncertain reasoning and regression analysis with the massive uncertain data, is also a challenge that must be faced. For the complex decision-making problems in actual applications, simple information fusion operators can not restore the real decision-making process. In addition, how to depict different types of uncertain information accurately and comprehensively requires a reasonable expansion of the classic HFS, which is conductive to improve the applicability of decision-making methods and reliability of results.

1.2 Current Situation of Related Research

1.2.1 Decision Making with Hesitant Fuzzy Information

In order to overcome the shortcomings of the existing hesitant fuzzy decision making methods which just rely too much on information fusion operators, scholars have developed distance measure and similarity measure under the hesitant fuzzy environment. Xu & Xia, (2011a) defined the generalized hesitant fuzzy Euclidean distance and generalized hesitant fuzzy Hamming distance respectively. Considering the importance of different attributes, they also defined the generalized hesitant fuzzy weighted distance measure, and further proposed a generalized hesitant fuzzy normalized distance measure. The corresponding similarity measures based on the above different distance measures were also proposed. Scholars also proposed some distance measures based on the entropy and cross entropy of hesitant fuzzy information (Xu & Xia, 2012) and the corresponding decision making methods.

Taking the advantages of HFSs in depicting uncertain information, scholars have extended some classical decision making methods to the hesitant fuzzy environment and developed many decision making methods based on the hesitant fuzzy information. According to the consistency of hesitant fuzzy information, Chen et al. (2015) developed the hesitant fuzzy ELECTRE (*Elimination Et Choix Traduisant La Realité*) II method. In addition, the TOPSIS (Technique for Order Preference by Similarity to an Ideal Solution) (Xu & Zhang, 2013), LINMAP (Linear Programming Techniques for Multidimensional Analysis of Preference) (Wan & Li, 2013),

PROMETHEE (Preference Ranking Organization Method for Enrichment Evaluations) (Liang et al., 2018) and VIKOR (VlseKriterijumska Optimizacija I Kompromisno Resenje) (Zhang & Wei, 2013) methods under the hesitant fuzzy environment have also been proposed. Those methods are widely applied in water resource assessment, energy policy selection, emergency decision making, strategic energy channel decision aid and other practical problems.

1.2.2 Research Status of Uncertain Reasoning

The process of deriving approximate reasonable results from the evidence and knowledge containing uncertain information is named as uncertain reasoning. The main methods include Dempster Shafer evidence theory, logic methods, probability methods, etc. Among them, the Bayesian Network (BN) conceptual model based on probability, which was proposed by Pearl (1988), a pioneer in the field of artificial intelligence and winner of Turing Award, is one of the most effective theoretical models in the field of uncertain reasoning. It is widely used in decision support, image processing, data fusion, machine learning and other fields. It combines graph theory and probability theory, and its network topology is a directed acyclic graph with directed links between random variables, which is used to depict the conditional dependence between attributes.

The key of building a BN from an intensive sample data set is structure learning, which refers to construct a directed network topology by the intensive training data set and prior knowledge. The main difficulty in the structure learning of BN is how to identify the arcs between network nodes and their directions accurately and quickly. The common method of structure learning is scoring search method, which means searching for the optimal network structure based on a defined score function in the search space. Since the structure learning from intensive data with hundreds of variables is a non-deterministic polynomial (NP) hard problem (Chickering, 1996), scholars have developed many scoring search methods. Cooper and Herskovits (1992) proposed a hill-climbing algorithm based on K2 score, which is a local optimization method. Chickering et al. (1995) introduced the Simulated Annealing (SA) algorithm for the structure learning of BN. It is a global optimization algorithm that converges to the global optimal solution with probability. Besides, some scholars have tried to apply the evolutionary algorithms to the structure leaning, such as Genetic Algorithm (GA) (Yan & Cercone, 2010), Artificial Bee Colony (ABC) Algorithm (Ji et al., 2013) and Ant Algorithm (Pinto et al., 2009). The existing algorithms have optimized the search space and improved the convergence speed. However, it is easy to fall into the local optimal solution. What is more, they cannot deal with intensive hesitant fuzzy data effectively and fail to determine the directions of arcs quickly and accurately.

In addition, with the increasing complexity of practical problems, some extended forms of BN have been proposed. For example, the weight information of each node to the root node is integrated into the calculation of conditional probability, named as weighted BN. Aiming at the change of variable information with time, a dynamic BN (Yang et al., 2010) model is also proposed. In addition, to manage with the uncertain information, some scholars put forward the concept of fuzzy BN (Kant & Bharadwaj, 2013) and BN under the intuitionistic fuzzy environment (Hao et al., 2018). They promoted the application of BN under the uncertain information environment.

At present, the practical problems and application of BN become more and more complex. The amount of uncertain data and state of nodes also expand rapidly. Therefore, how to manage with uncertain reasoning under complex models effectively is the focus and difficulty of BN research. However, a single exact value cannot reflect the uncertainty of evaluation, and the simple weighted averaging will lose the hesitant information of experts. Besides, the traditional BN cannot deal with massive uncertain data. Due to the complexity and uncertainty of practical problems, how to mine and analyze massive data to obtain scientific decision information requires effective information expression tool and analytical reasoning method. With the nonlinear evolution of events and the complexity of practical problems, there will be massive data with uncertainty, bringing more challenges to the application of the BN. In addition, for the situations that the membership function is multiple possible values, the related research is still very few.

1.2.3 Research Status of Regression Analysis

The regression analysis model is an effective method to study and evaluate the relationship between random variables. According to the number of independent variables, it can be divided into univeriate regression analysis and multivariate regression analysis. And based on the function expression of variable relationship, it can be divided into linear regression analysis and nonlinear regression analysis. The linear regression is one of the most well-known methods. Its core feature is to use the least square function of linear regression equation to model the relationship between independent variables and dependent variables. The logistic regression model is a generalized linear regression analysis model, which does not require the linear relationship between independent variables and dependent variables. It has been widely applied in different fields, such as disease diagnosis, economic forecasting, data mining and data analysis. In addition, scholars also developed the polynomial regression (Yazgi et al., 2017), stepwise regression (Kumar et al., 2019), ridge regression (Choi et al., 2019) and robust regression (Ying et al., 2011). After years of development, the regression analysis model has been the most mature statistical analysis method.

In addition, based on the nonlinear regression analysis, the general regression neural network (GRNN) has strong nonlinear mapping ability and learning efficiency, which is developed by simulating the structure of biological neural network. It has a good prediction result for the less sample data, which has been applied in artificial intelligence, medical diagnosis and data analysis.

However, the traditional regression analysis models rely too much on accurate data, which can not deal with the situations that the sample size is too small and fuzzy relationship between independent variables and dependent variables. In practical, due to the uncertainty and incomplete information, the observation results can not be measured with accurate values. In order to overcome those problems above, and consider the complexity of problems and the uncertainty of cognition, scholars adopt fuzzy theory to expand and improve the traditional regression analysis methods, and develop a variety of fuzzy regression analysis methods. It mainly includes three types: possibility regression analysis, fuzzy least square method and machine learning technology in fuzzy regression analysis.

Scholars have done lots of related work on fuzzy regression analysis, showing a good prospect. The regression analysis model under uncertain environment is a new research field, and the related theories need to be further developed and improved. How to further use large-scale uncertain data effectively, predict and analyze the relationship between variables, and improve the accuracy of regression analysis, are very important to provide more scientific and reasonable decision aid and support.

1.3 Preminaries

1.3.1 Hesitant Fuzzy Set

The HFS can deal with the situations that the experts hesitate to provide their evaluations and preferences. In this section, we review some basic knowledge about HFSs, including basic concepts, operational laws, aggregation operators and distance measures:

Definition 1.1 (Xia & Xu, 2011). Let X be a fixed set, then the HFS can be described as:

$$H = \{x, h(x)|x \in X\} \tag{1.1}$$

in which $h(x)$ consists of a set of some different values in [0,1]. Xu and Xia named $h(x)$ as a hesitant fuzzy element (HFE), and it denotes the membership degree consisting of several possible values.

Definition 1.2 (Xia & Xu, 2011). Let $h(x) = \{\gamma_i = i = 1, 2, \ldots, \#h\}$ be a HFE, then the score and the standard deviation degree of $h(x)$ are defined respectively as:

$$s(h(x)) = \frac{1}{\#h}\sum_{i-1}^{\#h}\gamma_i \tag{1.2}$$

$$\sigma(h(x)) = \sqrt{\frac{1}{\#h}\sum_{i-1}^{\#h}(\gamma_i - s(h))^2} \tag{1.3}$$

where $\#h$ indicates the number of the elements in $h(x)$.

Based on the score and standard deviation functions, the comparison between two HFEs can be conducted. Taking two HFEs $h_1(x)$ and $h_2(x)$ as example, we have:

(1) If $s(h_1(x)) > s(h_2(x))$, then $h_1(x) > h_2(x)$;
(2) If $s(h_1(x)) < s(h_2(x))$, then $h_1(x) < h_2(x)$;
(3) If $s(h_1(x)) = s(h_2(x))$ and $\sigma(h_1(x)) < \sigma(h_2(x))$, then $h_1(x) > h_2(x)$;
(4) If $s(h_1(x)) = s(h_2(x))$ and $\sigma(h_1(x)) > \sigma(h_2(x))$, then $h_1(x) < h_2(x)$;
(5) If $s(h_1(x)) = s(h_2(x))$ and $\sigma(h_1(x)) = \sigma(h_2(x))$, then we define that $h_1(x)$ is equivalent to $h_2(x)$, denoted as $h_1(x) \sim h_2(x)$.

1.3.2 Basic Operation Laws and Aggregation Operators

Inspired by the relationship between the intuitionistic fuzzy values (IFVs) and HFEs, Xia and Xu (2011) defined some basic operations of the HFEs. They also proposed some aggregation operators for hesitant fuzzy information.

Definition 1.3 (Xia & Xu, 2011). Let h, h_1 and h_2 be three HFEs, and h^c be the complementary set of h, $\lambda > 0$, then.

(1) $h^c = \cup_{\gamma\in h}\{1-\gamma\}$;
(2) $h_1 \cup h_2 = \cup_{\gamma_1\in h_1,\gamma_2\in h_2} \max\{\gamma_1,\gamma_2\}$;
(3)$h_1 \cap h_2 = \cup_{\gamma_1\in h_1,\gamma_2\in h_2} \min\{\gamma_1,\gamma_2\}$;
(4) $h^\lambda = \cup_{\gamma\in h}\{\gamma^\lambda\}$;
(5) $\lambda h = \cup_{\gamma\in h}\{1-(1-\gamma)^\lambda\}$;
(6) $h_1 \oplus h_2 = \cup_{\gamma_1\in h_1,\gamma_2\in h_2}\{\gamma_1+\gamma_2-\gamma_1\cdot\gamma_2\}$;
(7) $h_1 \otimes h_2 = \cup_{\gamma_1\in h_1,\gamma_2\in h_2}\{\gamma_1\cdot\gamma_2\}$.

Definition 1.4 (Xia & Xu, 2011). Let $h_i(i = 1, 2, \ldots, n)$ be a set of HFEs, then the hesitant fuzzy weighted averaging (HFWA) operator and the hesitant fuzzy weighted geometric (HFWG) operator are defined respectively as:

$$HFWA(h_1, h_2, \ldots, h_n) = \overset{n}{\underset{i=1}{\oplus}}(\omega_i h_i) = \cup_{\gamma_1\in h_1,\gamma_2\in h_2,\ldots,\gamma_n\in h_n}\left\{1-\prod_{i=1}^{n}(1-\gamma_i)^{\omega_i}\right\} \tag{1.4}$$

$$HFWG(h_1, h_2, \ldots, h_n) = \overset{n}{\underset{i=1}{\otimes}}(\omega_i h_i) = \cup_{\gamma_1\in h_1,\gamma_2\in h_2,\ldots,\gamma_n\in h_n}\left\{\prod_{i=1}^{n}\gamma_i^{\omega_i}\right\} \tag{1.5}$$

where $\omega = (\omega_1, \omega_2, \ldots, \omega_n)^{\mathrm{T}}$ is the corresponding weight vector of HFEs with $\omega_i \in [0, 1]$ and $\sum_{i=1}^{n}\omega_i = 1$

1.4 Aim and Focus of This Book

Since the concept of HFS was put forward, the related theory of HFS has been gradually enriched after more than ten years of development. It has provided a theoretical basis for the development of this book. However, the theory and application of HFS are not perfect, and the practical problems become more complex, which brings new challenges. The existing researches about decision making, uncertain reasoning and regression analysis still have some shortcomings:

(1) The existing hesitant fuzzy distance measure ignores the possible competitive relationship and background information between different alternatives. If the distance measure only focuses on the hesitant fuzzy information fusion of alternatives, it will obviously affect the result of distance measurement and even lead to wrong results. We need to study how to integrate the background information of alternatives and relationship of HFS. Besides, it is also necessary to consider the risk attitudes of decision makers.

(2) The existing research on uncertain reasoning under the hesitant fuzzy environment is insufficient. Most of the existing researchers rely on accurate data and information, but there are few studies on uncertain reasoning with a large number of uncertain data under the hesitant fuzzy environment. The existing methods of uncertain reasoning can't deal with uncertain data with multiple possible membership degrees. Therefore, it is necessary to develop more scientific and reasonable uncertain reasoning methods under the hesitant fuzzy environment.

(3) There are few researches on regression analysis under the hesitant fuzzy environment. The existing classical regression analysis methods are mature and widely applied. However, to some situations that there are few samples and uncertain information, it brings new challenges to the study of regression analysis. Most of the existing regression analysis methods can only deal with the deterministic data, and can not deal with the regression problems under the hesitant fuzzy environment. The regression analysis with hesitant fuzzy information is a new research field, and the related theories need to be further developed. Therefore, it is necessary to explore the regression analysis methods under the hesitant fuzzy environment further.

By analyzing the defects and shortcomings of the existing research, this book introduces some techniques of decision making, uncertain reasoning and regression analysis under the hesitant fuzzy environment. To overcome the ignorance of background information and competitive relationships between different alternatives, a new kind of distance measure, named as the hesitant fuzzy psychological distance measure is introduced in Chap. 2. Furthermore, a TODIM (TOmada deDecisão Iterativa Multicritério) method is also presented based on the proposed hesitant fuzzy psychological distance measure. Also, to make full use of the evaluation information and depict the process of comparison between different alternatives clearly, a process-oriented dynamic decision-making method is provided in Chap. 3. Consider that the uncertain information of risk factors varies with time, the concept of Dynamic Hesitant Fuzzy Bayesian Network (DHFBN) is introduced in Chap. 4. Then, an improved Particle Swarm Optimization (PSO) algorithm and the Expectation–Maximization (EM) algorithm are adopted for the structure learning and parameters learning of DHFBN respectively. Based o the learned optimal DHFBN, a dynamic reasoning and prediction method is introduced. Furthermore, uncertain information brings great challenges to regression analysis. So Chap. 5 introduces the generalized regression neural network (GRNN) based on an improved fruit fly optimization algorithm and the optimal logistic regression model based on maximum entropy estimation under the hesitant fuzzy environment. To improve the theory of HFS further, Chap. 6 presents a probabilistic hesitant fuzzy correlation coefficient and clustering algorithm. The concept of interval-valued probabilistic hesitant fuzzy set (IVPHFS) and the corresponding properties are also introduced.

References

Atanassov, K. T. (1986). Intuitionistic fuzzy sets. *Fuzzy Sets and Systems, 20*(1), 87–96.

Chen, N., & Xu, Z. S. (2015). Hesitant fuzzy ELECTRE II approach: A new way to handle multi-criteria decision making problems. *Information Sciences* 292: 175–197.

Chen, N., Xu, Z. S., & Xia, M. M. (2015a). The Electre I multi-criteria decision making method based on hesitant fuzzy sets. *International Journal of Information Technology and Decision Making, 14*, 621–657.

Chickering, D. M. (1996). *Learning Bayesian networks is NP-complete*. Springer.

Chickering, D. M., Geiger, D., & Heckerman, D. (1995). Heckerman. Learning Bayesian Networks: Search methods and experimental results. *General Information, 35*, 214–236.

Choi, S. H., Jung, H. Y., & Kim, H. (2019). Ridge fuzzy regression model. *International Journal of Fuzzy Systems, 21*(7), 2077–2090.

Cooper, G. F., & Herskovits, E. (1992). A Bayesian method for the introduction of probabilistic networks from data. *Machine Learning, 9*, 309–347.

Feng, X., Zhang, L., & Wei, C. (2018). The consistency measures and priority weights of hesitant fuzzy linguistic preference relations. *Applied Soft Computing, 65*.

Hao, Z. N., Xu, Z. S., Zhao, H., et al. (2018). A dynamic weight determination approach based on the intuitionistic fuzzy bayesian network and its application to emergency decision making. *IEEE Transactions on Fuzzy Systems, 26*(4), 1893–1903.

Ji, J., Wei, H., & Liu, C. (2013). An artificial bee colony algorithm for learning Bayesian Networks. *Soft Computing, 17*, 983–994.

Kant, V., & Bharadwaj, K. K. (2013). Integrating collaborative and reclusive methods for effective recommendations: A fuzzy Bayesian approach. *International Journal of Intelligent Systems, 28*(11), 1099–1123.

Kumar, S., Attri, S. D., & Singh, K. K. (2019). Comparison of lasso and stepwise regression technique for wheat yield prediction. *Journal of Agrometeorology, 21*(2), 188–192.

Li, D. Q., Zeng, W. Y., & Zhao, Y. B. (2015). Note on distance measure of hesitant fuzzy sets. *Information Sciences, 321*, 103–115.

Liang, R. X., Wang, J. Q., & Zhang, H. Y. (2018). Projection-based PROMETHEE methods based on hesitant fuzzy linguistic term sets. *International Journal of Fuzzy Systems, 20*(7), 2161–2174.

Liao, H. C., & Xu, Z. S. (2014). Subtraction and division operations over hesitant fuzzy sets. *Journal of Intelligent and Fuzzy Systems, 27*, 65–72.

Meng, F. Y., & Chen, X. H. (2015). Correlation coefficients of hesitant fuzzy sets and their application based on fuzzy measures. *Cognitive Computation, 7*, 445–463.

Pearl, J. (1988). *Probabilistic reasoning in intelligent systems: networks of plausible inference.* Morgan Kaufmann.

Pinto, P. C., Nagele, A., Dejori, M., et al. (2009). Using a local discovery ant algorithm for Bayesian Network structure learning. *IEEE Transportation on Evolutionary Computation, 13*, 767–779.

Torra, V., & Narukawa, Y. (2009). On hesitant fuzzy sets and decision. In *The 18th IEEE International Conference on Fuzzy Systems* (pp. 1378–1382), Jeju Island, Korea.

Torra, V. (2010). Hesitant fuzzy sets. *International Journal of Intelligent Systems, 25*, 529–539.

Wan, S. P., & Li, D. F. (2013). Fuzzy LINMAP approach to heterogeneous MADM considering comparisons of alternatives with hesitation degrees. *Omega, 41*(6), 925–940.

Wei, G. W. (2012). Hesitant fuzzy prioritized operators and their application to multiple attribute decision making. *Knowledge-Based Systems, 31*, 176–182.

Xia, M. M., & Xu, Z. S. (2011). Hesitant fuzzy information aggregation in decision making. *International Journal of Approximate Reasoning, 52*, 395–407.

Xu, Z. S., & Xia, M. M. (2011a). Distance and similarity measures for hesitant fuzzy sets. *Information Sciences, 181*, 2128–2138.

Xu, Z. S., & Xia, M. M. (2011b). On distance and correlation measures of hesitant fuzzy information. *International Journal of Intelligent Systems, 26*, 410–425.

Xu, Z. S., & Xia, M. M. (2012). Hesitant fuzzy entropy and cross-entropy and their use in multiattribute decision-making. *International Journal of Intelligent Systems, 27*(9), 799–822.

Xu, Z. S., & Zhang, X. L. (2013). Hesitant fuzzy multi-attribute decision making based on TOPSIS with incomplete weight information. *Knowledge-Based Systems, 52*, 53–64.

Yan, L. J., & Cercone, N. (2010). Bayesian Network modeling for evolutionary genetic structures. *Computers & Mathematics with Applications, 59*, 2541–2551.

Yang, G. S., Lin, Y. Z., & Bhattacharya, P. (2010). A driver fatigue rcognition model based on information fusion and dynamic Bayesian Network. *Information Sciences, 180*(10), 1942–1954.

Yazgi, D., Mohebalhoejeh, A. R., & Ghader, S. (2017). Using polynomial regression in designing the tie filters for the leapfrog time-stepping scheme. *Monthly Weather Review, 145*(5), 1779–1795.

Ying, K. C., Lin, S. W., Lee, Z. J., et al. (2011). A novel function approximation based on robust fuzzy regression algorithm model and particle swarm optimization. *Applied Soft Computing, 11*(2): 1820–1826.

Yu, D. J., Wu, Y. Y., & Zhou, W. (2011). Multi-criteria decision making based on Choquet integral under hesitant fuzzy environment. *Journal of Computational Information Systems, 7*, 4506–4513.

Yu, D. J., Wu, Y. Y., & Zhou, W. (2012). Generalized hesitant fuzzy Bonferroni mean and its application in multi-criteria group decision making. *Journal of Information and Computational Science, 9*, 267–274.

Zadeh, L. A. (1965). Fuzzy sets. *Information and Control, 8*(3), 338–353.

Zadeh, L. A. (1975). Concept of a linguistic variable and its application to approximate reasoning. *Information Sciences, 8*(3), 199–249.

Zhang, N., & Wei, G. W. (2013). Extension of VIKOR method for decision making problem based on hesitant fuzzy set. *Applied Mathematical Modelling, 37*(7), 4938–4947.

Zhu, B. (2013). Studies on consistency measure of hesitant fuzzy preference relations. *Procedia Computer Science, 17*, 457–464.

Zhu, B., Xu, Z. S., & Xu, J. (2017). Deriving a ranking from hesitant fuzzy preference relations under group decision making. *IEEE Transactions on Cybernetics, 44*, 1328–1337.

Chapter 2
TODIM Decision Making Method Based on the Hesitant Fuzzy Psychological Distance Measure

Traditional existing distance measures for hesitant fuzzy information are effective to depict the uncertainty and weight information of attributes, but fail to reflect the preferential relationships between attributes. The ignorance of background information and competitive relationships between different alternatives by traditional distances and similarity measurements may affect the result of distance measurement, as well as lead to wrong decision-making results in practical decision-making problems. Therefore, in this chapter, we introduce a new kind of distance measure to overcome those deficiencies, named as the hesitant fuzzy psychological distance measure. It not only captures the weight information of alternatives, but also the preferential relationships under the hesitant fuzzy environment. In addition, this chapter also introduces an improved similarity measure based on the above psychological distance measure for HFSs. Furthermore, a TODIM (TOmada deDecisão Iterativa Multicritério) method is also presented based on the hesitant fuzzy psychological distance measure. The specific implementation process of the introduced TODIM is also illustrated. Then the hesitant fuzzy psychological distance measure and the corresponding improved TODIM method are applied to the temporary rescue airport decision making problem of the arctic northwest passage to illustrate their advantages and efficiency. The results illustrate the validity of the hesitant fuzzy psychological measure and the corresponding TODIM method.

2.1 Review of the Related Work

Since the experts always make use of the distance to measure the similarity between alternatives, many different kinds of distance measures under the hesitant fuzzy environment have been proposed. Inspired by the famous Hamming distance and Euclidean distance, Xu and Xia (2011) defined the normalized Hamming distance and Euclidean distance for HFSs respectively. Li et al. (2015) introduced the concept

C. Song and Z. Xu, *Techniques of Decision Making, Uncertain Reasoning and Regression Analysis Under the Hesitant Fuzzy Environment and Their Applications*, Uncertainty and Operations Research, https://doi.org/10.1007/978-981-16-5800-6_2

of hesitant degree for hesitant fuzzy information, and based on which, they developed the distance measure for HFSs. Considering the importance degrees of different attributes, the generalized weighted distance measure for HFSs was also proposed (Xu & Xia, 2011). Furthermore, the entropy and cross-entropy for HFS (Xu & Xia, 2012) and the corresponding distance were also developed to improve the traditional forms.

Those kinds of distance measures for HFSs can manage the importance degrees of attributes, which have been applied in many practical problems. Nevertheless, few experts have considered the effect of preferential relationships under the hesitant fuzzy environment, i.e., the dominance of alternatives (Hong & Choi, 2000). Considering the preferential and competitive relationships of alternatives, it is wise to adopt the dominance and indifference vectors to calculate the distances (Huber et al., 1982). To begin with, a dimensional weight model (Wedel, 1991) consisting of the dominance and indifference vectors is developed to depict the preferential relationship. Furthermore, an improved form of dominance vector with weight information is also proposed. However, the above two methods just consider two attributes. Then, Berkowitsch et al. (2015) developed a generalized distance with multiple attributes for the preferential relationships in decision making. However, those distance measures only consider the preferential relationships, but ignore the uncertain information. Traditional existing distance measures for hesitant fuzzy information are effective to depict the uncertainty and weight information of attributes, but fail to reflect the preferential relationships between attributes.

Many experts have tried to manage this deficiency and provided several methods. Huang et al. (2012, 2013) extended the dominance relation to the rough set theory, which can simplify the information representation and reduce useless information. Wang et al. (2014) developed the dominance relation under the hesitant fuzzy environment and proposed a dominance-based outranking approach for hesitant fuzzy information. Farhadinia and Herrera-Viedma (2019) developed a sorting method based on the score function for hesitant fuzzy elements (HFEs) and the dominance-vector distance. Those studies mainly concentrate on the ranking methods of alternatives by investing the dominance relationship under the hesitant fuzzy environment, but ignore the detailed influences and dominance effect on the distances for HFSs. In addition, these traditional distance measures for hesitant fuzzy information cannot depict and reflect the competitive relationships clearly. The ignorance of background information and competitive relationships between different alternatives by traditional distances and similarity measurements may affect the result of distance measurement, as well as lead to wrong decision-making results in practical decision-making problems.

2.2 Distance and Similarity Measures for HFSs

In this section, we shall review the basic concepts of the distance measure and the similarity measure for HFSs.

Definition 2.1 (Xu & Xia, 2011). Let H_M and H_N be two HFSs, then the distance measure between H_M and H_N is defined as $D(H_M, H_N)$, which satisfies:

(1) $0 \leq D(H_M, H_N) \leq 1$;
(2) $D(H_M, H_N) = 0$, if $H_M = H_N$;
(3) $D(H_M, H_N) = D(H_N, H_M)$;
(4) If $H_M \subseteq H_N \subseteq H_O$, then $D(H_M, H_O) \geq D(H_M, H_N)$ and $D(H_M, H_O) \geq D(H_N, H_O)$.

Definition 2.2 (Xu & Xia, 2011). Let H_M and H_N be two HFSs, then the similarity degree between H_M and H_N can be depicted as $S(H_M, H_N)$, which satisfies:

(1) $0 \leq S(H_M, H_N) \leq 1$;
(2) $S(H_M, H_N) = 1$, if $H_M = H_N$;
(3) $S(H_M, H_N) = S(H_N, H_M)$;
(4) If $H_M \subseteq H_N \subseteq H_O$, then $S(H_M, H_O) \leq S(H_M, H_N)$ and $S(H_M, H_O) \leq S(H_N, H_O)$.

Definition 2.3 (Xu & Xia, 2011). Let H_M and H_N be two HFSs, then the generalized hesitant fuzzy weighted distance between H_M and H_N is defined as:

$$D(H_M, H_N) = \left[\sum_{i=1}^{n} w_i \left(\frac{1}{\#h_{x_i}} \sum_{j=1}^{\#h_{x_i}} \left|h_M^{\rho(j)}(x_i) - h_N^{\rho(j)}(x_i)\right|^{\lambda}\right)\right]^{\frac{1}{\lambda}} \tag{2.1}$$

where $H_M = \{x, h_M(x)|x \in X\}$ and $H_N = \{x, h_N(x)|x \in X\}$, w_i is the weight of $h(x_i)$, $w_i \in [0, 1]$ and $\sum_{i=1}^{n} w_i = 1$, $i = 1, 2, \ldots, n$, $h_M^{\rho(j)}(x_i)$ and $h_N^{\rho(j)}(x_i)$ are the j th largest values in $h_M(x_i)$ and $h_N(x_i)$, respectively. If $\lambda = 1$, then it reduces to the hesitant fuzzy weighted Hamming distance; if $\lambda = 2$, then it reduces to the hesitant fuzzy weighted Euclidean distance.

2.3 TODIM Method Based on the Hesitant Fuzzy Psychological Distance Measure

2.3.1 *Background of Psychological Distance*

The existing distance measures mainly depend on the information integration algorithms under all attributes, and then calculate the distance between them. However, it is obvious that the background information of alternatives is not integrated into the distance measure, which may lead to wrong decision-making results in the application. When alternatives are in different background information, the relationship between them and the distance measurement based on attribute space will also change (Nosofsky, 1986). The differences of weight and preferential relationships surely influence the distances between alternatives (Nosofsky & Zaki, 2002). In actual decision-making process, the experts always pay more attention to important attributes. This will certainly stretch their dimensions, and the distances will also be changed. The traditional distances cannot explain this phenomenon, because they neglect the competitive relationships of alternatives. In order to understand better, an example of the psychological distance measure for intuitionistic fuzzy information (Hao, 2018) is provided as Fig. 2.1.

To three intuitionistic fuzzy values (IFVs) A, B, C and their corresponding positions in the attribute space, suppose that the traditional Euclidean distance between the alternatives A and C and the alternatives A and B are exactly same. The directions $\overline{\text{CA}}$ and $\overline{\text{BC}}$ are regarded as indifference direction and dominance direction respectively. To the indifference direction, the alternatives are more competitive and similar with each other. But the dominance direction denotes the huge differences between alternatives along this direction, i.e., the cost that one DM gives up one attribute to another one (Rooderkerk et al., 2011), which always attracts more attention than the indifference direction. Therefore, the distance on dominance direction is stretched, but the distance on the indifference direction remains the same. So even though the Euclidean distances of the alternatives A and B are same, the psychological distances of the alternative B to C is much larger than A. It is obvious that the traditional Euclidean distance cannot depict and explain such preferential relationships of different alternatives.

To depict the distance measure of this kind of phenomenon under the hesitant fuzzy environment quantitatively, it is necessary to develop a novel psychological distance for HFSs. We can calculate the distance along the dominant and indifferent directions respectively to quantify the competition and domination between alternatives, and judge the relationship between the dominated relationships and similar degrees. The

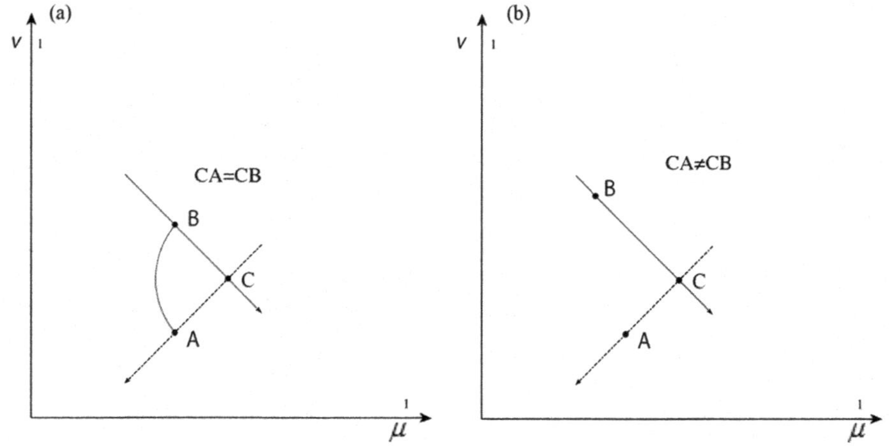

Fig. 2.1 The Euclidean distance **a** and the psychological distance, **b** for three alternatives A, B and C under intuitionistic fuzzy environment

detailed definition of hesitant fuzzy psychological distance measure will be presented in detail in the following section.

2.3.2 Hesitant Fuzzy Psychological Distance Measure and the Corresponding Similarity Measure

The HFS is effective to depict the uncertain preferences and information with several possible values of membership degree more comprehensively. Therefore, inspired by the definition of psychological distance measure for real number (Rooderkerk et al., 2011) and intuitionistic fuzzy information (Hao, 2018), this chapter generalizes the concept to the hesitant fuzzy environment and introduces a general hesitant fuzzy psychological distance.

For the decision making problems under the hesitant fuzzy environment, the attribute information of alternatives is depicted by HFSs. However, Li (2017) ignored that the alternatives usually had two opposite attributes in actual application, which usually led to mistakes. In addition, the normalization of hesitant fuzzy information is also necessary. Therefore, to begin with, we must transform all the attributes into the normalized type by the complement operators, i.e., the values of the benefit attributes remain the same, but the values of cost attributes should be transformed into the opposite values. Then the original HFSs should be normalized by the pessimistic principle. To simplify the calculation of indifference vector and remain the original information at the same time, an effective method is to compare each attribute with a certain arbitrary one, for example the first attribute (Berkkowitsh et al., 2015). Suppose that all the alternatives have n attributes which have been transformed into the normalized type by the complement operators. The corresponding weight vector for the n attributes is $w = (w_1, w_2, \ldots, w_n)^T, \sum_{i=1}^{n} w_i = 1$. Comparing each attribute with the first attribute, we can obtain $(n-1)$ indifference vectors as follows:

$$\beta_j = \begin{cases} -\frac{w_{j+1}}{w_1}, & i = 1 \\ \frac{w_1}{w_1}, & i = j+1 \quad (j = 1, \ldots, n-1) \\ 0, & others \end{cases} \tag{2.2}$$

Furthermore, the indifference matrix is composed of the above $(n-1)$ indifference vectors: $\beta = [\beta_1, \beta_2, \ldots, \beta_{n-1}]$. According to the orthogonality of dominance vector and indifference vector, we can obtain the corresponding dominance vector as:

$$\beta_n = \left(\frac{w_1}{w_1}, \frac{w_2}{w_1}, \ldots, \frac{w_n}{w_1} \right)^T \tag{2.3}$$

Then the normalized transformation basis is $T = \left[\frac{\beta_1}{\|\beta_1\|}, \frac{\beta_2}{\|\beta_2\|}, \ldots, \frac{\beta_{n-1}}{\|\beta_{n-1}\|}, \frac{\beta_n}{\|\beta_n\|}\right]$ and the transformed vector is $trans_{HFS} = T^{-1}D$, D denotes the hesitant fuzzy Euclidean distance vector. To ensure that the Euclidean distance along the dominance direction be attached with more importance and the indifference direction remain the same, the $n \times n$ diagonal matrix $A_w = \begin{bmatrix} 1 & \ldots & 0 \\ \vdots & \ddots & \vdots \\ 0 & \cdots & wd \end{bmatrix}$ is introduced. The parameter wd magnifies the stretching effect of dominance direction. Therefore, the general hesitant fuzzy psychological distance measure (Song et al., 2020) for HFSs is defined as follows:

$$D_{hf-psy} = \sqrt{\frac{1}{n \cdot w_d} \cdot trans'_{HFS} \cdot A_w \cdot trans_{HFS}} \tag{2.4}$$

where n denotes the number of attributes and $n \cdot w_d$ is the balancing coefficient to ensure that the proposed distance belongs to the interval [0,1].

Remark. When $w_1 = w_2 = \ldots = w_n$ and $w_d = 1$, the above hesitant fuzzy psychological distance will degenerate into the normalized Euclidean distance, which indicates that the Euclidean distance is a special case of the proposed hesitant fuzzy psychological distance.

Example 1 (Song et al., 2020): Suppose that there are three alternatives M, N and O, which are depicted by HFSs with two opposite attributes: $H'_M = \{(0.3, 0.4), (0.1)\}$, $H'_N = \{(0.8, 0.9), (0.1)\}$ and $H'_O = \{(0.6), (0.2, 0.3)\}$ respectively. Then we calculate the hesitant fuzzy Euclidean distance between the alternatives M and O and the distance between the alternatives N and O. The calculation result is $D_{Euc}(H_M, H_O) = D_{Euc}(H_N, H_O) = 0.212$, which indicates that the hesitant fuzzy Euclidean distance between the alternatives M and O is equal to the distance between N and O. To begin with, we should normalize the three alternatives as: $H_M = \{(0.3, 0.4), -(0.1, 0.1)\}$, $H_N = \{(0.8, 0.9), -(0.1, 0.1)\}$ and $H_O = \{(0.6, 0.6), -(0.2, 0.3)\}$ respectively. Suppose that the benefit attribute and the cost attribute are equally important, i.e., $w = (w_\mu, w_\upsilon)^T = (0.5, 0.5)^T$, then we can obtain the indifference vector and the dominance vector as $\beta_1 = \begin{pmatrix} -1 \\ 1 \end{pmatrix}$ and $\beta_2 = \begin{pmatrix} 1 \\ 1 \end{pmatrix}$ respectively. So the corresponding transforming basis matrix is

$$T = \left(\frac{\beta_1}{\|\beta_1\|}, \frac{\beta_2}{\|\beta_2\|}\right) = \begin{pmatrix} -\frac{1}{\sqrt{2}} & \frac{1}{\sqrt{2}} \\ \frac{1}{\sqrt{2}} & \frac{1}{\sqrt{2}} \end{pmatrix}$$

The hesitant fuzzy Euclidean distance vector between the alternatives O and M is $D_{OM} = \begin{pmatrix} -0.361 \\ 0.224 \end{pmatrix}$. Similarly, the hesitant fuzzy Euclidean distance vector between

Table 2.1 The hesitant fuzzy distances between the alternatives O and M and between the alternatives O and N with different values of wd

	$wd = 2$	$wd = 3$	$wd = 5$	$wd = 10$
D_{OM}	0.218	0.182	0.148	0.115
D_{ON}	0.297	0.295	0.294	0.293
$D_{ON} - D_{OM}$	0. 097	0. 113	0. 146	0.178

the alternatives O and N is $D_{ON} = \begin{pmatrix} 0.361 \\ 0.224 \end{pmatrix}$. So the transformed vectors for OM and ON are presented as follows respectively:

$$trans_{OM} = T^{-1} D_{OM} = \begin{pmatrix} 0.414 \\ -0.097 \end{pmatrix}$$

$$trans_{ON} = T^{-1} D_{ON} = \begin{pmatrix} -0.097 \\ 0.414 \end{pmatrix}$$

The two transformed vectors depict the transforming process of the competitive relationships. Take the $trans_{OM}$ as an example, if the DMs change from the HFS O to the HFS M, it is necessary to move 0.414 units and −0.097 units along the indifference direction and dominance direction respectively.

Furthermore, we can calculate the hesitant fuzzy psychological distance between the alternatives O and M, the alternatives O and N. In order to illustrate the stretching effect of dominance direction better, the hesitant fuzzy psychological distances with four difference values of the magnification parameter $wd(wd = 2, 3, 5, 10)$ are presented in Table 2.1 (Song et al., 2020).

The larger value of the parameter wd denotes the more attention of the dominance vector than the indifference vector. From Table 2.1, we can see that the hesitant fuzzy psychological distance between the alternatives O and M is always larger than that of the distance between the alternatives O and N with different values of the parameter wd. In addition, with the increase of wd, the difference value of the hesitant fuzzy psychological distance between the alternatives O and M and the distance between the alternatives O and N also increases. It indicates that the increasing value of wd magnifies the stretching effect of dominance information, and the difference between different alternatives will also be enlarged.

Furthermore, suppose that $\vartheta_{M,N}$ denotes the similarity measure and $d(M, N)$ denotes one certain kind of distance measure of the alternatives M and N, then the traditional similarity measure is expressed as $\vartheta_{M,N} = 1 - d(M, N)$. It can also be expressed as: $\vartheta_{M,N} = f(D(M, N))$, in which f denotes a decreased function. However, the traditional simple linear relationship cannot depict the real relationship between the distance measure and similarity measure. Consider that the exponential function is one of the most important models in practical application, this section adopts it as the basic decreased function and provides the definition of novel similarity measure for HFSs based on the hesitant fuzzy psychological distance measure as follows:

$$\vartheta_{M,N} = (\theta)^{D_{hf-psy}} \tag{2.5}$$

where θ is a basic parameter belongs to the interval (0,1), D_{hf-psy} denotes the hesitant fuzzy psychological distance measure between the alternatives M and N.

To illustrate relationship between the similarity measure and the hesitant fuzzy psychological distance measure, and understand the influence of the parameter θ better, a set of curves for the proposed similarity measure with different values of θ are also provided as the following Fig. 2.2 (Song et al., 2020).

From the above Fig. 2.2, it is obvious that the proposed similarity measure can depict the delicate difference and relationship better with the nonlinear decreased function. In addition, it makes full of background information of alternatives by the proposed hesitant fuzzy psychological distance measure. A smaller value of θ corresponds to a smoother curve of similarity, indicating a better capability of discrimination for the similarity measure. We can see that when the value of θ is smaller than 0.01, the values of similarity are very close to 0 at the point of 1. Besides, the variation in the interval that close to 1 is also very tiny. In general, the value of θ depends on the practical problems. To obtain a good recognition ability, the value of θ is supposed to be not larger than 0.01.

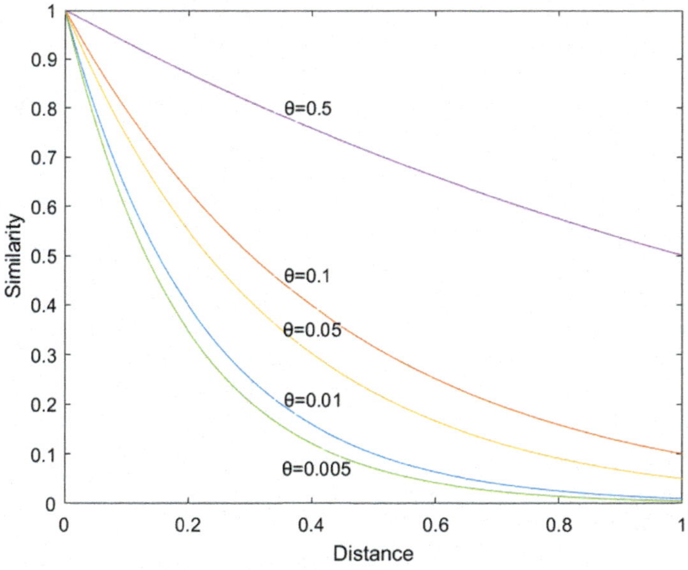

Fig. 2.2 The curves of similarity measure with different values of θ

2.3.3 TODIM Based on the Hesitant Fuzzy Psychological Distance Measure

The traditional decision making methods, such as TOPSIS (Liu & Zhang, 2013), LINMAP (Chen, 2013) and ELECTRE (Chhipi-Shrestha et al., 2017), are all based on the assumption that the DMs are completely rational. They ignore the psychological behaviors of the DMs in the decision-making process. However, in actual decision-making process, the DMs are usually not completely rational, and their behavior plays an important role in the actual decision-making process. The TODIM method is an interactive MADM method based on the prospect theory (Zhang & Xu, 2014), which considers the psychological behaviors of the DMs. Therefore, aiming at the actual decision making problems under the hesitant fuzzy environment, we introduce a TODIM method based on the hesitant fuzzy psychological distance.

Suppose that there are m alternatives with n attributes, denoted as x_i and a_j respectively, and the corresponding weight vector for the n attributes is $w = (w_1, w_2, \ldots, w_n)^T$, $\sum_{j=1}^{n} w_i = 1$, $i = 1, 2, \ldots, m$ and $j = 1, 2, \ldots, n$. Every alternative is depicted by HFSs, which contains the hesitant fuzzy information of all n attributes, expressed as $H(x_i) = \left(h_j(x_i)\right)$, $j = 1, 2, \ldots, n$. The collected evaluation information depicted by HFSs is all normalized by the pessimistic principle and all the attributes are transformed into the same type. Some basic concepts about the TODIM under the hesitant fuzzy environment are also presented as follows:

Definition 2.4 (Song et al., 2020). Suppose $w_{j*} = \max\left\{w_j | j = 1, 2, \ldots, n\right\}$, $j = 1, 2, \ldots, n$, then the corresponding attribute a_{j*} is denoted as the reference attribute. The relative weight of the attribute a_j to the reference attribute a_{j*} is defined as:

$$w_{j/j*} = w_j / w_{j^*} \tag{2.6}$$

where $w_j (j = 1, 2, \ldots, n)$ denote the weights of the attributes $a_j (j = 1, 2, \ldots, n)$.

Definition 2.5 (Song et al., 2020). Suppose that $D_{hf\text{-}psy}\left(h_j(x_i) h_j(x_k)\right)$ is the hesitant fuzzy psychological distance between the alternatives x_i and x_k in terms of the attribute a_j, $w_{j/j*}$ is the relative weight of the attribute a_j to the reference attribute a_{j*}, then the dominance degree of the alternative x_i over the alternative x_k in terms of the attribute a_j under the hesitant fuzzy environment is $\phi_j(x_i, x_k)$, which is defined as follows:

$$\phi_j(x_i, x_k) = \begin{cases} \sqrt{\left(w_{j/j^*} \cdot D_{hf-psy}\left(h_j(x_i), h_j(x_k)\right)\right) \Big/ \sum_j^n w_{j/j^*}} & h_j(x_i) > h_j(x_k) \\ 0 & h_j(x_i) \sim h_j(x_k) \\ -\frac{1}{\theta}\sqrt{\left(\left(\sum_j^n w_{j/j^*}\right) \cdot D_{hf-psy}\left(h_j(x_k), h_j(x_i)\right)\right) \Big/ w_{j/j^*}} & h_j(x_i) < h_j(x_k) \end{cases} \tag{2.7}$$

where θ denotes the attenuation factor of losses, $\theta > 0$. When $h_j(x_i) > h_j(x_k)$, then $\phi_j(x_i, x_k)$ denotes a gain of the comparison between the alternative x_i over the alternative x_k in terms of the attribute a_j; when $h_j(x_i) \sim h_j(x_k)$, then $\phi_j(x_i, x_k)$ denotes a nil; when $h_j(x_i) < h_j(x_k)$, then $\phi_j(x_i, x_k)$ denotes a loss.

Definition 2.6 (Song et al., 2020). Suppose that $\phi_j(x_i, x_k)$ is the dominance degree of the alternative x_i over the alternative x_k in terms of the attribute a_j under the hesitant fuzzy environment, then the dominance of the alternative x_i over the alternative x_k is defined as:

$$\phi(x_i, x_k) = \sum_{j=1}^{n} \phi_j(x_i, x_k) \tag{2.8}$$

where $i, k = 1, 2, \ldots, m,\ j = 1, 2, \ldots, n$.

Definition 2.7 (Song et al., 2020). Suppose that $\phi(x_i, x_k)$ is the dominance of the alternative x_i over the alternative x_k, then the overall prospect value of the alternative x_i is defined as:

$$\Phi(x_i) = \frac{\sum_{k=1}^{m} \phi(x_i, x_k) - \min_i\left\{\sum_{k=1}^{m} \phi(x_i, x_k)\right\}}{\max_i\left\{\sum_{k=1}^{m} \phi(x_i, x_k)\right\} - \min_i\left\{\sum_{k=1}^{m} \phi(x_i, x_k)\right\}} \tag{2.9}$$

where $i, k = 1, 2, \ldots, m,\ j = 1, 2, \ldots, n$.

The larger prospect value corresponds to a better alternative. Therefore, we can obtain the priority orders of the alternatives based on the overall prospect value $\Phi(x)$. The detailed implementation of the TODIM based on the hesitant fuzzy psychological distance is presented as follows (Song et al., 2020):

Step 1: Collect the evaluation information and construct the hesitant fuzzy decision matrix $H = \left(h_j(x_i)\right)_{m \times n}$.

Step 2: Select the reference attribute, and then calculate the relative weight of every attribute to the reference attribute.

Step 3: Determine the weight information for the attributes and set the weighted dominance effect parameter wd in preparation for obtaining the psychological distances.

Step 4: Calculate the hesitant fuzzy psychological distance between alternatives.

Step 5: Calculate the dominance degree between alternatives based on the hesitant fuzzy psychological distance.

Step 6: Calculate the overall prospect value of every alternative.

Step 7: Rank the alternatives based on the prospect values.

2.4 Application to the Temporary Rescue Airport Decision Making Problem

This section will apply the hesitant fuzzy psychological distance measure and the corresponding TODIM to the temporary rescue airport decision making problem of the Arctic Northwest Passage in detail (Song et al., 2020).

The temporary rescue airport decision making problem is very complex that contains many uncertainties, including cultural, economic, facilities, medical and political factors. Many of those factors are difficult to depict with accurate data. In addition, the DMs must consider all the factors and provide the preference and consultation information. Furthermore, if the alternative temporary rescue airports are very similar in some attributes, it will bring more difficult for the DMs to reach a certain consensus and make a decision with sound reliability. Consider the advantages of HFS theory in managing uncertainties and depicting the experts' cognition, it is reasonable to adopt the HFS to solve the temporary rescue airport decision making problems. To determine the best airport concerning the emergencies, we use the proposed hesitant fuzzy psychological distance measure and the related improved TODIM method.

Take the temporary rescue airports of the Arctic Northwest Passage as an example to evaluate the performance of the proposed model (Song et al., 2020), it is known to us all that the Arctic Northwest Passage is located in the cold area of high latitude (Reimnitz et al., 2011). The natural environment is also bad and changeable, which brings great security threats to the navigation of ships. It is prone to casualties, oil spill and other emergencies (Eicken et al., 2011). At the same time, there are many challenges of insufficient emergency rescue facilities and limited professional rescuers in the Arctic region. The construction and selection of temporary rescue airport can save resources effectively, making it more efficient and convenient in maritime emergency rescue. Consider the scale and facilities of airport around the Northwest Passage, we select five airports as candidates: Iqaluit Airport, Lesolute Bay Airport, Nasaswago Airport, Tuktoyatuk Airport and Nuuk Airport. To simplify the temporary rescue airport selection problem, we mainly consider that economics, the safety of airports, the medical condition, the emergency capability of airports. Suppose that the decision information is expressed in terms of HFSs, then the original decision matrix of different temporary rescue airports and the corresponding normalized decision matrix based on the pessimist principle are provided in Tables 2.2 and 2.3 respectively. Then we solve the similarity problems and the priority orders of the alternative routes step by step as follows (Song et al., 2020).

Suppose that the corresponding weight vector of four attributes about the temporary rescue airport decision making problem is $w = (0.2, 0.3, 0.3, 0.2)^T$, and the weight dominance effect parameter is $wd = 5$. Then we calculate the hesitant fuzzy psychological distances and the generalized weighted Euclidean distances between different airports respectively. The calculation results of the two kinds of distances are presented respectively as follows (Tables 2.4 and 2.5).

Table 2.2 The original decision matrix of different temporary rescue airports

	Economics	Safety	Medical condition	Emergency capability
A: Iqaluit Airport	(0.1, 0.2)	(0.8)	(0.2, 0.3)	(0.4, 0.6)
B:Lesolute Bay Airport	(0.2)	(0.4, 0.5, 0.6)	(0.1)	(0.5, 0.6)
C:Nasaswago Airport	(0.3, 0.4)	(0.7, 0.9)	(0.4, 0.5)	(0.2, 0.4, 0.5)
D:Tuktoyatuk Airport	(0.2, 0.4)	(0.2, 0.3)	(0.2, 0.3)	(0.5, 0.6)
E: Nuuk Airport	(0.4, 0.5)	(0.7, 0.9)	(0.2, 0.4)	(0.5, 0.6, 0.7)

Note All attribute values have already been transformed into the same type

Table 2.3 The normalized decision matrix of different temporary rescue airports

	Economics	Safety	Medical condition	Emergency capability
A: Iqaluit Airport	(0.1, 0.2)	(0.8, 0.8, 0.8)	(0.2, 0.3)	(0.4, 0.4, 0.6)
B:Lesolute Bay Airport	(0.2, 0.2)	(0.4, 0.5, 0.6)	(0.1, 0.1)	(0.5, 0.5, 0.6)
C: Nasaswago Airport	(0.3, 0.4)	(0.7, 0.7, 0.9)	(0.4, 0.5)	(0.2, 0.4, 0.5)
D: Tuktoyatuk Airport	(0.2, 0.4)	(0.2, 0.2, 0.3)	(0.2, 0.3)	(0.5, 0.5, 0.6)
E: Nuuk Airport	(0.4,0.5)	(0.7,0.7,0.9)	(0.2, 0.4)	(0.5, 0.6, 0.7)

Table 2.4 The hesitant fuzzy psychological distances of different temporary rescue airports

	A	B	C	D	E
A	0	0.045	0.028	0.141	0.029
B	0.045	0	0.073	0.037	0.052
C	0.028	0.073	0	0.129	0.026
D	0.141	0.037	0.129	0	0.126
E	0.029	0.052	0.026	0.126	0

Table 2.5 The generalized weighted Euclidean distances of different temporary rescue airports

	A	B	C	D	E
A	0	0.197	0.162	0.321	0.163
B	0.197	0	0.268	0.183	0.227
C	0.162	0.268	0	0.326	0.144
D	0.321	0.183	0.326	0	0.306
E	0.163	0.277	0.144	0.306	0

The minimum values of the hesitant fuzzy psychological distances and the weighted Euclidean distances are 0.026 and 0.144 respectively, i.e., the distance between the airports C and E. They both indicate that the most similar alternative airports are the Nasaswago Airport and Nuuk Airport. Furthermore, the maximum value of the hesitant fuzzy psychological distances is 0.141, implying that the most different airports are the Iqaluit Airport and Tuktoyatuk Airport. However, as for the weighted Euclidean distances, the most different airports are the Nasaswago Airport and Tuktoyatuk Airport with the largest value of 0.326.

After that, we can also calculate the proposed similarity measure between the alternative airports based on the above results of the hesitant fuzzy psychological distances. To begin with, suppose that $\theta = 0.01$ and $wd = 5$. Then we can calculate the similarity measure based on the exponential function and hesitant fuzzy psychological distance measure in Table 2.6. What is more, the traditional similarity measure is also provided based on the results of weighted Euclidean distances in Table 2.7.

According to the calculation results of the similarity measure in Table 2.6, the most similar alternatives are the airports C and E, which are also consistent with the results of hesitant fuzzy psychological distance. In addition, the minimum value of the proposed similarity measure is 0.522. It also corresponds to the largest value of the hesitant fuzzy psychological distances. Furthermore, the values of the proposed similarity measure vary from 0.522 to 0.887, whose range is almost two times wider than that of the traditional similarity measure based on the weighted Euclidean distance and the linear basis decreased function. Besides, the category in Table 2.7 is not that

Table 2.6 The simplified similarity between different airports based on the hesitant fuzzy psychological distance measure and the exponential function

	A	B	C	D	E
A	1	0.813	0.879	0.522	0.875
B	0.813	1	0.714	0.843	0.787
C	0.879	0.714	1	0.552	0.887
D	0.522	0.843	0.552	1	0.560
E	0.875	0.787	0.887	0.560	1

Table 2.7 The similarity between different airports based on the weighted Euclidean distance and the linear basis decreased function

	A	B	C	D	E
A	1	0.803	0.838	0.679	0.837
B	0.803	1	0.732	0.817	0.773
C	0.838	0.732	1	0.674	0.856
D	0.679	0.817	0.674	1	0.694
E	0.837	0.773	0.856	0.694	1

apparent than those in Table 2.6. It is obvious that the proposed similarity measure categorizes the airports into three obvious types, i.e., the much similar ones, the moderate ones and the most different ones. However, there are many categories according to the similarity classification in Table 2.7, which is not conductive for the DMs to make a choice. The main reason for the differences is that the introduction of exponential function, which enlarges the detailed information in similarity. Besides, the hesitant fuzzy psychological distance also makes contribution to make full use of original uncertain information and depicts the competitive relationships better. It reduces the difficulty in making a decision and avoids the defect of traditional Euclidean distance.

Later, we will consider to obtain the priority orders of the temporary rescue airports. The original decision matrix indicates the comprehensive information for these airports. To begin with, we compare every two alternative airports in terms of each attribute based on the normalized decision matrix of different temporary rescue airports. By calculating the score and the deviation degrees, we can obtain the comparison results as follows (Table 2.8).

After that, we can select the reference attribute a_{j*} with the largest value of the weight $w_{j*} = \max\{w_j | j = 1, 2, \ldots, n\} = 0.3$, and calculate the relative weight $w_{j/j*}$ of other attributes a_j to the reference attribute a_{j*}. Suppose that $\theta = 1$ without the loss of generality, then based on the calculation results of the hesitant fuzzy psychological distance between alternative airports, we can obtain the dominance degree $\phi_j(x_i, x_k)$ of the airport x_i over the airport x_k under the attribute a_j, which are presented as follows (Tables 2.9, 2.10, 2.11 and 2.12).

After that, we can obtain the overall dominance degree of the airport x_i over the airport x_k by integrating the dominance degree $\phi_j(x_i, x_k)$, which is presented as follows (Table 2.13).

Furthermore, we can calculate the overall prospect value of the alternative airport based on the overall dominance degree, presented as follows (Table 2.14).

Table 2.8 The pairwise comparison of temporary rescue airports under different attributes

	Economics	Safety	Medical condition	Emergency capability
A/B	$h_1(x_1) < h_1(x_2)$	$h_2(x_1) > h_2(x_2)$	$h_3(x_1) > h_3(x_2)$	$h_4(x_1) < h_4(x_2)$
A/C	$h_1(x_1) < h_1(x_3)$	$h_2(x_1) > h_2(x_3)$	$h_3(x_1) < h_3(x_3)$	$h_4(x_1) > h_4(x_3)$
A/D	$h_1(x_1) < h_1(x_4)$	$h_2(x_1) > h_2(x_4)$	$h_3(x_1) < h_3(x_4)$	$h_4(x_1) < h_4(x_4)$
A/E	$h_1(x_1) < h_1(x_5)$	$h_2(x_1) > h_2(x_5)$	$h_3(x_1) < h_3(x_5)$	$h_4(x_1) < h_4(x_5)$
B/C	$h_1(x_2) < h_1(x_3)$	$h_2(x_2) < h_2(x_3)$	$h_3(x_2) < h_3(x_3)$	$h_4(x_2) > h_4(x_3)$
B/D	$h_1(x_2) < h_1(x_4)$	$h_2(x_2) > h_2(x_4)$	$h_3(x_2) < h_3(x_4)$	$h_4(x_2) \sim h_4(x_4)$
B/E	$h_1(x_2) < h_1(x_5)$	$h_2(x_2) < h_2(x_5)$	$h_3(x_2) < h_3(x_5)$	$h_4(x_2) < h_4(x_5)$
C/D	$h_1(x_3) > h_1(x_4)$	$h_2(x_3) > h_2(x_4)$	$h_3(x_3) > h_3(x_4)$	$h_4(x_3) < h_4(x_4)$
C/E	$h_1(x_3) < h_1(x_5)$	$h_2(x_3) \sim h_2(x_5)$	$h_3(x_3) > h_3(x_5)$	$h_4(x_3) < h_4(x_5)$
D/E	$h_1(x_4) < h_1(x_5)$	$h_2(x_4) < h_2(x_5)$	$h_3(x_4) < h_3(x_5)$	$h_4(x_4) < h_4(x_5)$

Table 2.9 The dominance degree of different airports in terms of attribute a_1

	A	B	C	D	E
A	0	−0.077	−0.219	−0.173	−0.329
B	0.035	0	−0.173	−0.155	−0.280
C	0.044	0.035	0	0.015	−0.110
D	0.035	0.031	−0.077	0	−0.173
E	0.066	0.056	0.022	0.035	0

Table 2.10 The dominance degree of different airports in terms of attribute a_2

	A	B	C	D	E
A	0	0.091	0.029	0.166	0.029
B	−0.454	0	−0.394	0.079	−0.394
C	−0.147	0.079	0	0.156	0
D	−0.829	−0.394	−0.781	0	−0.781
E	−0.147	0.079	0	0.156	0

Table 2.11 The dominance degree of different airports in terms of attribute a_3

	A	B	C	D	E
A	0	0.046	−0.292	0	−0.102
B	−0.230	0	−0.516	−0.230	−0.326
C	0.058	0.103	0	0.058	0.046
D	0	0.046	−0.292	0	−0.102
E	0.020	0.065	−0.230	0.020	0

Table 2.12 The dominance degree of different airports in terms of attribute a_4

	A	B	C	D	E
A	0	−0.112	0.034	−0.112	−0.188
B	0.022	0	0.051	0	−0.112
C	−0.172	−0.257	0	−0.257	−0.318
D	0.022	0	0.051	0	−0.112
E	0.038	0.022	0.064	0.022	0

Table 2.13 The overall dominance degree of different airports

	A	B	C	D	E
A	0	−0.052	−0.448	−0.119	−0.590
B	−0.627	0	−1.032	−0.306	−1.112
C	−0.217	−0.040	0	−0.028	−0.382
D	−0.772	−0.317	−1.099	0	−1.168
E	−0.023	0.222	−0.144	0.233	0

Table 2.14 The overall dominance degree of different airports

Airport	A	B	C	D	E
$\Phi(x_i)$	0.589	0.077	0.738	0	1

The larger overall prospect value $\Phi(x)$ denotes a better alternative. Thus, we can obtain the priority orders of the five airports as: E > C > A > B > D. So the best alternative airport is the Nuuk Airport.

In addition, we also make a comparison with the aggregation techniques of hesitant fuzzy information to analyze the results thoroughly. Suppose that the weights of attributes remain the same. This section adopts the hesitant fuzzy weighted averaging (HFWA) aggregation operator to aggregate the hesitant fuzzy information of the five alternative airports. The aggregation results of the hesitant fuzzy information of every alternative airports and their corresponding score function values are presented in Table 2.15 as follows:

Therefore, the priority orders of the five airports are E > C > A > B > D, and the best alternative airport is also the Nuuk Airport, which is same to our model.

The comparison results indicate that our method obtains the same optimal temporary rescue airport with that of traditional aggregation technique. The aggregation results of hesitant fuzzy information validate the efficiency and precision of the new hesitant fuzzy psychological distance and similarity measure we propose from another aspect. In view of the similarity results, the alternative airports C and E, A and C, A and E are the most similar, which are also consistent with the priority orders of the presented TODIM and aggregation techniques. However, it is obvious that our method enlarges this competitive relationship. The similarity measures based on the hesitant fuzzy psychological distance makes the results more distinguishable and sensitive to similar information by the introduction of decreased exponential function. In practical problems, the similarity of alternatives may be higher, which makes it more difficult for the DMs to provide the optimal choice. The traditional methods are based on the strict assumption that the DMs are completely rational and fail to consider the psychological and behavior factors in the decision making process. As has been discussed before, the traditional HFWA operator only manages with the hesitant fuzzy information along the dimension of attributes, ignoring the competitive relationship between alternatives. Besides, the aggregation of HFSs may also lead to overload information, which makes the computation more difficult and complicated.

The hesitant fuzzy psychological distance measure supposes that different alternatives could be exchanged on the dominance direction to reflect the competitive relationships between alternatives. The introduction of parameter wd magnifies the stretching effect of dominance direction and rebuilds the dominant competition. Based on which, we also present a corresponding non-linear similarity measure for hesitant fuzzy information and a TODIM method. It integrates the idea of prospect theory, and considers the psychological and behavioral factors of the DMs in decision making problems better. By combining the advantages of HFSs in depicting

Table 2.15 The aggregated hesitant fuzzy information of the alternative airports and the corresponding score function values

Airport	A	B	C	D	E
Aggregated hesitant fuzzy information	(0.490,…,0.559)	(0.308,…,0.414)	(0.468,…,0.680)	(0.272,…,0.393)	(0.488,…,0.706)
Score function values	0. 525	0. 361	0.583	0.335	0. 605

uncertain information and psychological distance measure in enlarging competitive relationship, the presented TODIM can obtain a more reliable and logical results. The experimental results validate the accuracy and efficiency of the presented TODIM.

2.5 Remarks

Since most existing distance measures of HFSs ignore the background information of the alternative set and the deficiency in practical decision making problems, this chapter introduces the concept of hesitant fuzzy psychological distance measure. It considers the differences of hesitant fuzzy information under different attributes and their competitive relationship at the same time. Based on which, we further present a new hesitant fuzzy similarity measure. It introduces the exponential function to enlarge the detailed information in similarity. It is nonlinear and more distinguishable with a better recognition ability. Furthermore, a TODIM method based on the hesitant fuzzy psychological distance measure under the hesitant fuzzy environment is presented. Then the above TODIM is applied to the temporary rescue airport decision making problem of the Arctic Northwest Passage, which verifies the validity and reliability of the presented TODIM method.

References

Berkowitsch, N. A. J., Scheibehenne, B., Rieskamp, J., et al. (2015). A generalized distance function for preferential choices. *British Journal of Mathematical & Statistical Psychology, 68*, 310–325.

Chen, T. Y. (2013). An interval-valued intuitionistic fuzzy LINMAP method with inclusion comparison possibilities and hybrid averaging operations for multiple criteria group decision making. *Knowledge-Based Systems, 45*, 134–146.

Chhipi-Shrestha, Cyan K., Hewage, K. Sadiq, R. (2017). Selecting sustainability indicators for small to medium sized urban water systems using fuzzy ELECTRE. *Water Environment Research* 89, 238-249.

Eicken, H., Jones, J., Meyer, F., et al. (2011). Environmental security in Arctic ice-covered seas: From strategy to tactics of hazard identification and emergency response. *Marine Technology Society Journal, 45*, 37–48.

Farhadinia, B., & Herrera-Viedma, E. (2019). Sorting of decision-making methods based on their outcomes using dominance-vector hesitant fuzzy-based distance. *Soft Computing*, 23, 1109–1121.

Hao, Z. N. (2018). *Several intuitionistic fuzzy multi-attribute decision making methods and their applications*. Army Engineering University of PLA.

Hong, D. H., & Choi, C. H. (2000). Multi-criteria fuzzy decision-making problems based on vague set theory. *Fuzzy Sets and Systems, 114*, 103–113.

Huang, B., Li, H. X., & Wei, D. K. (2012). Dominance-based rough set model in intuitionistic fuzzy information systems. *Knowledge-Based Systems, 28*, 115–123.

Huang, B., Wei, D. K., Li, H. X., et al. (2013). Using a rough set model to extract rules in dominance-based interval-valued intuitionistic fuzzy information systems. *Information Sciences, 221*, 215–229.

Huber, J., Payne, J. W., Puto, C. (1982). Adding asymmetrically dominated alternatives-violations of regularity and the similarity hypothesis. *Journal of Consumer Research, 9*, 90–98.

Li, C. Q. (2017). *Study on hesitant fuzzy distance measures and clustering methods*. Army Engineering University of PLA.

Li, D., Zeng, W., & Zhao, Y. (2015). Note on distance measure of hesitant fuzzy sets. *Information Sciences, 321*, 103–115.

Liu, F., & Zhang, W. G. (2013). TOPSIS-based consensus model for group decision-making with incomplete interval fuzzy preference relationships. *IEEE Transactions on Cybernetics, 44*, 1283–1294.

Nosofsky, R. M. (1986). Attention, similarity and the identification-categorization relationship. *Journal of Experimental Psychology: General, 115*, 39–57.

Nosofsky, R. M., & Zaki, S. R. (2002). Exemplar and prototype models revisited: Response strategies, selective attention and stimulus generalization. *Journal of Experimental Psychology: Learning, Memory and Cognition, 28*, 924–940.

Reimnitz, E., Marincovich, L., McCormick, M., et al. (2011). Suspension freezing of bottom sediment and biota in the Northwest Passage and implications for Arctic Ocean sedimentation. *Canadian Journal of Earth Sciences, 29*, 693–703.

Rooderkerk, R. P., Van heerde, H. J., & Bijmolt, T. H. A. (2011). Incorporating context effects into a choice model. *Journal of Marketing Research, 48*, 767–780.

Song, C. Y., Xu, Z. S., & Hou, J. (2020). An improved TODIM method based on the hesitant fuzzy psychological distance measure. *International Journal of Machine Learning and Cybernetics* published online.

Wang, J. Q., Wang, D. D., Zhang, D. D., et al. (2014). Multi-criteria outranking approach with hesitant fuzzy sets. *Or Spectrum, 36*, 1001–1019.

Wedel, D. H. (1991). Distinguishing among models of contextually induced preference reversals. *Journal of Experimental Psychology: Learning, Memory and Cognition, 17*, 767–778.

Xu, Z. S., & Xia, M. M. (2011). Distance and similarity measures for hesitant fuzzy sets. *Information Sciences, 181*, 2128–2138.

Xu, Z. S., & Xia, M. M. (2012). Hesitant fuzzy entropy and cross-entropy and their use in multi-attribute decision making. *International Journal of Intelligent Systems, 27*(2012), 799–822.

Zhang, X. L., & Xu, Z. S. (2014). The TODIM analysis approach based on novel measured functions under hesitant fuzzy environment. *Knowledge-Based Systems, 61*, 48–58.

Chapter 3
Dynamic Decision Making Method Based on the Hesitant Fuzzy Decision Field Theory

Most existing methods based on HFSs only focus on the final integrated information by different kinds of aggregation operators, but fail to provide the detailed comparisons between alternatives. They are essentially result-oriented static decision-making methods, based on which, the decision-making results may be inconsistent with reality. The decision field theory (DFT) is a dynamic decision-making method and can better simulate the uncertain decision-making process. In this chapter, we introduce a dynamic decision making method named as hesitant fuzzy decision field theory (HFDFT), which integrates the HFS into DFT.

3.1 Review of the Related Work

Since the excellent properties of HFSs in quantitative decision-making problems, many scholars have studied HFS theory and obtained a series of research achievements. For example, Yu et al. (2011) defined a hesitant fuzzy Choquet integral operator and applied it to solve MAGDM problems with unknown weights, Wei (2012) proposed a priority integration operator for hesitant fuzzy information, and Yu et al. (2012) put forward a generalized hesitant fuzzy Bonferroni method to solve the MAGDM problems. Besides, Chen et al. (2015) proposed a hesitant fuzzy ELECTRE I method and applied it to deal with the MAGDM problems under hesitant fuzzy environment. The method is developed based on the concept of hesitant fuzzy concordance and hesitant fuzzy discordance, which are provided based on score function and deviation degree.

As for fuzzy MAGDM, Chen and Hwang (1992) pointed out that the key of solving it is to determine the weights of attributes, and select the appropriate information integration operators to calculate the fuzzy utility values of alternatives. After that, the optimal alternative is obtained by comparing and sorting the fuzzy utility values. Most existing studies on hesitant fuzzy MAGDM methods are carried out based on

C. Song and Z. Xu, *Techniques of Decision Making, Uncertain Reasoning and Regression Analysis Under the Hesitant Fuzzy Environment and Their Applications*,
Uncertainty and Operations Research, https://doi.org/10.1007/978-981-16-5800-6_3

Chen and Hwang's summary. The development of various hesitant fuzzy integration operators lays the mathematical foundation of the integration of hesitant fuzzy data. Besides, the introduction of various HFS sequencing theories makes it possible to sort and compare hesitant fuzzy information.

Most existing methods based on HFSs only focus on the final integrated information by different kinds of aggregation operators. They ignore the influence of time of consideration on the decision-making results and fail to provide the detailed comparisons between alternatives. They are essentially result-oriented static decision-making methods. However, many studies indicate that there is a functional relationship between preference intensity and time (Payne et al., 1988; Jamieson & Petrusic, 1977). Besides, experts need to consider decision-making time, decision scenarios and variation of different factors, which will affect the results over time. Thus, compared with traditional static decision-making methods, dynamic decision-making methods are more applicable and logical.

The research on human dynamic decision making based on psychological theory (Toda, 2010) and computer simulations of complicated decision-making tasks (Scheibehenne et al., 2013) has promoted the development of dynamic decision-making theory, which is important to solve the MAGDM problems. Scholars have carried out some studies on the dynamic decision-making processes and put forward the corresponding models and theories. For instance, Gonzalez et al. (2010) proposed the instance-based learning theory (IBLT), which improves the accumulation of cases based on the results of the action and makes decisions based on the accumulated experience. They also provided the decision-making process of dynamic decision tasks. Saaty (2005) elaborated his idea for the development of dynamic decision making. Busemeyer and Pleskac (2009) deeply studied the connection and application range of various theories and methods in dynamic decision making, including Expected Multi Utility Theory, Game Theory, Bayesian Inference, Decision Tree, Markov Logic Network and so on.

The research findings on dynamic decision making can be mainly divided into two types: normative decision making and behavioral decision making (Hao & Xu, 2017). Normative decision-making theory demonstrates the possibility of the optimal decision by theoretical analysis. The studies on behavioral decision making focus on exploring the behavioral characteristics and laws of experts in the dynamic process through empirical methods. Combining normative decision-making theory and behavioral decision-making theory, Busemeyer and Townsend (1993) proposed the concept of decision field theory (DFT), which applied the diffusion to the study of human decision-making behaviors. The DFT method is a process-oriented dynamic decision-making method, and it can simulate the motivational process and cognitive process of uncertain decision making (Busemeyer & Diederich, 2002). Besides, the DFT method can accurately predict the selection probability and present the relationship between preference intensity and time.

3.2 Hesitant Fuzzy Decision Field Theory

The DFT is a dynamic decision-making method and can better simulate the uncertain decision-making process. Sometimes, when evaluating alternatives, experts can't reach a certain consensus or provide a common measure of the membership degree with sound reliability. In such cases, the HFS is an effective tool to depict hesitant preferences and uncertain knowledge of the experts. Therefore, to avoid the loss of information, this section introduces the concept of hesitant fuzzy decision field theory (HFDFT), which integrates the HFS into the DFT. Then, the group decision-making method based on HFDFT is presented and a specific implementation process for the HFDFT method is also illustrated.

3.2.1 *Classical DFT Method*

The DFT method, which can capture experts' cognitive decision-making behaviors, is a dynamic decision-making method. It can simulate the uncertain decision-making process and the cognitive process better and accurately predict the relationship between the probability of selection and preference with time.

The main idea of DFT method is to calculate the momentary valences of alternatives based on the weights and the given attributes, which are inputted into the decision system. Then, the momentary preferences are obtained by integrating the decision system and valences along with the time. The final result is produced by the motor system after accumulating the preferences. The detailed process is illustrated in Fig. 3.1.

Suppose that $P(t)$ is the preference information at the time t, then we can obtain the preference information at the next moment $t + s$ by the following equation (Busemeyer & Townsend, 1993):

$$P(t + s) = SP(t) + V(t + s) \tag{3.1}$$

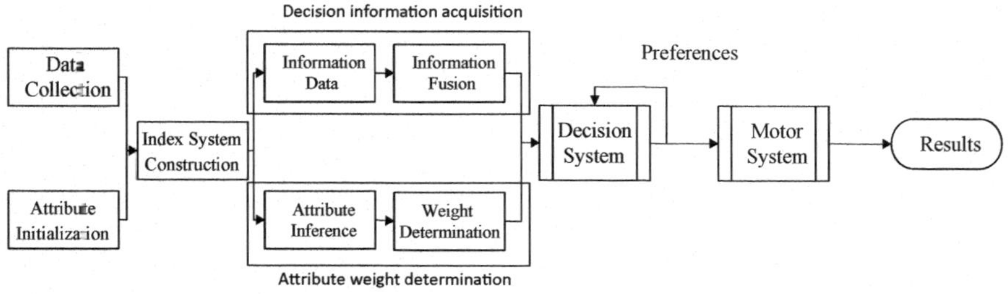

Fig. 3.1 The detailed process of DFT

in which s is a little time step.

The feedback matrix S, satisfying $0 \leq S_{ij} \leq 1$, indicates the competitive effects between alternatives in the process of decision making. It is symmetric and reflects the interactive relationship between alternatives. In order to ensure the stability and convergence of computations, the eigenvalues of S should be less than 1 in general.

The valence vector represents the psychological expectations of experts for each alternative. The momentary valence $V_i(t)$ reflects the advantages or disadvantages of ith alternative to the others in a certain attribute at the time t. We can obtain the valence vector by the following formula:

$$V(t) = CM\,W(t) \tag{3.2}$$

where the contrast matrix $C = \begin{cases} 1, i = j \\ -\dfrac{1}{n-1}, i \neq j \end{cases}$, the decision matrix M consists of complete preference information, W is the corresponding weight vector.

3.2.2 *Hesitant Fuzzy Decision Field Theory*

Uncertainty and imprecision widely exist in practical decision-making problems. To depict the randomness and hesitant information more comprehensively, the HFS is proposed with the membership degree consisting of several possible values.

Similar to the traditional DFT method, we elaborate the basic process of the HFDFT method. To begin with, we identify the main attributes and establish an index system. Some experts are invited to evaluate the alternatives from different aspects by using HFSs. Then, in the situations that attribute weights are uncertain, we need to calculate the weight vector based on the hesitant fuzzy information. Finally, the feedback matrix and the corresponding parameters are redefined and calculated under hesitant fuzzy environment, presented as follows:

Definition 3.1 (Song et al., 2019). Let C be the contrast matrix, M^* be the hesitant fuzzy decision matrix that contains the preference information of the experts, $W(t)$ be the weight vector of attributes, then the hesitant fuzzy valence vector is defined as:

$$V^*(t) = C \otimes M^* \otimes W(t) \tag{3.3}$$

where $C = \begin{cases} 1, i = j \\ -\dfrac{1}{n-1}, i \neq j \end{cases}$ and $M^* \otimes W(t)$ is the weighted evaluation information of the alternatives, calculated by the basic operation laws of HFSs.

Definition 3.2 (Song et al., 2019). The feedback matrix S^* depicts the memorizing effect of competitive relationship between different alternatives, consisting of self-connection and interconnection. The diagonal elements indicate the degree of self-influences for a specific alternative, and the off-diagonal elements represent the competitive influences between alternatives. Let I be the identity matrix, D^* be the distance degree matrix, φ and δ be the related parameters, then the feedback matrix based on Gaussian function under the hesitant fuzzy environment is defined as:

$$S^* = I - \varphi \cdot e^{-\delta \cdot D^{*2}} \tag{3.4}$$

where φ belongs to [0,1], δ belongs to [0.01, 1000]. The parameter φ indicates the competitive influence between alternatives, which should be smaller than one. The parameter δ depicts the discriminable capability. The more similar the alternatives are, the larger the value of δ should be. What's more, the distance degree matrix D^* is calculated by using the hesitant fuzzy weighted Euclidean distance.

Definition 3.3 (Song et al., 2019). Let $P^*(t)$ be the hesitant fuzzy preference information at the time t, S^* be the feedback matrix under the hesitant fuzzy environment, and V^* be the hesitant fuzzy valence vector, then the hesitant fuzzy preference information at the next moment $t + s$ is defined as follows:

$$P^*(t + s) = S^* P^*(t) + V^*(t + s) \tag{3.5}$$

in which s is a little time step. It is obvious that the hesitant fuzzy preference $P^*(t)$ can be calculated by the dynamic process with time. The positive preference value indicates a tendency for a certain alternative, and the largest preference value corresponds to the best alternative.

3.2.3 Group Decision Making Based on the Hesitant Fuzzy Decision Field Theory

When dealing with practical decision-making problems, we usually need to invite a group of experts to evaluate the alternatives from different aspects. To improve the application of the HFDFT method in solving the MAGDM problems, the group decision-making method based on the HFDFT is developed. As for the process-oriented decision theory in the group decision-making process, the key is to integrate preference information of different experts effectively. After integrating the preference information of different experts, the group decision-making method based on the HFDFT can reflect the original decision-making process and the final decision results is also obtained. The general group decision-making process based on the HFDFT is presented in detail as follows (Song et al., 2019):

For a MAGDM problem, we assume that $P = \{p_1, p_2, \ldots, p_k\}$ is a group of experts, and $\zeta = (\zeta_1, \zeta_2, \ldots, \zeta_k)^T\left(\zeta \geq 0, \sum_{j=1}^{k} \zeta_j = 1\right)$ is the corresponding weight vector of the experts. Then, $S = \{Si|i = 1, 2, \cdots, m\}$ is a finite set of alternatives, and $c = \{c_1, c_2, \ldots, c_n\}$ is a set of attributes. The corresponding weight vector of attributes is $\omega = (\omega_1, \omega_2, \ldots, \omega_n)^T$, $\omega \geq 0$, $\sum_{i=1}^{n} \omega_n = 1$. By collecting the hesitant fuzzy information provided by the experts, we can construct the hesitant fuzzy decision matrix $H_l = \left(h_{ij}^{(l)}\right)_{m\times n}$ $(l = 1, 2, \ldots, k)$, where $h_{ij}^{(l)}$ is the evaluation value of the alternative Si on the attribute c_j provided by the l th expert. $h_{ij}^{(l)}$ is the HFE consisting of several possible values.

With the individual hesitant fuzzy decision matrix of each expert, the HFWA operator in Chap. 1 is adopted to integrate the preference information provided by all the experts, denoted as $h_{ij} = HFWA\left(h_{ij}^{(1)}, h_{ij}^{(2)}, \ldots, h_{ij}^{(k)}\right), i = 1, 2, \ldots, m, j = 1, 2, \ldots, n$. The collective hesitant fuzzy decision matrix is $H = \left(h_{ij}\right)_{m\times n}$.

The attribute weights are usually directly provided by the experts. However, in the process of emergency decision making, sometimes the weight vector of attributes is either uncertain or incompletely known. Hence, it is significant to study the MAGDM problems with completely unknown or incompletely known attribute weight information.

According to the relationship and constraints of different attributes, we can obtain the weight information of attributes by a linear programming model (Xu, 2007) based on the score function, which is presented as follows (Song et al., 2019):

Model 1

$$\begin{cases} \max(s_i(\omega)) = \sum_{j=1}^{n} \omega \cdot s_{ij} \\ s.t.\ \ \omega = \Lambda \\ \sum_{j=1}^{n} \omega_j = 1 \end{cases} \tag{3.6}$$

where $s_{ij} = s\left(d_{ij}\right) = \frac{1}{\#h_{ij}} \sum_{\sigma=1}^{\#h_{ij}} \gamma_\sigma$ $(i = 1, 2, \ldots, m; j = 1, 2, \ldots, n)$, Λ represents all possible weight sets that can be determined by the known weight information.

In general, there are several kinds of relationships among the weights of attributes as follows (Xu & Cai, 2012):

$$\begin{cases} \{\omega_i \geq \omega_j\} \\ \{\omega_i - \omega_j \geq \delta_i\} \quad \delta_i > 0 \\ \{\omega_i \geq \delta_i \omega_j\} \quad 0 \leq \delta_i \leq 1 \\ \{\delta_i \leq \omega_i \leq \delta_i + \varepsilon_i\} \ 0 \leq \delta_i < \delta_i + \varepsilon_i \leq 1 \end{cases} \tag{3.7}$$

By solving Model 1, the optimal weight solution corresponding to the alternative Si is obtained: $\omega^{(i)} = \left(\omega_1^{(i)}, \omega_2^{(i)}, \ldots, \omega_n^{(i)}\right)^T$. After obtaining the group hesitant fuzzy decision matrix and the corresponding weight vector of the attributes, we acquire the feedback matrix under hesitant fuzzy environment and the hesitant fuzzy valence vector. Subsequently, the hesitant fuzzy preference information of each alternative is calculated. Based on the preference values of alternatives, we can choose the optimal alternative. The specific implementation process is illustrated in Fig. 3.2 (Song et al., 2019).

The HFDFT method combines the advantages of the HFSs in describing fuzzy information and the advantages of the DFT in dealing with cognitive decision-making problems, which will surely provide more reliable decision-making results. On the one hand, the introduction of HFSs can make up for the deficiency of the DFT in

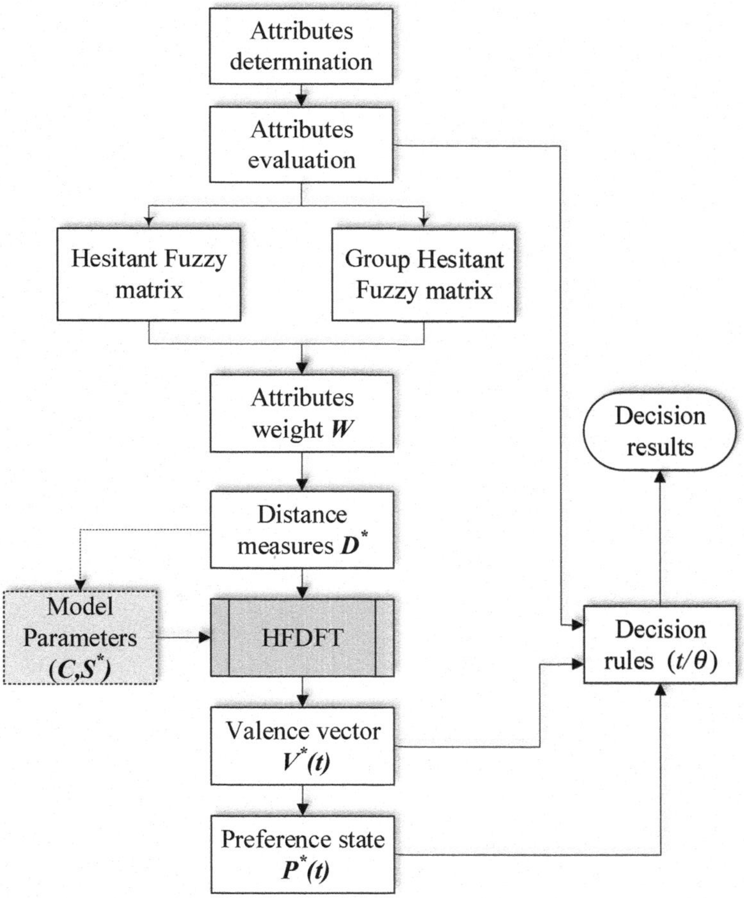

Fig. 3.2 The general implementation procedure for the HFDFT

dealing with group dynamic decision-making problems to some extent. On the other hand, the HFDFT has transformed the traditional hesitant fuzzy MADM from single information integration to a dynamic comparative reasoning process. And the hesitant fuzzy information is fully utilized in the comparison process at every moment. In addition, the HFDFT method also takes into account the influence of the background information of each alternative on the experts' preferences.

3.3 Application to the Route Selection of the Arctic Northwest Passage Based on the HFDFT Method

3.3.1 Case Study

The Arctic is the most sensitive area to global climate change. In recent years, with the accelerated melting of the sea ice in Arctic (Sou & Flato, 2009), the impact of ice barriers on the opening of the Arctic waterways has gradually weakened. The Northwest Passage is a channel connecting the Pacific and the Atlantic oceans through the Arctic Ocean along the northern coast of North America and Canadian Arctic Islands. It is the shortest route that connects Asia and eastern North America. What's more, the Northwest Passage can shorten the transport route prominently, which will bring huge economic benefits. Therefore, the opening of the Northwest Passage is of great importance to the shipping industry. At present, some scholars have studied the navigation environment, navigation management, strategic planning and laws of the Northwest Passage. However, there are few studies on emergency response to marine emergencies in the Arctic region. For the long-term development and utilization of the Arctic region, it is necessary to evaluate risk of the routes of the Arctic Northwest Passage.

The Northwest Passage has been divided into six major routes by the Arctic Council in The Arctic marine shipping assessment 2009 report (Brigham & Mccalla, 2009), and the specific route planning is presented in Table 3.1 (Song et al., 2019).

The identification and determination of indicators is the primary task, which directly affects the rationality of the evaluation process. There are many factors that influence the navigation of ships. In this section, we mainly focus on the marine environment and geographical environment, which are complicated and changeable. From the perspective of the marine environment, the Northwest Passage is located in the cold area of high latitude which is covered with ice and snow most of the year, and most straits are blocked by sea ice all the year round. Meanwhile, the Arctic with low temperature harms ships and crews. Besides, strong winds, thick fog and other bad weather in the Arctic threaten the navigation of ships. Geographically, the Northwest Passage, along with its intricate islands, straits, bays, and icebergs, is considered to be one of the most dangerous waterways in the world. Complex terrain and other uncertainties also increase the safety risks to navigation.

Table 3.1 The routes of the Arctic Northwest passage

Route number	Passing area (from east to west)
S1	Lancaster Sound–Barrow Strait–Viscant Melville Sound–Prince of Wales Strait–Amundsen Gulf
S2	Lancaster Sound–Barrow Strait–Viscant Melville Sound–M'Clure Strait
S3	Lancaster Sound–Barrow Strait–Peel Sound–Larsen Strait–Victoria Strait–Queen Maud Bay–Dease Strait–Coronation G.– Dolphin Channel–Amundsen Gulf
S4	Lancaster Sound–Prince Regent Inlet–The Strait of Peter–Victoria Strait–Queen Maud Bay–Dease Strait–Coronation G.– Dolphin Channel–Amundsen Gulf
S5	Foxe Channel–Foxe Basin–Gulf of Boothia–The Strait of Peter
S6	Lancaster Sound–Barrow Strait–Viscant Melville Sound–McClintock Chan–Victoria Strait–Dease Strait–Coronation G.– Dolphin Channel–Amundsen Gulf

Table 3.2 The index system for evaluating route risk of the Northwest Passage

Object	Attribute
Route risk evaluation	Sea ice c_1
	Visibility c_2
	Strong wind c_3
	Islands and reefs c_4
	Water depth and width c_5

According to the analysis above, we can determine the main factors influencing the route selection of the Northwest Passage in the Arctic. The constructed index system is presented in Table 3.2 (Song et al., 2019).

From the perspective of decision-making analysis, the route selection of the Northwest Passage involves many uncertainties. It is difficult to provide accurate quantitative preference information. In many situations, it depends on the consultation information provided by the experts. Therefore, we make full use of the advantages of the HFS in uncertain information description and use the HFDFT method to evaluate the routes of the Arctic Northwest Passage.

We note that the attribute indicators are divided into two types: positive attribute and negative attribute. The larger the value of the positive attribute is, the safer the route should be. In contrast, the higher the value of the negative attribute is, the more dangerous the route should be. These two types of attributes usually have different measurement. We need to transform them into the dimensionless indicators or the indicators with the same dimension to ensure the consistency and compatibility. To prevent the adverse consequences of different types of attributes, we define the transformation function to normalize the hesitant fuzzy information.

Definition 3.4 (Torra, 2010; Xia & Xu, 2011). To a hesitant fuzzy set $H = \{x, h(x)|x \in X\}$, the normalized HFS is defined as:

$$H(x)^N = f(H(x)) = \begin{cases} H(x) & \textit{for positive attribute} \\ neg(H(x)) & \textit{for negative attribute} \end{cases} \tag{3.8}$$

where $neg(H(x)) = \text{neg}\{x, h(x)|x \in X\} = \{x, 1 - h(x)|x \in X\}$ is the negation operation of $H(x)$.

For convenience, we assume that all the HFSs discussed in the following sections have been normalized. The hesitant fuzzy decision matrix consisting of normalized HFSs is denoted as normalized hesitant fuzzy decision matrix.

We denote the set of the attribute indicators as $c = \{c_j|j = 1, 2, \ldots, n\}$ and the set of the routes as $S = \{Si|i = 1, 2, \ldots, m\}$. According to the data of sea ice and wind speed (ERA-Interim, 1979), the data of islands and reefs (ETOPO1), the data of water depth and width (ETOPO1) and the data of visibility (ISCCP Cloud Data), four experts are invited to evaluate six major routes of the Arctic Northwest Passage concerning all the indicators. Their assessment values are expressed as HFSs. Then we construct the original hesitant fuzzy decision matrix of each expert $H_l = \left(h_{ij}^{(l)}\right)_{m\times n}$ $(l = 1, 2, 3, 4)$ (see Tables 3.3, 3.4, 3.5 and 3.6). Besides, the attributes in Tables 3.3, 3.4, 3.5 and 3.6 are normalized. The weight vector of the four experts is $\zeta = (0.2, 0.3, 0.3, 0.2)^T$. We integrate the decision matrices of each expert by the

Table 3.3 The hesitant fuzzy decision matrix H_1 of the expert P_1

Routes properties	Sea ice	Visibility	Strong wind	Islands and reefs	Water depth and width
S1	{0.3}	{0.1, 0.2}	{0.2}	{0.3}	{0.4, 0.6}
S2	{0.2, 0.3}	{0.1}	{0.4}	{0.2, 0.4}	{0.8}
S3	{0.5}	{0.2}	{0.4, 0.5}	{0.2}	{0.5, 0.8}
S4	{0.8}	{0.6}	{0.7}	{0.5}	{0.6}
S5	{0.5, 0.6}	{0.8}	{0.5, 0.6}	{0.4}	{0.2}
S6	{0.7}	{0.5}	{0.7}	{0.2}	{0.6}

Table 3.4 The hesitant fuzzy decision matrix H_2 of the expert P_2

Routes properties	Sea ice	Visibility	Strong wind	Islands and reefs	Water depth and width
S1	{0.2}	{0.1}	{0.6}	{0.5}	{0.2}
S2	{0.1}	{0.4, 0.5}	{0.5}	{0.4}	{0.6}
S3	{0.2}	{0.5}	{0.2}	{0.4, 0.6}	{0.3}
S4	{0.6}	{0.8}	{0.4}	{0.6}	{0.4}
S5	{0.7}	{0.4, 0.5}	{0.5}	{0.2, 0.4}	{0.5}
S6	{0.4}	{0.3}	{0.5, 0.6}	{0.3}	{0.2}

Table 3.5 The hesitant fuzzy decision matrix H_3 of the expert P_3

Routes properties	Sea ice	Visibility	Strong wind	Islands and reefs	Water depth and width
S1	{0.4, 0.5}	{0.2}	{0.3}	{0.3}	{0.5}
S2	{0.3}	{0.5}	{0.5}	{0.6}	{0.7}
S3	{0.5}	{0.4, 0.6}	{0.6}	{0.5}	{0.4}
S4	{0.7}	{0.6}	{0.5}	{0.6}	{0.5, 0.6}
S5	{0.8}	{0.3}	{0.7}	{0.4}	{0.3}
S6	{0.5}	{0.4}	{0.6}	{0.4}	{0.6}

Table 3.6 The hesitant fuzzy decision matrix H_4 of the expert P_4

Routes properties	Sea ice	Visibility	Strong wind	Islands and reefs	Water depth and width
S1	{0.6}	{0.5}	{0.3, 0.4}	{0.1}	{0.2}
S2	{0.4}	{0.6}	{0.3}	{0.2}	{0.6}
S3	{0.6}	{0.3}	{0.5}	{0.4}	{0.2}
S4	{0.5, 0.6}	{0.6}	{0.4}	{0.6}	{0.5}
S5	{0.3}	{0.4}	{0.5}	{0.4}	{0.6}
S6	{0.4, 0.5}	{0.5, 0.6}	{0.4}	{0.4, 0.6}	{0.5, 0.6}

HFWA operator and construct the collective hesitant fuzzy decision matrix H (see Table 3.7).

For actual group decision-making problems, one of the most important considerations is the weight vector of the attributes. After discussions and consultations, four

Table 3.7 The collective hesitant fuzzy decision matrix H

Routes properties	Sea ice	Visibility	Strong wind	Islands and reefs	Water depth and width
S1	{0.378, 0.411}	{0.228, 0.246}	{0.392, 0.411}	{0.335}	{0.344, 0.395}
S2	{0.248, 0.268}	{0.432, 0.462}	{0.445}	{0.404, 0.437}	{0.681}
S3	{0.449}	{0.379, 0.451}	{0.442, 0.462}	{0.398, 0.467}	{0.358, 0.466}
S4	{0.665, 0.681}	{0.675}	{0.505}	{0.582}	{0.495, 0.528}
S5	{0.651, 0.667}	{0.496, 0.522}	{0.571, 0.589}	{0.346, 0.4}	{0.419}
S6	{0.505, 0.523}	{0.416, 0.441}	{0.562, 0.59}	{0.334, 0.386}	{0.485, 0.508}

experts reach a consensus for weight information of the attributes, which is depicted by a set of linear inequality as follows:

$$\Delta=\begin{cases} \omega_1 \leq 0.25 \\ 0.1 \leq \omega_2 \leq 0.2 \\ 0.2 \leq \omega_3 \leq 0.3 \\ \omega_5 \leq 0.2 \\ \omega_3 - \omega_2 \geq \omega_4 - \omega_5 \\ \omega_4 \geq \omega_1 \\ \omega_3 - \omega_1 \leq 0.1 \\ 0.1 \leq \omega_4 \leq 0.4 \\ \sum_{i=1}^{n} \omega_i = 1 (i = 1, 2, 3, 4, 5) \end{cases}$$

Therefore, we can calculate the optimal weight vector of the attributes, and the result is $\omega=(0.2113, 0.1801, 0.2315, 0.2618, 0.1153)^T$. Based on the collective hesitant fuzzy decision matrix H, we can obtain that the contrast matrix as:

$$C = \begin{bmatrix} 1 & -0.2 & -0.2 & -0.2 & -0.2 & -0.2 \\ -0.2 & 1 & -0.2 & -0.2 & -0.2 & -0.2 \\ -0.2 & -0.2 & 1 & -0.2 & -0.2 & -0.2 \\ -0.2 & -0.2 & -0.2 & 1 & -0.2 & -0.2 \\ -0.2 & -0.2 & -0.2 & -0.2 & 1 & -0.2 \\ -0.2 & -0.2 & -0.2 & -0.2 & -0.2 & 1 \end{bmatrix}$$

The parameters of the feedback matrix under hesitant fuzzy environment are set to $\varphi=0.15$ and $\delta=20$, then the feedback matrix S^* is obtained as:

$$S^* = \begin{bmatrix} 0.75 & -0.03 & -0.03 & -0.01 & -0.02 & -0.02 \\ -0.03 & 0.75 & -0.02 & -0.01 & -0.01 & -0.01 \\ -0.03 & -0.02 & 0.75 & -0.02 & -0.015 & -0.033 \\ -0.01 & -0.01 & -0.02 & 0.75 & -0.04 & -0.02 \\ -0.02 & -0.01 & -0.015 & -0.04 & 0.75 & -0.038 \\ -0.02 & -0.01 & -0.033 & -0.02 & -0.038 & 0.75 \end{bmatrix}$$

After 1000 times' simulations, we obtain the preferences of six alternative routes for the Northwest Passage in the Arctic, and the prediction results are illustrated in Fig. 3.3.

It is obvious that the route **S4** is the best alternative, which is consistent with The Arctic marine shipping assessment 2009 report published by the Arctic Council. The preference probabilities of different alternative routes vary with time, and the preference of route **S4** is more obvious over time. We can find that the proposed HFDFT method can not only depict the hesitant information and experts' preferences more

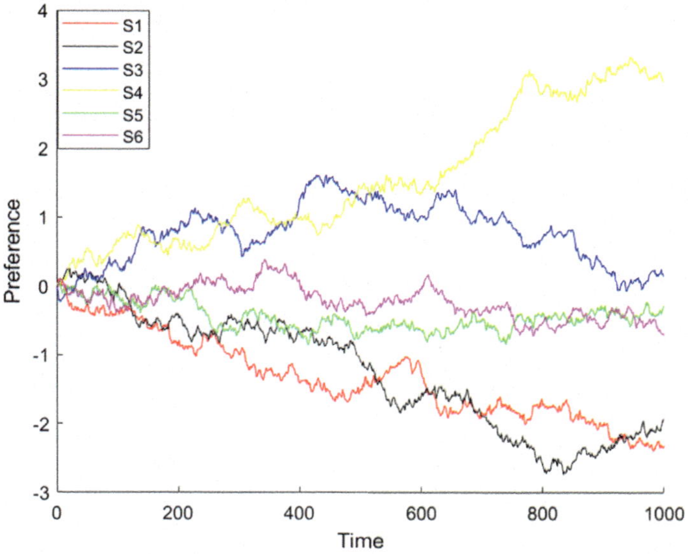

Fig. 3.3 The hesitant fuzzy decision field theory predictions for the six alternative routes

clearly, but also describe the background information of alternatives and illustrate the original decision-making process. It is a process-oriented dynamic decision-making method, which is closer to the actual decision-making circumstance and can provide the decision-making results accurately.

3.3.2 Comparisons with the Existing Methods for HFSs

To illustrate the advantages and effectiveness of the proposed HFDFT method, we compare it with two existing methods under the hesitant fuzzy environment. The one is to compare the routes by the scores of collective hesitant fuzzy information, the other one is to compare the routes by the correlation coefficients between each route and the ideal alternative. For comparing effectively and understanding conveniently, in this section we adopt the collective hesitant fuzzy decision matrix H in Table 3.7 and the corresponding weight vector $\omega=(0.2113, 0.1801, 0.2315, 0.2618, 0.1153)^T$ as the evaluation information.

First, we obtain the overall preferences of the collective hesitant fuzzy information for the six routes through the HFWA operator (see Table 3.8). After aggregating the evaluation information expressed as HFEs in Table 3.8, the scores of each route are calculated and presented in Table 3.9. It can be seen that the route **S4** is the best alternative.

To compare all the routes by the correlation coefficients, we first review some basic concepts about the novel correlation coefficient between HFSs (Liao et al., 2015). The

Table 3.8 The preferences of the collective hesitant fuzzy information for the routes by HFWA operator

Routes	Overall preference values
S1	{0.3413, 0.3441, 0.3462, 0.3475, 0.3489, 0.3489, 0.3502, 0.3516,0.3522, 0.3536, 0.3549, 0.355, 0.3564, 0.3577, 0.3596, 0.3624}
S2	{0.432, 0.4352, 0.4375, 0.4404, 0.4407, 0.4436, 0.4458, 0.449}
S3	{0.4118, 0.4168, 0.4242, 0.4248, 0.429, 0.4296, 0.4303, 0.4351, 0.4368, 0.4416, 0.4423, 0.4428, 0.447, 0.4475, 0.4545, 0.4591}
S4	{0.5948, 0.598, 0.599, 0.6021}
S5	{0.5111, 0.5157, 0.5159, 0.5159, 0.5205, 0.5205, 0.5207, 0.522, 0.5252, 0.5265, 0.5267, 0.5267, 0.5312, 0.5312, 0.5314, 0.5358}
S6	{0.4618, 0.4646, 0.466, 0.466, 0.4688, 0.4688, 0.4699, 0.4702, 0.4727, 0.473, 0.4731, 0.4741, 0.4741, 0.4759, 0.4768, 0.4769, 0.4772, 0.4772, 0.4782, 0.48, 0.48, 0.481, 0.4811, 0.4813, 0.4838, 0.4841, 0.4852, 0.4852, 0.4879, 0.4879, 0.4892, 0.4919}

Table 3.9 The scores of the collective hesitant fuzzy information for the six routes

Routes	S1	S2	S3	S4	S5	S6
Scores	0.3519	0.4405	0.4358	0.5985	0.5236	0.477

novel correlation coefficient doesn't add any value so that it can reserve the original information to the greatest extent. Moreover, the values of the novel correlation matrix vary from negative values to positive ones, and the novel correlation coefficient can depict the relationship between different alternatives better.

Definition 3.5 (Liao et al., 2015). Let $H = \{x_i, h(x_i)|x_i \in X, i = 1, 2, \ldots, n\}$ and $M = \{x_i, m(x_i)|x_i \in X, i = 1, 2, \ldots, n\}$ be two HFSs on the reference set X, and $\omega = (\omega_1, \omega_2, \ldots, \omega_n)^T$ be the corresponding weight vector of $x_i \in X (i = 1, 2, \ldots, n)$ with $\omega_i \in [0, 1]$, $i = 1, 2, \ldots, n$ and $\sum_{i=1}^{n} \omega_i = 1$. The weighted correlation coefficient between the HFSs H and M is defined as:

$$\rho_{\omega HFS}(H, M) = \sum\nolimits_{k=1}^{n} \left(\omega_i \overline{h}(x_i) - \overline{H}_{\omega}\right) \cdot \left(\omega_i \overline{m}(x_i) - \overline{M}_{\omega}\right) \quad (3.9)$$

where $\overline{h}(x_i) = \frac{1}{l_{Hi}} \sum_{j=1}^{l_{Hi}} \gamma_{Hij}$, $\overline{m}(x_i) = \frac{1}{l_{Mi}} \sum_{j=1}^{l_{Mi}} \gamma_{Mij}$, $\overline{H}_{\omega} = \sum_{i=1}^{n} \omega_i \overline{h}(x_i)$, $\overline{M}_{\omega} = \sum_{i=1}^{n} \omega_i \overline{m}(x_i)$.

The ideal route is denoted as RT^* with the evaluation information $\{(1)(1), (1), (1), (1)\}$. Then, we can calculate the weighted correlation coefficients between the ideal route RT^* and each route. The calculation results are shown in Table 3.10. We can see that the route **S4** is the best one.

By comparing the proposed HFDFT method with the two existing methods, we note that the best route derived by using our method is the same as that derived by the traditional methods. The proposed method can not only depict the uncertain

Table 3.10 The weighted correlation coefficient between the ideal route and the six alternative routes

$\rho_{\omega HFS}(RT^*, S1)$	$\rho_{\omega HFS}(RT^*, S2)$	$\rho_{\omega HFS}(RT^*, S3)$	$\rho_{\omega HFS}(RT^*, S4)$	$\rho_{\omega HFS}(RT^*, S5)$	$\rho_{\omega HFS}(RT^*, S6)$
1.1226	1.3677	1.3978	1.9018	1.6416	1.5109

information more delicately, but also display the dynamic decision-making process. However, the traditional methods only depend on the final score function values and the correlation coefficient values. Besides, the proposed method can make use of the original data and the experts' evaluation information effectively, and it depicts the process of comparison between different routes clearly. The two traditional methods are result-oriented static decision-making methods, and they only compare different alternatives by the final integrated information. The results derived by the two traditional methods are too absolute and inconsistent with reality. Therefore, the HFDFT method can simulate the process of the experts' consideration and comparison through the contrast matrix and the feedback matrix. The results derived by our method, containing much more probabilistic information and varying with time, are more logical and reasonable.

The HFDFT method conducts a comprehensive comparative analysis of different alternatives by the input decision-making matrix and various parameters. After that, it obtains and accumulates the dynamic preference values with decision-making time of different alternatives, which avoids the shortcomings of the existing methods that just depend on the information integration by integration operators at a certain time. By analyzing the principles of the existing methods, we can find that they usually ignore the longitudinal dynamic comparisons between alternatives concerning different attributes, and it will result in the local optimal decision-making results easily. The process-oriented dynamic DFT method can make up for this deficiency. Therefore, the HFDFT method, which combines the HFSs and the DFT, has more advantages in dealing with the MAGDM problems.

What's more, we need to consider the choice of decision rules for the HFDFT method. If the decision rule is the decision time, then we should stop to analyze and calculate when the accumulation time of the decision process reaches the specified time threshold. At this time, the alternative with the largest preference values is chosen as the optimal one. At present, there is no general standard and in-depth theoretical research on the choice of threshold in practical applications. Actually, the threshold usually depends on the empirical information of the experts, which may result in some contingency and randomness. To improve the practicality of the HFDFT method, we set a larger time threshold for less time-sensitive MCDM problems. Although this may spend some computation time, it can ensure that the HFDFT method provides more accurate and reliable decision-making results.

3.4 Remarks

The traditional DFT method is a process-oriented dynamic decision-making method, which can simulate the motivational process and the cognitive process of uncertain decision making. Besides, the DFT method can accurately predict the selection probability and the relationship between preference intensity and time, which has been widely applied in decision-making problems. However, it is never easy for the experts in a group to reach a certain consensus of the membership degree with sound reliability when evaluating the alternatives. In order to avoid the loss of information, in this chapter, we introduce the HFS theory, with the membership degree consisting of several possible values, which can depict the uncertain knowledge and hesitant fuzzy preferences more comprehensively and accurately. After that, we introduce a new dynamic decision-making method named as hesitant fuzzy decision field theory (HFDFT). We also provide the hesitant fuzzy momentary preference function and other parameters in the HFDFT. Then, the group decision-making method based on the HFDFT is presented in this chapter. A specific implementation process for the HFDFT method to deal with actual evaluation problems is illustrated. The HFDFT can not only depict the experts' preferences more delicately, but also describe the background information of alternatives at the same time. It illustrates the original decision-making process better and is more reasonable than traditional hesitant fuzzy decision-making methods. Besides, the presented HFDFT method can make full use of the evaluation information and depict the process of comparison between different alternatives clearly. Since it can simulate the process of experts' consideration and comparison by the contrast matrix and feedback matrix, it is obvious that the results are more logical, which contain more probabilistic information and vary with time. Finally, the HFDFT method is applied to the route selection problem of Arctic Northwest Passage, which demonstrates the accuracy and rationality of our method in dealing with practical MAGDM problems. Besides, two traditional methods based on the score function and the correlation coefficient of the hesitant fuzzy information are introduced for comparisons to further illustrate the advantages of HFDFT method.

References

Brigham, L., Mccalla, R., et al. (2009). *Arctic marine shipping assessment 2009 report*. Cambridge University Press.

Busemeyer, J. R., & Diederich, A. (2002). Survey of decision field theory. *Mathematical Social Sciences, 43*, 345–370.

Busemeyer, J. R., & Pleskac, T. J. (2009). Theoretical tools for understanding and aiding dynamic decision making. *Journal of Mathematical Psychology, 53*, 126–138.

Busemeyer, J. R., & Townsend, J. T. (1993). Decision field theory: A dynamic-cognitive approach to decision making in an uncertain environment. *Psychological Review, 100*, 432–459.

Chen, S. J., & Hwang, C. L. (1992). Multiple attribute decision making—An overview. In *Fuzzy multiple attribute decision making: Methods and applications*. Springer.

Chen, N., Xu, Z. S., & Xia, M. M. (2015). The ELECTRE I multi-criteria decision making method based on hesitant fuzzy sets. *International Journal of Information Technology and Decision Making, 14*, 621–657.

Gonzalez, C., Lerch, J. F., & Lebiere, C. (2010). Instance-based learning in dynamic decision making. *Cognitive Science, 27*, 591–635.

Hao, Z. N., & Xu, Z. S. (2017). Novel intuitionistic fuzzy decision making models in the framework of decision field theory. *Information Fusion, 33*, 57–70.

Jamieson, D. G., & Petrusic, W. M. (1977). Preference and the time to choose. *Organizational Behavior and Human Performance, 19*(1), 56–67.

Liao, H. C., Xu, Z. S., & Zeng, X. J. (2015). Novel correlation coefficients between hesitant fuzzy sets and their application in decision making. *Knowledge-Based Systems, 82*, 115–127.

Payne, J. W., Bettman, J. R., & Johnson, E. J. (1988). Adaptive strategy selection in decision. *Journal of Experimental Psychology Learning Memory and Cognition, 14*, 534–552.

Satty, T. L. (2005). Making and validating complex decisions with the AHP/ANP. *Journal of Systems Science and Systems Engineering, 14*, 1–36.

Scheibehenne, B., Rieskamp, J., & Wagenmakers, E. J. (2013). Testing adaptive toolbox models: A Bayesian hierarchical approach. *Psychological Review, 120*(1), 39–64.

Song, C. Y., Zhang, Y. X., Xu, Z. S., et al. (2019). Route selection of the Arctic Northwest Passage based on hesitant fuzzy decision field theory. *IEEE Access, 7*, 19979–19989.

Sou, T., & Flato, G. (2009). Sea ice in the Canadian Arctic Archipelago: Modeling the past (1950–2004) and the future (2041–60). *Journal of Climate, 22*, 2181–2198.

The European Center for Medium-Range Weather Forecasts (ECMEF). *ERA-Interim* (Jan 1979–present). http://apps.ecmwf.int/datasets/

The National Geophysical Data Center (NGDC). ETOPO1. http://maps.ngdc.noaa.gov/viewers/wcs-client/

The National Oceanic and Atmospheric Administration (NOAA). *ISCCP Cloud Data*. https://www.ncdc.noaa.gov/data-access/satellite-data/satellite-data-access-datasets

Toda, M. (2010). The design of a fungus eater: A model of human behavior in an unsophisticated environment. *Systems Research and Behavioral Science, 7*, 164–183.

Torra, V. (2010). Hesitant fuzzy sets. *International Journal of Intelligent Systems, 25*, 529–539.

Wei, G. W. (2012). Hesitant fuzzy prioritized operators and their application to multiple attribute decision making. *Knowledge-Based Systems, 31*, 176–182.

Xia, M. M., & Xu, Z. S. (2011). Hesitant fuzzy information aggregation in decision making. *International Journal of Approximate Reasoning, 52*, 395–407.

Xu, Z. S. (2007). Multi-person multi-attribute decision making models under intuitionistic fuzzy environment. *Fuzzy Optimization and Decision Making, 6*, 221–236.

Xu, Z. S., & Cai, X. Q. (2012). *Intuitionistic fuzzy information aggregation*. Springer.

Yu, D. J., Wu, Y. Y., & Zhou, W. (2011). Multi-criteria decision making based on Choquet integral under hesitant fuzzy environment. *Journal of Computational Information Systems, 7*, 4506–4513.

Yu, D. J., Wu, Y. Y., & Zhou, W. (2012). Generalized hesitant fuzzy Bonferroni mean and its application in multi-criteria group decision making. *Journal of Information and Computational Science, 9*, 267–274.

Chapter 4
Uncertain Reasoning Algorithm Under the Hesitant Fuzzy Environment

The Bayesian Network (BN) is one of the most effective theoretical models in the fields of uncertain reasoning. With the nonlinear evolution of events and the complexity of practical problems, there will be massive data with uncertainty, bringing more challenges to the application of the BN. To deal with different kinds of uncertain knowledge and hesitancy in the uncertain nreasoning process, this chapter introduces the concept of Dynamic Hesitant Fuzzy Bayesian Network (DHFBN) to solve uncertain reasoning problems under the hesitant fuzzy environment. It combines the advantages of hesitant fuzzy sets (HFSs) in depicting information and Bayesian Network (BN) in uncertain reasoning. Then, an improved Particle Swarm Optimization (PSO) algorithm and the Expectation–Maximization (EM) algorithm are adopted for the structure learning and parameters learning of DHFBN respectively. Based on the learned optimal DHFBN, a dynamic reasoning and prediction method is developed. Furthermore, a case about the optimal port investment decision making problem of "Twenty-First-Century Maritime Silk Road" is presented to illustrate the application of the proposed method. Finally, we also conduct a comparative experiment to testify the validity and advantages of the method in detail.

4.1 Motivations and Background

The Twenty-First-Century Maritime Silk Road (Silk Road for short) is a new trade initiative (Len, 2015). It helps strengthen communication and promote economic cooperation and the peaceful development of the global economy (Zhang, 2016). The ocean is the natural link of economy, trade and cultural exchanges between countries. With the changes in global politics and trade, it is of great importance to construct the Silk Road to guarantee free trade. It enhances the exchanges between neighboring countries and regions, and connects ASEAN, South Asia, West Asia, North Africa and Europe. Aiming to develop the economic and trade integration of

C. Song and Z. Xu, *Techniques of Decision Making, Uncertain Reasoning and Regression Analysis Under the Hesitant Fuzzy Environment and Their Applications*, Uncertainty and Operations Research, https://doi.org/10.1007/978-981-16-5800-6_4

the Asia, Europe and Africa, the Silk Road develops strategic cooperative economic zones oriented to the South China Sea, the Pacific and the Indian Ocean (Karim, 2015).

Most of the ports along the Silk Road are important international trade transport nodes. The investment and construction of ports along the Silk Road is one of the most important issues (Cheng & Liang, 2007). However, influenced by different levels of economic development, some countries along the Silk Road have limited financial resources and cannot provide sovereign guarantees. Besides, there are still other problems, such as imperfect laws and regulations, inefficient governments, imperfect credit systems and large fluctuation of exchange rates. These problems will lead to higher capital costs, higher credit risks and the lower levels of cross-border financial cooperation (Chen & Han, 2016). The political stability and social security of the invested countries also attract much attention. In addition, the investment cycle of ports is very long and the amount of investment is huge, which requires an effective risk assessment. There is a great demand for the investment of port, but also facing many risks at the same time (Chen & Yang, 2017).

Since the optimal investment port decision making problem is complicated and influenced by many factors with unknown mechanism, many scholars have made efforts to study the investment of ports. Musso et al. (2006) studied the profitability and economic impact of port investment. He also pointed out the importance of port investment in modern economy. Zhang (2018) made an in-depth research of the climate and marine environment of the Silk Road. Stephane et al. (2011) assessed impacts of climate change, sea level rise and storm surge risk in ports. Besides, some scholars have tried to apply various methods to port investment from different perspectives, such as fuzzy integer programming model (Allahviranloo and Afandizadeh, 2008), fuzzy set theory and evidential reasoning approach (Mokhtari et al., 2012) and Multiple Criteria Decision Making (MCDM) methods (Chou, 2007; Fei & Deng, 2019). These existing methods consider different attributes of port investment. However, in real life problems, the evaluation information may be massive hesitant and uncertain information in complicated environment. The above methods fail to achieve dynamic risk evaluation results with time. What's more, static evaluation results are inconsistent with the facts.

The risk is a quantitative measure of the adverse effects that may occur during the development of an event (Sharpe, 2012). The port investment is affected by many factors, including the natural environment (Liu et al., 2017a), politics, religion, and so on. This may bring great uncertainties to the security of port investment along the Silk Road (Qiao et al., 2019). These risk factors of port investment are dynamically changing. In addition, there is no clear analytical mode to depict the interaction between various risk factors. The mechanism is also unclear. To evaluate the investment risk, it is of great importance to deal with different kinds of uncertain information comprehensively and systematically. The uncertain information comes from different sources in various forms. Besides, it is necessary to predict changes of the investment risk in time. By the scientific and quantitative risk assessment, we can conduct risk warming and management. The Bayesian Network (BN) is an effective uncertain reasoning method. Since Pearl (1988) proposed the BN based on the Bayesian Formula, many scholars have thoroughly studied it and found excellent properties of the BN. And it has been applied in different fields, such as information prediction (Borsuk et al., 2004; Bradford et al, 2006), reasoning (Cheng and Druzdzel, 2011), uncertainty analysis (Hosack et al., 2008) and classification (Friedman, 1997; Bielza & Li, 2011). However, a single exact value cannot reflect the uncertainty of evaluation, and the simple weighted averaging will lose the hesitant information of experts. Besides, the traditional BN cannot deal with massive uncertain data. Therefore, in this chapter, we can combine the great potential of the hesitant fuzzy set (HFS) (Torra, 2010; Torra & Narukawa, 2009; Xia & Xu, 2011) in depicting massive uncertain knowledge and advantages of BN in uncertain reasoning. Considering the uncertain information of risk factors varies with time in real life, Song et al., (2019) introduced the concept of Dynamic Hesitant Fuzzy Bayesian Network (DHFBN) to manage port investment problems under the hesitant fuzzy environment. First, based on the definition of hesitant fuzzy event (HF-event) and the corresponding probability, the concept of Hesitant Fuzzy Bayesian Network (HFBN) is defined. Furthermore, to depict the correlation of continuous time, they combined the HFBN with time dimension and develop the DHFBN. It is a dynamic probabilistic reasoning model, which is capable of processing temporal information with uncertainties. The DHFBN not only inherits the advantages of HFS and BN, but also considers the influence of time factor. Then the improved PSO algorithm (Song et al., 2019) and the improved Expectation–Maximization (EM) algorithm can be adopted to manage structure learning problems and parameter learning problems respectively under the hesitant fuzzy environment. At last, we can conduct reasoning and prediction by DHFBN with the learned optimal structure and parameters. The advantages of the DHFBN are summarized as follows (Song et al., 2019):

(1) The DHFBN makes full use of massive uncertain information with more flexibility, and it remains the original information better.
(2) The DHFBN obtains a global optimal structure and parameters with the higher efficiency and accuracy, and it depicts the evolution of massive hesitant fuzzy variables in time series better.
(3) The DHFBN is an effective model to solve the complicated risk assessment problems under the hesitant fuzzy environment, and it obtains the dynamic prediction results, which are more consistent with reality.

4.2 Preliminaries

Definition 4.1 (Liao et al., 2015). Let $M = \{\langle x, m(x_i)\rangle | x_i \in X\}$ be a HFS on the reference set X with $m(x_i) = \{\gamma_{ik} | k = 1, 2, \ldots, l_i\}$, then the means of $m(x_i)$ and M are:

$$\overline{m}(x_i) = \frac{1}{l_i} \sum_{k=1}^{l_i} \gamma_{ik} \tag{4.1}$$

$$\overline{M} = \{\langle x, \overline{m}(x_i)\rangle | x_i \in X\} \tag{4.2}$$

where l_i denotes the number of elements in $m(x_i)$, $i = 1, 2, \ldots, n$.

The Bayesian Network (BN) is a widely used theoretical model in the field of uncertain knowledge representation and reasoning (Jensen, 1997). It combines the graph theory and the probability theory. A BN is a directed acyclic graph (DAG) consisting of random variables and the directed links between random variables. The DAG depicts conditional dependencies between attributes.

The core of BN is the Bayesian formula, which is defined as follows (Jensen, 1997):

$$P(A_i|B) = \frac{P(B|A_i)P(A_i)}{\sum_{i=1}^{n} P(B|A_i)P(A_i)} \tag{4.3}$$

where $P(A_i) > 0, A_iA_j = \emptyset, \cup_{i=1}^{n} A_i = \Omega, i \neq j, i = 1, 2, \ldots, n$.

4.3 Dynamic Hesitant Fuzzy Bayesian Network

The Bayesian Network (BN) is one of the most effective theoretical models in risk assessment and uncertain decision making, which combines the advantages of probability theory and graph theory. However, the classical BN can't deal with cognitive uncertain information well, such as hesitant fuzzy information. Considering the uncertainty of decision-making environment and the limitations of empirical knowledge, it is usually difficult to reach a certain consensus with sound reliability. The HFS is an effective tool to depict the uncertain knowledge comprehensively and avoid the loss of information with the membership degree consisting of several possible values. In order to introduce the HFS into BN, this section gives the definitions of hesitant fuzzy event (HF-event) and probability of HF-event. Based on which, the concept of Hesitant Fuzzy Bayesian Network (HFBN) is also proposed. After that, this section introduces the concept of DHFBN, which combines the time dimension with HFBN. It integrates the causality with uncertain information between different times, and conducts dynamic analysis and prediction under the hesitant fuzzy environment.

4.3.1 Hesitant Fuzzy Event

Suppose that HFEs have the same length and they are arranged in ascending order according to their values. If two HFEs do not have the same length, then we add the minimum value of the shorter HFE based on the pessimistic principle (Chen et al., 2013) till they have the same length. Inspired by probabilities of the fuzzy event

(Zadeh, 1968) and the intuitionistic fuzzy event (IF-event) (Hao et al., 2018), this section also provides the definition of the hesitant fuzzy event (HF-event) and its probability as follows:

Definition 4.2. Let (X, S, P) be a probability space, in which S is the σ-field of Borel sets in X and P is a probability measure over X, then a HF-event in X is a HFE M in X whose membership function $m(x)$ is Borel measurable. And probability of HF-event M is defined as $P(M) = \bigcup_{j=1}^{l_M} \left\{ \sum_{\gamma \in X} P(\gamma) \cdot \gamma_M^j(x) \right\}$, where $P(\gamma)$ is the corresponding probability of the basic event γ_M, $\gamma_M^j(x)$ is the jth element in $h_M(x)$ and $P_j(M) = \sum_{\gamma \in X} P(\gamma) \cdot \gamma_M^j(x)$.

Remark 1. If a HF-event degenerates into a fuzzy event, then the probability of HF-event also degenerates into the probability of a fuzzy event.

Definition 4.3 (Song et al., 2019)**.** Let M and N be two HF-events over X, and $P_j(N) > 0 (j = 1, 2, \ldots, l)$, then the conditional probabilities of M under N is defined as:

$$P(M|N) = \frac{P(M \cap N)}{P(N)} = \left\{ P_j(M|N), j = 1, 2, \ldots, l \right\} \tag{4.4}$$

where $P_j(M|N) = \frac{P_j(M \cap N)}{P_j(N)}$.

Definition 4.4 (Song et al., 2019)**.** Let M and N be two HF-events over X. If $P(M \cap N) = P(M) \cdot P(N)$, then M and N are called independent. Besides, it is obvious that $P(M|N) = P(M)$ if the HF-events M and N are independent.

Theorem 1 (Song et al., 2019)**.** Suppose that $M_i (i = 1, 2, \ldots)$ are different HF-events over X. If $M_i \cap M_j = \emptyset$ $(i \neq j)$, then $P\left(\cup_{i=1}^{\infty} M_i\right) = \sum_{i=1}^{\infty} P(M_i)$.

Proof When $i \neq j$, then $M_i \cap M_j = \emptyset$, $\forall j \in \{1, 2, \ldots, l\}$, then $\underset{i=1}{\overset{\infty}{\vee}} \gamma_{M_i}^j = \sum_{i=1}^{\infty} \gamma_{M_i}^j$. So based on Definition 4.2, it is obvious that:

$$\begin{aligned} P\left(\bigcup_{i=1}^{\infty} M_i\right) &= \bigcup_{j=1}^{l} \left\{ \sum_{\gamma \in X} P(\gamma) \cdot \bigvee_{i=1}^{\infty} \gamma_{M_i}^j \right\} = \bigcup_{j=1}^{l} \left\{ \sum_{\gamma \in X} P(\gamma) \cdot \sum_{i=1}^{\infty} \gamma_{M_i}^j \right\} \\ &= \bigcup_{j=1}^{l} \left\{ \sum_{i=1}^{\infty} \sum_{\gamma \in X} P(\gamma) \cdot \gamma_{M_i}^j \right\} = \bigcup_{j=1}^{l} \left\{ \sum_{i=1}^{\infty} P_j(M_i) \right\} = \sum_{i=1}^{\infty} P(M_i) \end{aligned}$$

Theorem 2 (Song et al., 2019)**.** Suppose that $M_i (i = 1, 2, \ldots)$ are different HF-events over X and $P_j\left(\cap_{i=1}^{n} M_i\right) > 0 (j = 1, 2, \ldots, l)$, then:

$$P\left(\bigcap_{i=1}^{n} M_i\right) = P(M_1) \cdot P(M_2|M_1) \cdot \ldots \cdot P(M_n|M_1 \cap \ldots \cap M_{n-1})$$

Proof If $n = 2$, then according to Definition 4.3, $P(M_1 \cap M_2) = P(M_1) \cdot P(M_2|M_1)$. Suppose that the above equation holds when $n = m$, then $P\left(\cap_{i=1}^{m} M_i\right) = P(M_1) \cdot P(M_2|M_1) \cdot \ldots \cdot P(M_m|M_1 \cap \ldots \cap M_{m-1})$. So when $n = m + 1$, then

$$P\left(\bigcap_{i=1}^{m+1} M_i\right) = P\left(M_{m+1}\middle|\bigcap_{i=1}^{m} M_i\right) \cdot P\left(\bigcap_{i=1}^{m} M_i\right)$$
$$= P(M_1) \cdot P(M_2|M_1) \cdot \ldots \cdot P(M_{m+1}|M_1 \cap \ldots \cap M_m).$$

Thus, for every number n, $P\left(\bigcap_{i=1}^{n} M_i\right) = P(M_1) \cdot P(M_2|M_1) \cdot \ldots \cdot P(M_n|M_1 \cap \ldots \cap M_{n-1})$.

Theorem 3 (Song et al., 2019). Suppose that $M_i (i = 1, 2, \ldots)$ are different HF-events over X, then $M_i \cap M_j = \emptyset$ if $i \neq j$. $\forall j \in \{1, 2, \ldots, l\}$, $\forall i \in \{1, 2, \ldots\}$, $P_j(M_i) > 0$, then $\forall M \leq \cup_{i=1}^{\infty} M_i$. So $P(M) = \sum_{i=1}^{\infty} P(M_i) \cdot P(M|M_i)$.

Proof When $i \neq j$, $M_i \cap M_j = \emptyset$. Hence $(M_i \cap M) \cap \left(M_j \cap M\right) = \emptyset$. Since $M \leq \cup_{i=1}^{\infty} M_i$, then we have $M = M \cap \left(\cup_{i=1}^{\infty} M_i\right)$. Thus based on Theorem 1, it is easy to obtain that:

$$P(M) = P\left(M \cap \left(\bigcup_{i=1}^{\infty} M_i\right)\right) = P\left(\bigcup_{i=1}^{\infty} (M \cap M_i)\right)$$
$$= \sum_{i=1}^{\infty} P(M \cap M_i) = \sum_{i=1}^{\infty} P(M|M_i) \cdot P(M_i).$$

Theorem 4 (Song et al., 2019). Suppose that $M_i (i = 1, 2, \ldots)$ are different HF-events over X. If $i \neq j$, then $M_i \cap M_j = \emptyset$. And $\forall j \in \{1, 2, \ldots, l\}$, $\forall i \in \{1, 2, \ldots\}$,$P_j(M_i) > 0$. $\forall M \leq \cup_{i=1}^{\infty} M_i$ and $P_j(M_i) > 0 (j = 1, 2, \ldots, l)$, then

$$P(M_i|M) = \frac{P(M|M_i) \cdot P(M_i)}{\sum_{k=1}^{\infty} P(M|M_k) \cdot P(M_k)}$$

Proof According to Theorems 2 and 3, we have $P(M_i|M) = \frac{P(M_i \cap M)}{P(M)} = \frac{P(M_i) \cdot P(M|M_i)}{P(M)}$ and $P(M) = \sum_{k=1}^{\infty} P(M_k) \cdot P(M|M_k)$, so $P(M_i|M) = \frac{P(M|M_i) \cdot P(M_i)}{\sum_{k=1}^{\infty} P(M|M_k) \cdot P(M_k)}$.

4.3.2 *Hesitant Fuzzy Bayesian Network*

Similar to the traditional BN, this section proposes the concept of the Hesitant Fuzzy Bayesian Network (HFBN) based on the HF-event and the corresponding probability.

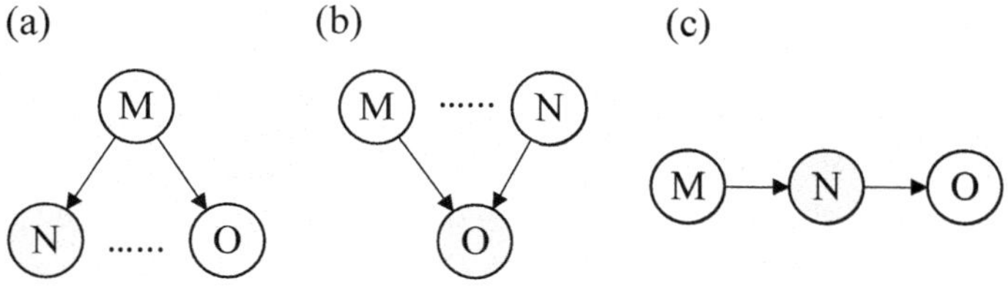

Fig. 4.1 Three kinds of connections in the HFBN

Definition 4.5 (Song et al., 2019). Let V be a set consisting of finite nodes, every node denotes a hesitant fuzzy random variable and is corrected by an arc, then a directed acyclic graph (DAG) is constructed by the set V of HF-events and the corresponding directed links, which is named as the Hesitant Fuzzy Bayesian Network (HFBN).The nodes denote different HF-events, which are linked by directed arcs. The direction of the arcs represents the dependence between two hesitant fuzzy variables. Besides, the probabilities of the HF-events are presented in the form of HFSs.

Theorem 5 (Song et al., 2019). In the HFBN, if the probability in every node take the form of HFEs, then the final deduced probabilities are also in the form of HFEs.

Proof There are three kinds of connections in the BN: (a) diverging connections; (b) converging connections; (c) serial connections (Fig. 4.1).

(a) Diverging connections:

Suppose that M is the parent node, N and O are its children nodes. Let $P\big(M_j\big) = P\big(e_{M_j}\big)$ be the probability of M at a certain status e_{M_j} $(j = 1, 2, \cdots, n)$. Then the probability of N at a certain status e_N can be calculated by:

$$\begin{aligned} P(e_N) &= P(M) \cdot P(N|M\,) = P(N \cap M) \\ &= \sum_{i=1}^{n} P(N \cap M_i) = \sum_{i=1}^{n} P(N|M_i\,) \cdot P(M_i) \end{aligned}$$

Similarly, it is easy to prove that the final calculation result $P(e_N)$ also takes the form of HFE.

(b) Converging connections:

Suppose that M and N are the parent nodes, O is their child node. The probability of the child node O at a certain statue e_O can be calculated by:

$$P(e_O) = \sum_{i=1}^{n} (P(O|M\,) \cdot P(M), \ldots, P(O|N\,) \cdot P(N)) \quad (4.5)$$

It is obvious that the probability of the child node O at a certain statue e_O and all other status takes the form of HFE.

(iii) Serial connections:

Suppose that e^{child} and e^{parent} are the evidences from the children nodes and the parent nodes respectively, M is the parent node of N, N is the parent node of O. Then the probability of node N at a certain statue e_N depends on the parent nodes e^{parent} and children nodes e^{child} (Duda et al., 2014), which could be depicted as:

$$P(e_N) \propto P\left(e^{child}\left|e_N\right.\right) \cdot P\left(e_N\left|e^{parent}\right.\right) \tag{4.6}$$

where $P\left(e^{child}\left|e_N\right.\right) = P\left(e_{O_1}, e_{O_2}, \cdots, e_{O_{|O|}}\left|e_N\right.\right) = P\left(e_{O_1}\left|e_N\right.\right) \cdot P\left(e_{O_2}\left|e_N\right.\right) \cdot \ldots \cdot P\left(e_{O_{|O|}}\left|e_M\right.\right)$ and $P\left(e_N\left|e^{parent}\right.\right) = \sum_{i=1}^{m} P\left(e_N\left|e_{M_i}\right.\right)$ respectively. Then

$$P(e_N) \propto \left(P\left(e_{O_1}\left|e_N\right.\right) \cdot P\left(e_{O_2}\left|e_N\right.\right) \cdot \ldots \cdot P\left(e_{O_{|O|}}\left|e_M\right.\right)\right) \cdot \left(\sum_{i=1}^{m} P\left(e_N\left|e_{M_i}\right.\right)\right) \tag{4.7}$$

where $P\left(e_{O_j}\left|e_N\right.\right)$,$P(e_N|e_M)$, and $P(e_M)$ are HFEs. Thus, $P(e_N)$ is also a HFE.

According to the above analysis of three different kinds of connections in BN, it is proven that if all the probabilities in the nodes take the form of HFEs, then the final deduced probabilities are also in the form of HFEs.

4.3.3 Dynamic Hesitant Fuzzy Bayesian Network

Based on the introduction of HFBN, this section combines the time dimension with HFBN, and proposes the concept of Dynamic Hesitant Fuzzy Bayesian Network (DHFBN). The HFBN is a DAG, which consists of hesitant fuzzy variables and the directed links between hesitant fuzzy variables. The DHFBN is an extension of HFBN in time dimension. It can be depicted by a binary $\langle B_0, B_{\rightarrow}\rangle$, in which B_0 denotes the initial network and $B_{\rightarrow}$ denotes the transition network. The transition network $B_{\rightarrow}$ defines the transition probability distribution between nodes at different times, which consists of two or more HFBNs.

Given a hesitant fuzzy variable set $M = (M_1, M_2, \ldots, M_n)$ and a limited time $(0, 1, \ldots, T)$, then the joint probability distribution is defined as:

$$P(M^0, M^1, \ldots, M^T) = P(M^0) \cdot \prod_{t=1}^{T} \prod_{i=1}^{n} P\left[M_i^t \middle| \pi\left(M_i^t\right)\right] \tag{4.8}$$

where M_i^t denotes the node i at the time t and $\pi\left(M_i^t\right)$ is the parent node of M_i^t.

The DHFBN can simulate complex dynamic systems well. It integrates the causality with hesitant fuzzy information between different times and conducts a dynamic analysis and prediction under the hesitant fuzzy environment. The DHFBN can depict the causal relationship between hesitant fuzzy variables and the evolution process of hesitant fuzzy variables in time series. The initial network of DHFBN denotes the state of the network, the transition network reflects the dependence between adjacent time, and the conditional probability between nodes measures the strength of dependence.

4.4 Structure Learning Algorithm of Bayesian Network Based on the Hesitant Fuzzy Information Flow

Generally, the construction of BN is determined by the knowledge of experts. But it cannot ensure the objectivity and reliability. Many researchers hope to construct BN by the observed data and further try to learn network structures completely without prior knowledge of experts. However, how to identify the arcs between network nodes and their directions accurately is the main difficulty. One possible way is to search for the optimal network structure based on a defined score function in the search space (Schwarz, 1978), which is a non-deterministic polynomial (NP) hard problem (Chickering, 1996; Malone, 2015; Yang et al., 2013).

In order to manage the complexity of practical problems with massive uncertain information, this section adopts an improved Particle Swarm Optimization (PSO) algorithm for the structure learning of the BN based on the hesitant fuzzy information flow (HFIF) (Song et al., 2019). By conducting the global causal analysis and an unconstrained optimization model, we can obtain the initial structure and the optimized search space with the most significant causality. Furthermore, the optimized PSO algorithm can determine the directions of arcs and search for the approximate global optimal structure with higher accuracy and efficiency. Based on which, the initial network and the transfer network are obtained. That is to say, they constitute a complete DHFBN structure (Fig. 4.2).

Remark 1. It is noted that the detailed process about the improved PSO algorithm will be introduced in detail in the following section (Song et al., 2019).

In practice, the structure of BN is often unknown. The primary task is to find the most appropriate topology based on the given training data set. The structure learning mainly includes two parts: score function and search algorithm. The information flow can better depict the causal relationship between two attributes and it has

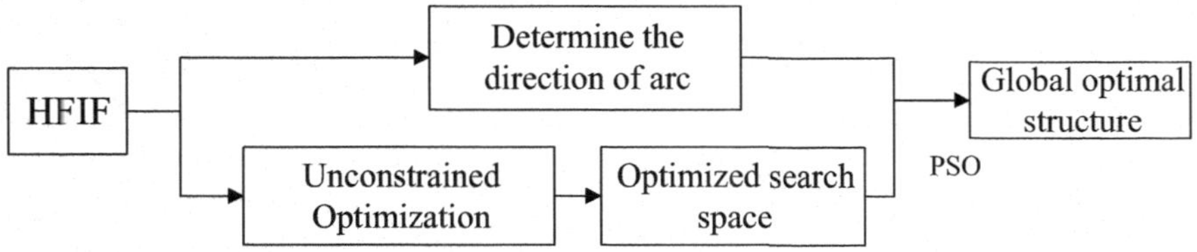

Fig. 4.2 The process of the improved PSO algorithm

been widely applied to the structure learning of BN. However, with the nonlinearity of the evolution and the complexity of practical problems, there will be massive data with uncertainty that brings more challenges to the application of the BN. In such cases, the HFS is an effective tool to depict large amounts of uncertain information with the membership degree consisting of multiple possible values. For the structure learning with massive uncertain information, this section first defines the concept of HFIF. Then, an unconstrained optimization model is constructed to find the initial structure of BN. By integrating the mutation operation and cross over operation of the GA into the updated formulas of the PSO algorithm, the improved PSO algorithm combined with HFIF is further developed for the structure learning of BN. A specific implementation process of the structure learning based on the improved PSO algorithm under hesitant fuzzy environment is also presented.

4.4.1 Hesitant Fuzzy Information Flow

The HFS is used to depict hesitant information in practical problems. To describe the causal relationship between two hesitant fuzzy variable sequences, a physical notion called hesitant fuzzy information flow (HFIF) is developed. It measures the causal relationship by the time rate from a hesitant fuzzy variable sequence to the other one. The information exchange between two hesitant fuzzy variables reflects strength and direction of the causality. Inspired by the concept of IF (Liang, 2014), HFIF is defined as follows:

Definition 4.6 (Song et al., 2019). Given two time series of hesitant fuzzy information $H_1 = \{\langle x, h_1(x_i)\rangle | x_i \in X\}$ and $H_2 = \{\langle x, h_2(x_i)\rangle | x_i \in X\}$ $(i = 1, 2, \ldots, n)$, the rate of HFIF from the series H_1 to the series H_2 is:

$$T(h)_{1\to 2} = \frac{Cov(H_2, H_2)Cov(H_1, H_2)Cov\big(H_1, \dot{H}_2\big) - Cov^2(H_1, H_2)Cov\big(H_2, \dot{H}_2\big)}{Cov^2(H_2, H_2)Cov(H_1, H_1) - Cov(H_2, H_2)Cov^2(H_1, H_2)} \tag{4.9}$$

where $Cov(H_1, H_2)$ is the covariance between H_1 and H_2, and $\dot{H}_2$ is the difference approximation of $\frac{dH_2}{dt}$ by the Euler forward scheme. It is obvious that $\dot{H}_{2,i} = \frac{H_{2,i+k} - H_{2,i}}{k\Delta t}$, where Δt denotes the time step, $k = 1$ for general time series, and $k = 2$ for chaotic and densely sampled series.

Then, a method to normalize the HFIF is also developed. Based on a two-dimensional dynamic system $\frac{dH_2}{dt} = F(H_2, t) + B(H_2, t)\dot{W}$, where F and B are arbitrary nonlinear functions of H_2, and $\dot{W}$ is a two-dimensional vector of white noise, the change rate of the marginal entropy H_2^* of H_2 has been proven:

$$\frac{dH_2^*}{dt} = -E\left(F_{H_2}\frac{\partial \log \rho_{H_2}}{\partial \overline{h}_{H_2}(x)}\right) - \frac{1}{2}E\left(g_{11}\frac{\partial^2 \log \rho_{H_2}}{\partial \overline{h}_{H_2}^2(x)}\right) \tag{4.10}$$

where E is the expectation function, ρ_{H_2} is the marginal density of H_2, and $g_{ij} = \sum_k b_{ik}b_{jk}$. Based on Eq. (4.10), we obtain that:

$$\begin{aligned}-E\left(F_{H_2}\frac{\partial \log \rho_{H_2}}{\partial \overline{h}_{H_2}(x)}\right) &= -E\left[\frac{1}{\rho_{H_2}}\frac{\partial(F_{H_2}\rho_2)}{\partial \overline{h}_{H_2}(x)} - \frac{\partial F_{H_2}}{\partial \overline{h}_{H_2}(x)}\right] \\ &= E\left(\frac{\partial F_{H_2}}{\partial \overline{h}_{H_2}(x)}\right) - E\left[\frac{1}{\rho_{H_2}}\frac{\partial(F_{H_2}\rho_{H_2})}{\partial \overline{h}_{H_2}(x)}\right]\end{aligned} \tag{4.11}$$

Equation (4.10) can be rewritten as

$$\begin{aligned}\frac{dH_2^*}{dt} &= E\left(\frac{\partial F_{H_2}}{\partial \overline{h}_{H_2}(x)}\right) + T(h)_{1\to 2} \\ &+ \left[-\frac{1}{2}E\left(\frac{1}{\rho_{H_2}}\frac{\partial^2 g_{11}\rho_{H_2}}{\partial \overline{h}_{H_2}^2(x)}\right) - \frac{1}{2}E\left(g_{11}\frac{\partial^2 \log \rho_{H_2}}{\partial \overline{h}_{H_2}^2(x)}\right)\right]\end{aligned} \tag{4.12}$$

where $T(h)_{1\to 2}$ denotes the rate of hesitant fuzzy information flowing from H_1 to H_2: $T(h)_{1\to 2} = -E\left[\frac{1}{\rho_{H_2}}\frac{\partial(F_{H_2}\rho_{H_2})}{\partial \overline{h}_{H_2}(x)}\right] + \frac{1}{2}E\left(\frac{1}{\rho_{H_2}}\frac{\partial^2 g_{11}\rho_{H_2}}{\partial \overline{h}_{H_2}^2(x)}\right)$. Equation (4.12) consists of three parts: the change of H_2^* due to H_2 itself, the rate of HFIF from H_1 to H_2 and the stochastic effect H_2^{*noise}. Then it is obvious that:

$$-\frac{1}{2}E\left(\frac{1}{\rho_{H_2}}\frac{\partial^2 g_{11}\rho_{H_2}}{\partial \overline{h}_{H_2}^2(x)}\right) - \frac{1}{2}E\left(g_{11}\frac{\partial^2 \log \rho_{H_2}}{\partial \overline{h}_{H_2}^2(x)}\right) = \frac{dH_2^{*noise}}{dt} \tag{4.13}$$

Without loss of generality, it is assumed that all the variables are subject to the original Gaussian distribution and $F = f + AN + BB^T$, where $f = (f_1, f_2)^T$, $A = (a_{ij})_{i,j=1,2}$ and $B = (b_{ij})_{i,j=1,2}$ are three constant matrices. Then

$$\rho_{H_2} = \frac{1}{\sqrt{2\pi}\sigma_{H_2}}\exp\left[-\frac{\left(\overline{h}_{H_2}(x) - \mu_{H_2}\right)^2}{2\sigma_{H_2}^2}\right] \tag{4.14}$$

Based on Eq. (4.13) and Eq. (4.14), it is obvious that:

$$\frac{dH_2^{*noise}}{dt} = \frac{1}{2}\frac{g_{11}}{\sigma_{H_2}} \tag{4.15}$$

The normalized hesitant fuzzy information flow (NHFIF) is defined as:

$$\tau(h)_{1\to 2}=\frac{absT(h)_{1\to 2}}{abs(T(h)_{1\to 2})+abs\left(\frac{dH_2^{*noise}}{dt}\right)} \tag{4.16}$$

where abs is the absolute value function and $\tau(h)_{1\to 2} \in [0, 1]$. Compared with the normalization formula, we delete the term $\left|E\left(\frac{\partial F_{H_2}}{\partial \bar{h}_{H_2}(x)}\right)\right|$, which measures the contribution itself, because that it makes the results of relative causal relationships too small. The larger the value of $\tau(h)_{1\to 2}$ is, the more obvious the effect of H_1 on H_2 will be. If $\tau(h)_{1\to 2} = 1$, then the series H_1 does completely cause the series H_2; if $\tau(h)_{1\to 2} = 0$, then H_1 is not the cause; if $\tau(h)_{1\to 2} \to 0$, then the series H_1 is not an important factor in the occurrence and development of the series H_2, and the direct causal relationship between H_1 and H_2 is weak. Particularly, when the significance level is 0.05, the causal relationship between H_1 and H_2 is significant if $\tau(h)_{1\to 2} > 0.01$.

According to the above analysis, the HFIF is suitable for the structure learning of BN under hesitant fuzzy environment. The value of the HFIF reflects the strength of the dependence between network nodes. The directions of the structural arcs can be identified by the HFIF. Therefore, a holistic learning of the network structure under hesitant fuzzy environment is achieved based on the HFIF.

4.4.2 Unconstrained Optimization Model

The unconstrained optimization model is a method to find the local minimum point of the multivariate function. It occupies an important position in the research of nonlinear programming. For the structure learning of BN, an unconstrained optimization model based on the HFIF is constructed to find the optimal adjacency matrix, i.e., the initial structure of BN.

In general, the structure of BN with n random variables is depicted by an adjacency matrix $B = \left(b_{ij}\right)_{n\times n}$. If $b_{ij}=1$, then $\mathbb{N}_i$ is a parent node of $\mathbb{N}_j$. If $b_{ij}= 0$, then there is no arc between the nodes $\mathbb{N}_i$ and $\mathbb{N}_j$. A function to measure the global causality of BN based on HFIF and the adjacency matrix is defined as follows:

Definition 4.7 (Song et al., 2019). Let $B = \left(b_{ij}\right)_{n\times n}$ be an adjacency matrix, $\tau(h)_{i\to j}$ be the HFIF, and $\mathbb{N}_i$ be the node in the structure, then the function to measure the global causality of BN is:

$$R(B,\alpha) = \sum_{i=1}^{n}\sum_{j=1,j\neq i}^{n} \tau(h)_{i\to j}\cdot b_{ij} \tag{4.17}$$

where α is the significance level, n is the number of nodes in the network structure, $b_{ij}=1$ or $b_{ij}=0$. The value of $R(B, \alpha)$ indicates the significance level of the causal relationships in the network structure. Therefore, an unconstrained optimization model can be constructed below (Song et al., 2019):

Model 1

$$\max R(B, \alpha) = \sum_{i=1}^{n} \sum_{j=1, j \neq i}^{n} \tau(h)_{i \to j} \cdot b_{ij}$$

By solving Model 1, the optimal adjacency matrix is obtained, i.e., the initial network structure. The directed arcs in the initial structure are the candidate arcs of the optimal BN structure. The optimized search space of the structure with the most significant causality is also obtained.

4.4.3 Improved PSO Algorithm for the Structure Learning of Bayesian Network

It is a challenge to search for the optimal structure of BN from all possible network structure spaces, which is also a NP-hard problem and has been widely studied. A popular method is to search for the optimal structure through different search algorithms based on the score function. Song et al., (2019) adopted the Bayesian Information Criterion (BIC) as the score function, which is more balanced between accuracy and complexity. For the training dataset DS consisting of N samples, the BIC of DS is $BIC(DS) = LL(DS) - \frac{1}{2}(\ln N)|\theta|$. $LL(DS)$ is the likelihood function for a graph structure, $|\theta| = \sum_{i=1}^{n} q_i(r_i - 1)$, in which q_i provides the number of possible configurations for the parents of the ith variable, and r_i is the number of different states of the ith variable, and n is the number of variables in each sample.

PSO algorithm is a global random search algorithm based on swarm intelligence, which is inspired by simulating the behavior of birds foraging. In recent years, many scholars have applied the PSO algorithm to the structure learning of the BN. Gheisari and Meybodi (2016) proposed a PSO-based algorithm to solve the structure learning problem of BN, and developed a new discrete method to update the velocity and position of the particles based on the genetic operations. It ensures the particles to obtain the optimal solution and avoids the invalid solutions by a cycle removing procedure. Besides, the modified depth first search algorithm (colored-DFS) is also introduced in the search procedure to detect the cycles. However, there is great uncertainty in determining the arcs' directions in the structure. Besides, it is difficult to identify all the arcs and their directions. Therefore, Song et al. (2019) improved the PSO algorithm and proposed a method for structure learning based on the HFIF. To achieve this, it is necessary to review some basic knowledge about the PSO algorithm first. In the PSO algorithm, every potential solution to the optimization problem is a particle in the search space. The particle has a fitness value determined by an

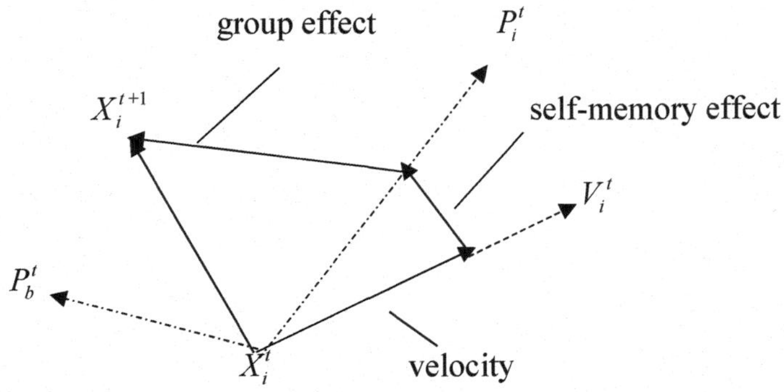

Fig. 4.3 The way to update particle position

optimized function. Each particle has a velocity that determines the direction and distance it flies. Then, the particle, following the current optimal particle, searches in the solution space.

As illustrated in Fig. 4.3 (Song et al., 2019), for the D-dimension of the search space consisting of p particles, $X_i = (X_{i1}, X_{i2}, \ldots, X_{iD})$ and $P_i = (P_{i1}, P_{i2}, \ldots, P_{iD})$ are the position and best previous position of the i-th particle respectively, $V_i = (V_{i1}, V_{i2}, \ldots, V_{iD})$ is the velocity of the i-th particle, and P_b is the best particle in the swarm. The particles can update their velocity and position by the following formulas:

$$V_i^{t+1} = \omega \times V_i^t + c_1 r_1 \left(P_i^t - X_i^t\right) + c_2 r_2 \left(P_b^t - X_i^t\right) \tag{4.18}$$

$$X_i^{t+1} = X_i^t + V_i^{t+1} \tag{4.19}$$

According to the formulas above, the particles can update their velocity and position based on genetic operations by the following formulas:

$$X_i^{t+1} = N_3\left(N_2\left(N_1\left(X_i^t, \omega\right), c_1\right)c_2\right) \tag{4.20}$$

$$W_i^{t+1} = N_1\left(X_i^t, w\right) = \begin{cases} M\left(X_i^t\right), r_1 < w \\ X_i^t, \quad others \end{cases} \tag{4.21}$$

$$S_i^{t+1} = N_2\left(W_i^{t+1}, c_1\right) = \begin{cases} C_p\left(W_i^{t+1}\right), r_2 < c_1 \\ W_i^{t+1}, \quad others \end{cases} \tag{4.22}$$

$$X_i^{t+1} = N_3\left(S_i^t, c_2\right) = \begin{cases} C_g\left(S_i^t\right), r_3 < c_2 \\ S_i^t, \quad others \end{cases} \tag{4.23}$$

where w is the mutation probability, r_1, r_2 and r_3 are random numbers between 0 and 1, $S = \{0, 1\}$. N_1 is the mutation operation. N_2 and N_3 are the crossover operations, which denote the cognitive personal experience and cooperative global experience of the particles respectively. c_1 and c_2 are two acceleration constants, which mean the crossover probability with personal optimal solution and the crossover probability with global optimal solution respectively. It should be noted that the detailed explanation and pseudo codes of the mutation operation and cross operation are provided in Appendix.

Then, the main idea of the improved PSO algorithm for the structure leaning of BN is illustrated. As discussed above, the initial network structure and the search space with the most significant causality are obtained by solving the unconstrained optimization model. It means that the arcs in the search space can only be randomly generated in the arcs of the initial network. Besides, the arcs in the initial network structure are determined by the HFIF and they are the candidate arcs of the optimal BN structure. By optimizing the search space and identifying the arcs and their directions, the global optimal structure can be obtained. The specific implementation process of the improved PSO algorithm is presented in Algorithm 1 (Song et al., 2019).

Algorithm 1

Input: A set of variables n and a set of massive hesitant fuzzy data $DS(h)$.

Step 1. Set the level of significance in the analysis of the HFIF.

Step 2. Calculate the HFIF of each pair of nodes $\left(\mathbb{N}_i, \mathbb{N}_j\right)$ based on Eq. (4.16), and conduct significance test and causal analysis.

Step 3. Construct the unconstrained optimization problem, identify all the arcs and their directions, and then obtain the initial structure.

Step 4. Generate the initial valid population randomly in the optimized search space, and calculate the BIC value of each particle.

Step 5. Update the personal optimal solution of each particle.

Step 6. Update the position and velocity of each particle and verify the new particle.

Step 7. Recalculate the BIC value of each particle and update the global optimal solution.

Step 8. Check whether if the termination condition is satisfied. If it is satisfied, then end the run. Otherwise, return to Step 5.

Output: Optimal BN structure S.

The improved PSO algorithm combines the advantages of the HFIF in determining causal relationship and the advantages of PSO in searching for the global optimal solution. The introduction of the HFIF can make up for the great uncertainty caused by PSO in determining the arcs and their directions to some extent. On the other hand, the improved PSO algorithm searches the optimal BN structure from the optimized solution space, which is more reasonable than the traditional PSO algorithm that searches the optimal BN structure from all possible structures. Besides, the improved PSO algorithm can manage the structure learning problems with massive uncertain information under hesitant fuzzy environment with high efficiency, and it obtains the global optimal structure.

4.5 Parameter Learning and Inference Prediction

This section uses two classical networks, ASIA network and BOBLO network to illustrate the feasibility and application of the improved PSO algorithm based on HFIF in structure learning of BN. A comparative analysis with three traditional algorithms to validate the advantages of the proposed algorithm is also conducted (Song et al., 2019).

4.5.1 *Databases and Measure of the Performance*

The ASIA network is a simple network consisting of eight binary nodes and eight arcs, and the BOBLO network is a system with twenty three variables and twenty four arcs. They are two benchmark network models for testing structure learning algorithms. According to the given structure and probability table, sample the training dataset with 500 and 5000 cases respectively. The original data are transformed into the corresponding hesitant fuzzy information by the following linear transformation:

$$\gamma_i = \frac{x_i - \min(x)}{\max(x) - \min(x)} \tag{4.24}$$

where $x_i (i = 1, 2, \ldots, n)$ are the original data concerning each attribute. To avoid the randomness of the search algorithms, repeat each simulation experiment ten times and take the average of ten simulation experiments as the final result. In addition, Hamming distance is used to evaluate the performance of algorithm (Raftery et al., 2017): $HD = L + R + O$, in which L, R and O be the numbers of the added, the deleted and the reversed arcs, respectively, to make the learned network being consistent with the standard network. The smaller HD indicates the better learned network. If $HD = 0$, then the learned structure is the optimal.

4.5.2 *Experimental Results and Analysis*

The HFIF is an effective tool to depict the causal relationship between two hesitant fuzzy variable sequences. In order to understand better, this section takes the ASIA network as an example. Then the NHFIF matrices of ASIA network (see Tables 4.1 and 4.2) is calculated, in which the direction of each NHFIF is from the row variable to the column variable (Song et al., 2019).

In Table 4.1, $\tau(h)_{Smoking \to LungCancer} = 0.232 > 0.01$ and $\tau(h)_{LungCancer \to Smoking} = 0.006 > 0$. Confidence test shows that there exists a significant causal relationship between "Smoking" and "Lung Cancer", and "Smoking" is the cause of "Lung Cancer". Thus, there may be a directed arc from "Smoking" to "Lung Cancer"

Table 4.1 The normalized hesitant fuzzy information flow matrix of ASIA network with 500 samples

HFIF	Smoking	Bronchities	LungCancer	VisitAsia	TB	TBorCancer	Dys	Xray
Smoking	–	0.136	0.232	0.001	0.000	0.215	0.129	0.006
Bronchitis	0.013	–	0.003	0.002	0.004	0.002	0.082	0.004
LungCancer	0.006	0.004	–	0.002	0.006	0.182	0.056	0.185
VisitAsia	0.002	0.001	0.002	–	0.168	0.052	0.048	0.005
TB	0.006	0.005	0.006	0.000	–	0.008	0.006	0.016
TBorCancer	0.028	0.006	0.007	0.002	0.002	–	0.193	0.202
Dys	0.009	0.001	0.004	0.002	0.001	0.006	–	0.009
Xray	0.025	0.001	0.003	0.003	0.000	0.002	0.022	–

Table 4.2 The normalized hesitant fuzzy information flow matrix of ASIA network with 5000 samples

HFIF	Smoking	Bronchities	LungCancer	VisitAsia	TB	TBorCancer	Dys	Xray
Smoking	–	0.183	0.259	0.004	0.001	0.226	0.146	0.004
Bronchitis	0.016	–	0.004	0.003	0.012	0.008	0.132	0.001
LungCancer	0.007	0.008	–	0.004	0.006	0.165	0.087	0.328
VisitAsia	0.003	0.002	0.006	–	0.198	0.052	0.056	0.001
TB	0.002	0.004	0.014	0.001	–	0.016	0.016	0.041
TBorCancer	0.026	0.003	0.063	0.011	0.054	–	0.217	0.258
Dys	0.010	0.052	0.004	0.005	0.005	0.004	–	0.012
Xray	0.032	0.000	0.068	0.019	0.005	0.067	0.022	–

in the BN. Besides, Table 4.1 shows that $\tau(h)_{Bronchitis \to TB} = 0.004 < 0.01$ and $\tau(h)_{TB \to Bronchitis} = 0.005 < 0.01$. It means that the causal relationship between "Brochitis" and "TB" is not significant, and there is no arc between them. As seen in Tables 4.1 and 4.2, other NHFIFs can be interpreted in a similar way.

In addition, it is obvious that the NHFIF matrix in Table 4.2 is generally consistent with the matrix in Table 4.1, which indicates that depicting the causal relationship by NHFIF is effective. With the increase of the sample size, the causal relationship will become more significant. For example, $\tau(h)_{Smoking \to LungCancer} = 0.232$ in Table 4.1 and $\tau(h)_{Smoking \to LungCancer} = 0.259$ in Table 4.2. The causal relationship between "Smoking" and "Lung Cancer" becomes more significant as the sample size increases.

After that, the global causal measures based on HFIF is constructed and the unconstrained optimization model is solved. By determining directions of the arcs and significance level of the HFIF, the optimal adjacency matrix A is obtained as:

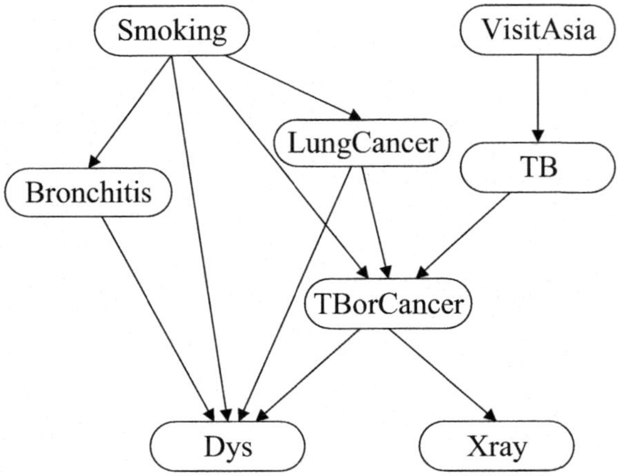

Fig. 4.4 The initial network structure

$$A = \begin{bmatrix} 0\,1\,1\,0\,0\,1\,1\,0 \\ 0\,0\,0\,0\,0\,0\,1\,0 \\ 0\,0\,0\,0\,0\,0\,1\,0 \\ 0\,0\,1\,0\,1\,0\,0\,0 \\ 0\,0\,0\,0\,0\,1\,0\,0 \\ 0\,0\,0\,0\,0\,0\,1\,1 \\ 0\,0\,0\,0\,0\,0\,0\,0 \\ 0\,0\,0\,0\,0\,0\,0\,0 \end{bmatrix}$$

The corresponding initial structure is presented in Fig. 4.4. Furthermore, the optimized search space with the most significant causality is obtained, which means that the arcs in the search space can only be randomly generated in the arcs of the initial network. After optimizing the search space, the PSO algorithm is used for search learning. The global optimal structure with efficiency and precision can be determined. For the sample with the size of 5000, the network structure learned by the improved PSO algorithm is consistent with the standard ASIA network. The score convergence curves and learning structures of the sample with different sizes are presented in Figs. 4.5 and 4.6, respectively (Song et al., 2019).

4.5.3 Comparisons with Traditional Algorithms for Structure Learning

To illustrate the advantages of the proposed algorithm, this section compares it with three traditional algorithms under the hesitant fuzzy environment: GA, PSO algorithm and Hill-climbing algorithm. By running these four algorithms ten times separately, we can compare the accuracy and running time of the four algorithms in

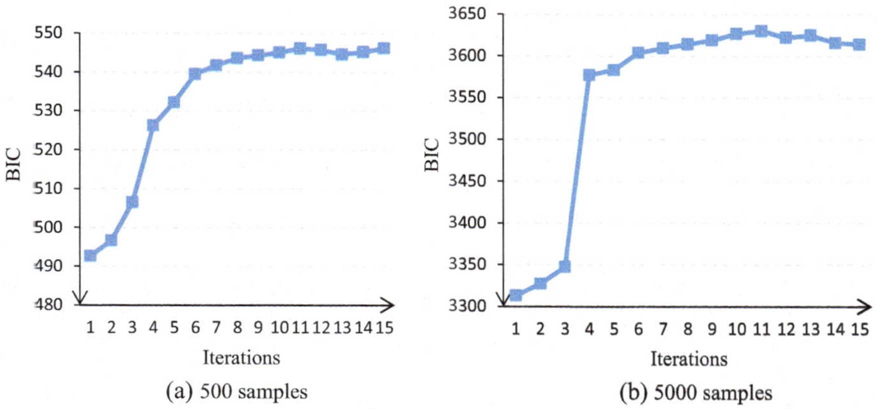

Fig. 4.5 The score convergence curves with different sizes of samples

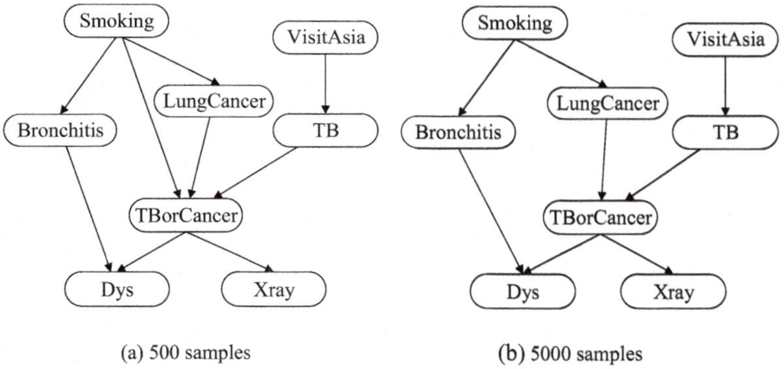

Fig. 4.6 The learning structures with different sizes of samples

structure learning. The comparison results are presented in Tables 4.3, 4.4, 4.5 and 4.6 (Song et al., 2019).

We can see that: (1) To the ASIA network, the improved PSO algorithm can learn a better structure when the sample size is 500 and 5000 respectively. Besides, the improved PSO algorithm derives a better structure as the sample size increases.

Table 4.3 The learning results of ASIA network with 500 samples

Algorithm	L	R	O	HD	Time(s)
Improved PSO	1.6	0.4	0.6	2.6	2.37
GA	0.9	1	1.8	3.7	3.29
PSO	5.2	2.2	2.5	9.9	8.59
Hill-climbing	5.6	1.9	3.8	11.3	35.64

Table 4.4 The learning results of ASIA network with 5000 samples

Algorithm	L	R	O	HD	Time(s)
Improved PSO	0.1	0.1	0	0.2	6.61
GA	0.8	0.6	1.3	2.7	9.59
PSO	3.1	1.7	2.5	7.3	23.28
Hill-climbing	3.7	1.6	3.9	9.2	115.34

Table 4.5 The learning results of BOBLO network with 500 samples

Algorithm	L	R	O	HD	Time(s)
Improved PSO	3.4	5.1	2.8	11.3	23.31
GA	6.8	11.2	6.1	24.1	49.62
PSO	11.4	19.5	8.7	39.6	652.84
Hill-climbing	16.3	28.5	9.3	54.1	3175.22

Table 4.6 The learning results of BOBLO network with 5000 samples

Algorithm	L	R	O	HD	Time(s)
Improved PSO	1.7	0.6	0.9	3.2	328.80
GA	3.5	2.8	2.6	8.9	989.97
PSO	4.5	3.4	6.2	14.1	2405.59
Hill-climbing	8.3	4.9	8.5	21.7	7621.25

When the simple size is 5000, our algorithm has prominent advantages over other algorithms. To the BOBLO network, those four algorithms perform poor in accuracy with the sample size of 500. In terms of network complexity, the sample size is too small to fit the data and structure correctly. When the sample size is 5000, the improved PSO algorithm can learn a better structure and has advantages in accuracy and efficiency over other algorithms. (2) Compared with the traditional PSO algorithm and Hill-climbing algorithm, the improved PSO algorithm has a great improvement in accuracy and efficiency of the BN structure learning. (3) Compared with GA, the improvement in search time of the improved PSO algorithm is not very obvious. However, the proposed algorithm has certain advantages in structure accuracy, especially in reducing reversion of the directed arcs. It means that the improved PSO algorithm based on HFIF has better performance in determining the directions of arcs. The score convergence curves of ASIA network by different algorithms with 500 samples are presented in Fig. 4.7.

We can see that the improved PSO algorithm is obviously superior to the traditional algorithms under hesitant fuzzy environment. The improved PSO algorithm optimizes the initial search space based on the global causal analysis of HFIF. It avoids invalid searches on the network and improves the accuracy and efficiency of structure learning. However, the traditional algorithms usually search for all possible

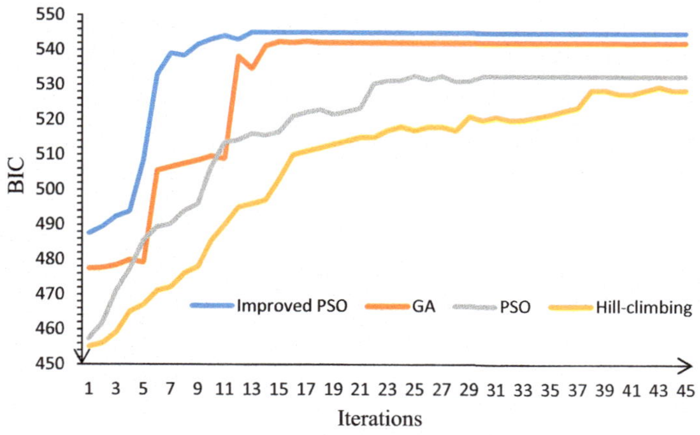

Fig. 4.7 The score convergence curves of ASIA network with 500 samples by different algorithms

network structures based on the score function, which makes it difficult to find the global optimal solution in a limited time. Besides, the proposed algorithm makes full use of the original massive data with uncertainty. It also depicts the causal relationship between different attributes clearly. While the traditional algorithms perform poor in determining causal relationship. The results derived by the traditional algorithms may be the local optimal solutions, which are inconsistent with reality. Therefore, the presented algorithm can achieve effective global search through some operations. The learning structure derived by the presented algorithm is more logical and closer to the global optimal structure.

The PSO is an effective global random search algorithm to solve the structure learning problem of BN, which updates the velocity and position of particles based on the genetic operations. It avoids the invalid solutions by a cycle removing procedure and ensures that the particles obtain the optimal solution. However, the traditional PSO algorithm cannot deal with massive hesitant fuzzy data and fails to determine the directions of arcs quickly and accurately. Therefore, this chapter improves the PSO algorithm and propose a new method for structure learning based on the HFIF. It combines the advantages of HFS in depicting large amounts of uncertain data and the advantages of HFIF in determining the causality. By solving the unconstrained optimization model and optimizing the search space, we can obtain the initial network structure. It avoids the low efficiency of the existing algorithms in searching for possible structures, and it also simplifies the search procedure. The improved PSO algorithm determines the arcs and the directions of the arcs synchronously, and then it finds the global optimal solution by following the current searched optimal particle in the optimized search space. The experimental results validate the efficiency and precision of the improved PSO algorithm.

4.5.4 Parameter Learning of Dynamic Hesitant Fuzzy Bayesian Network

After constructing the structure of DHFBN, the core step is the parameter learning, which determines the accuracy and efficiency of the DHFBN in practical applications. Therefore, it is particularly important to select an appropriate parameter learning algorithm. However, the loss of sample data often occurs in practice, which makes the process of parameter learning difficult. Besides, the complexity of events with uncertain information brings more challenges. The Expectation–Maximization (EM) algorithm (Bailey & Elkan, 1995; Zhang et al., 2002) is a commonly used parameter learning algorithm. The main idea of EM algorithm is: if the parameters are known, then the optimal latent variables can be inferred from the training data; otherwise, if the latent variables are known, then it is easy to calculate the maximum likelihood estimation of parameters. However, the traditional EM algorithm cannot deal with hesitant fuzzy information. In this section, we introduce an improved EM algorithm to find the maximum likelihood estimation of parameters under the hesitant fuzzy environment (Song et al., 2019).

Given a hesitant fuzzy observed variable set M and a hesitant fuzzy latent variable set Z, Θ denotes the related parameter set. The maximum likelihood function of Θ is defined as:

$$LL(\Theta|M, Z) = \ln P(\overline{M}, \overline{Z}|\Theta) \tag{4.25}$$

Since M and Z are expressed by HFSs, and Z is latent variable, the above function cannot be solved directly. We can calculate the means of HFSs M and Z to maximize the logarithmic marginal likelihood function of the observed set M:

$$LL(\Theta|M) = \ln P(\overline{M}|\Theta) = \ln \sum\nolimits_{Z} P(\overline{M}, \overline{Z}|\Theta) \tag{4.26}$$

where $\overline{M}$ and $\overline{Z}$ are the means of HFSs M and Z respectively. After that, we perform the following steps iteratively (Song et al., 2019):

(1) Infer the expectation of the hesitant fuzzy latent variable set Z based on Θ^t(denoted as Z^t);
(2) Calculate the maximum likelihood estimation of the parameter set Θ based on the observed hesitant fuzzy variable set M and Z^t(denoted as Θ^{t+1}).

Furthermore, if we calculate the probability distribution $P(\overline{Z}|\overline{M}, \Theta^t)$ of the hesitant fuzzy latent variable set Z based on the parameter set Θ^t, instead of the expectation of Z. Then the two steps of the improved EM algorithm are presented (Song et al., 2019):

(1) Expectation: Infer the probability distribution $P(\overline{Z}|\overline{M}, \Theta^t)$ based on the current parameter set Θ^t, and calculate the mathematical expectation of the logarithmic likelihood function $LL(\Theta|M, Z)$ about Z:

$$Q(\Theta|\Theta^t) = \mathrm{E}_{Z|M,\Theta^t} LL(\Theta|M, Z) \quad (4.27)$$

(2) Maximization: search for the parameter set that maximizes the above likelihood expectation:

$$\Theta^{t+1} = \arg\max_{\Theta} Q(\Theta|\Theta^t) \quad (4.28)$$

After that, the new parameters are re-applied to the Expectation step until they converge to the local optimal solution.

The improved EM algorithm can manage the parameter learning problems with massive uncertain information under hesitant fuzzy environment. Firstly, we initialize the probability distribution of each node, including the prior probability, the observation probability and the transition probability. Then, we learn the parameters by the improved EM algorithm based on the given reasoning mechanism and the given training data set. That is, we modify the initial conditional probability distribution iteratively to obtain the most consistent probability distribution with the objective training data. At last, the optimal probability distribution with higher accuracy and efficiency is obtained.

4.5.5 *Reasoning and Prediction of Dynamic Hesitant Fuzzy Bayesian Network*

The reasoning and prediction of BN is to update the status of network nodes based on the changes of current or future information. By updating and transferring information by the causal relationship between nodes, we can infer the state distribution of the target node. To improve the efficiency of all reasoning algorithms, the BNT toolbox (Pauplin & Jiang, 2012; Ross & Eduardo, 2007) adopts engine mechanism. Different engines can transform, refine and solve models according to different algorithms.

The toolbox BNT provides a variety of reasoning engines, mainly includes: Joint Tree Inference (Meara, 2010), Global Joint Tree Inference (Liu et al., 2017b), Variable Elimination Inference (Rafael et al., 2016) and Brief Propagation Inference (Dolder et al., 2014). The Joint Tree algorithm is the fastest one at present, especially for sparse networks. In this section, we construct the Joint Tree Inference by DHFBN, and then input the evidence data. The probability distribution of the target node can be further inferred. The flow chart of Joint Tree Inference is presented as follows (Song et al., 2019) (Fig. 4.8).

The pre-processed data serve as the input evidence of the network, and the output is the probability distribution at different times, which achieves dynamic reasoning and prediction. The DHFBN combines the advantages of the HFS in depicting uncertain information and the advantages of BN in reasoning. One the one hand, the improved PSO algorithm can search for the optimal structure from the optimized search space with high efficiency and accuracy. On the other hand, the introduction of time factor

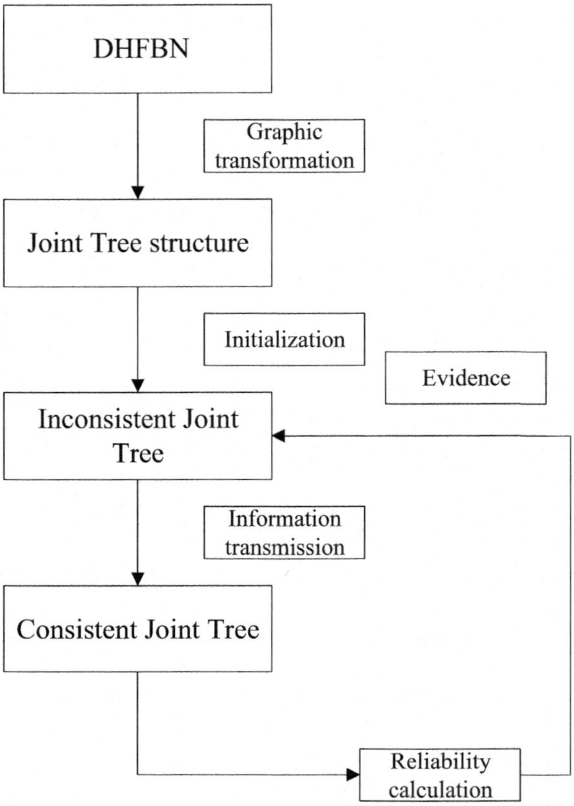

Fig. 4.8 The flow chart of Joint Tree Inference (Song et al. 2020)

considers the relevance of information at different times and can make up for the defects of the traditional methods in processing time series information. In addition, the DHFBN can make full use of the massive uncertain information and better depict the evolution of hesitant fuzzy variables in time series.

4.6 Case Study

In this section, we make a case study of an optimal investment port decision making problems of "Twenty-First-Century Maritime Silk Road" based on the proposed DFHBN. So we start with the background of the problem, present the calculation process and results, and further make some comparisons (Song et al., 2019).

4.6.1 Background of the Optimal Investment Port Decision Making Problems of "Twenty-First-Century Maritime Silk Road"

The "Twenty-First-Century Maritime Silk Road" ("Silk Road" for short) is an overseas investment strategy and development plan proposed by China in recent years, which involves more than 80 countries along the line and covers nearly 60 percent of the global economy. It has brought new opportunities for the development of the world economy and helped promote economic integration and trade facilitation along the Silk Road. However, while bringing opportunities and providing a better investment platform, there are also some potential risks and challenges of overseas. The decision making problem under such a circumstance is challenging because it involves lots of dynamic meteorological data and uncertain risk indices, which are also not only ambiguous but also difficult to quantify. Fortunately, the proposed DHFBN provides an effective dynamic and quantified method for these decision making problems.

As an important transport corridor of the Silk Road and hub of the global transport network system, the port is playing an increasingly prominent role in international trade and logistics. The construction of ports will be a potential investment focus. Investors and enterprises inevitably worry that most ports are doubled due to dynamic natural environment, domestic political stability, financial risks and other safety problems, putting the interests of investors at risk. Most of the information available for these attributes is uncertain and is difficult to quantify, which hinders the evaluation and the decision making process of the DMs.

Suppose that an enterprise decides to invest one of the four ports, Chittagong (P_1), Colombo (P_2), Karachi (P_3) and Djibouti (P_4). The relevant core attributes include the natural environment risk (*NER*), social security risk (*SSR*), religious risk (*RR*), cultural difference risk (*CDR*), safety environment (*SE*), the country's political stability (*PS*), the local infrastructure condition (*LIC*) and the credit risk (*CR*). However, the values of the above factors are changing dynamically with great uncertainty. From the perspective of decision analysis, this problem involves many uncertain factors and it is difficult to obtain accurate quantitative information. It depends more on the consultation information provided by experts. The hesitant fuzzy decision theory provides an effective tool to manage massive uncertain information. This section uses 132 sets of simulation samples [adapted from (Yang et al., 2016)] to illustrate the proposed model. Then, we can make decision analysis by the proposed DHFBN to the optimal port decision making problem, which will provide an effective decision support for investors.

4.6.2 Calculations and Results Analysis

Step 1. Normalize the simulation samples.

Suppose that the training sample is the hesitant fuzzy evaluations of 120 months from 2007 to 2016, and the test sample is the hesitant fuzzy evaluations of 12 months in 2017. The time interval between adjacent networks is one month. We denote the set of ports as $P = \{P_i | i = 1, 2, \ldots, m\}$ and the set of attributes as $A = \{NER, SSR, RR, CDR, SE, PS, LIC, CR\}$. For these four ports, P_1, P_2, P_3, P_4, parts of the hesitant fuzzy evaluation matrix $H^t = \left[h_{ij}^t\right]_{m \times n}$ $(t = 1, 2, \ldots, 132)$ are presented as follows, where h_{ij}^t denotes the hesitant fuzzy evaluation of the attribute j for the port i at the time t, and the higher evaluation values indicate the higher risk.

$$H^1 = \begin{array}{c} \\ P_1 \\ P_2 \\ P_3 \\ P_4 \end{array} \begin{array}{cccccccc} NER & SSR & RR & CDR & SE & PS & LIC & CR \\ \{0.5,0.7\} & \{0.4,0.5\} & \{0.2\} & \{0.6,0.7\} & \{0.6\} & \{0.6,0.8,0.9\} & \{0.6\} & \{0.5,0.6\} \\ \{0.3,0.4\} & \{0.2,0.3,0.4\} & \{0.1,0.2\} & \{0.4,0.6\} & \{0.3,0.4\} & \{0.7\} & \{0.5,0.7\} & \{0.8\} \\ \{0.7,0.8\} & \{0.5\} & \{0.2,0.3\} & \{0.5,0.6\} & \{0.5\} & \{0.5\} & \{0.7,0.9\} & \{0.4,0.5,0.6\} \\ \{0.1,0.2\} & \{0.3,0.5\} & \{0.1\} & \{0.2,0.3,0.4\} & \{0.2\} & \{0.5,0.6\} & \{0.7,0.8\} & \{0.6\} \end{array}$$

$$H^2 = \begin{array}{c} \\ P_1 \\ P_2 \\ P_3 \\ P_4 \end{array} \begin{array}{cccccccc} NER & SSR & RR & CDR & SE & PS & LIC & CR \\ \{0.5,0.6\} & \{0.5\} & \{0.2,0.3\} & \{0.5,0.7\} & \{0.6\} & \{0.7,0.8,0.9\} & \{0.5\} & \{0.4,0.5\} \\ \{0.2,0.3,0.4\} & \{0.3,0.4\} & \{0.2,0.4\} & \{0.6\} & \{0.4,0.5\} & \{0.6,0.7\} & \{0.6,0.7\} & \{0.7\} \\ \{0.6\} & \{0.6,0.7\} & \{0.4,0.5,0.6\} & \{0.6,0.7\} & \{0.3,0.4\} & \{0.3\} & \{0.5,0.8\} & \{0.6\} \\ \{0.1\} & \{0.3,0.5,0.6\} & \{0.2\} & \{0.2,0.4\} & \{0.2\} & \{0.4,0.5\} & \{0.6\} & \{0.3,0.4\} \end{array}$$

…

$$H^{132} = \begin{array}{c} \\ P_1 \\ P_2 \\ P_3 \\ P_4 \end{array} \begin{array}{cccccccc} NER & SSR & RR & CDR & SE & PS & LIC & CR \\ \{0.8,0.9\} & \{0.3,0.4\} & \{0.2\} & \{0.6,0.7\} & \{0.6\} & \{0.6,0.8,0.9\} & \{0.6\} & \{0.5,0.6\} \\ \{0.1,0.2\} & \{0.7,0.8,0.9\} & \{0.1,0.2\} & \{0.4,0.6\} & \{0.3,0.4\} & \{0.7\} & \{0.5,0.7\} & \{0.8\} \\ \{0.1\} & \{0.6,0.7\} & \{0.2,0.3\} & \{0.5,0.6\} & \{0.5\} & \{0.5\} & \{0.7,0.9\} & \{0.4,0.5,0.6\} \\ \{0.2,0.3\} & \{0.4,0.6\} & \{0.1\} & \{0.2,0.3,0.4\} & \{0.2\} & \{0.5,0.6\} & \{0.7,0.8\} & \{0.6\} \end{array}$$

Step 2. Learn the structure of DHFBN.

Combining the advantages of HFIF and PSO algorithm, we adopt the improved PSO algorithm to learn the structure of DFHBN under the hesitant fuzzy environment. By constructing an unconstrained optimization model based on the causal analysis of HFIF, we obtain the initial structure and optimize the search space. In addition, the arcs and their directions can be determined by HFIF simultaneously based on the initial structure, which indicates that we can obtain the global optimal structure with higher accuracy and efficiency. Then the initial network and transition network, which combines the complete DHFBN of port investment, are presented in Fig. 4.9.

Step 3. Learn the parameters of DHFBN.

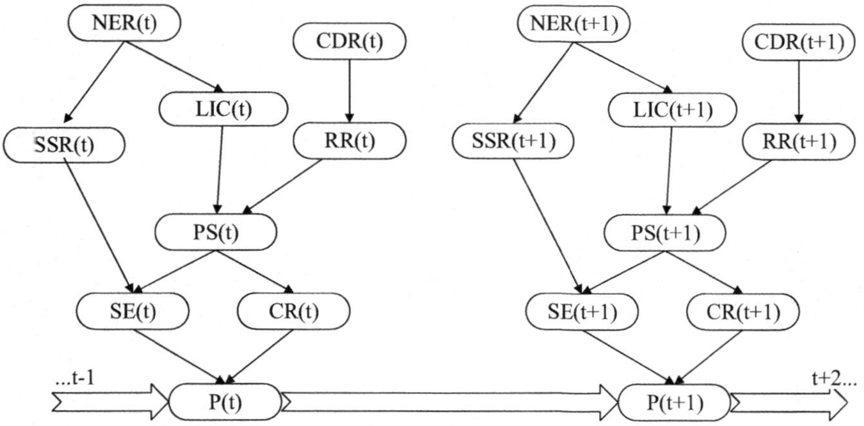

Fig. 4.9 The complete DHFBN structure of port investment

Table 4.7 The distribution of transition probability of the port P_2

P(t + 1)|P(t)	High(t + 1)	Medium(t + 1)	Low(t + 1)
High(t)	0.7125	0.2436	0.0439
Medium(t)	0.1823	0.6325	0.1852
Low(t)	0.0865	0.2018	0.7117

After constructing complete DHFBN structure, we use the training data to learn parameters by the EM algorithm. First, each node of the network is assigned a random probability distribution, including prior probability, observation probability and transition probability. Then, based on the input hesitant fuzzy training data, the EM algorithm is used to update and iterate the probability distribution of each node and finally the probability distribution is determined. Taking the port P_2 as an example, we present the transition probability of P_2 in Table 4.7 (Song et al., 2019).

Step 4. Predict the risk of port investment by the learned DHFBN.

Input the evaluation indicators of test sample to the learned DHFBN, and the probability distribution of investment risk is obtained through reasoning and forecasting. The prediction result of the port P_2 is presented in Fig. 4.10 (Song et al., 2019).

Step 5. Output the dynamic prediction results of the four ports.

According to the consultation information in the form of HFS and the learned DHFBN, we can obtain the dynamic risks of the four ports over time. The investors can make corresponding investment policies and strategies based on the dynamic prediction results to avoid and reduce the loss of enterprises and national investment.

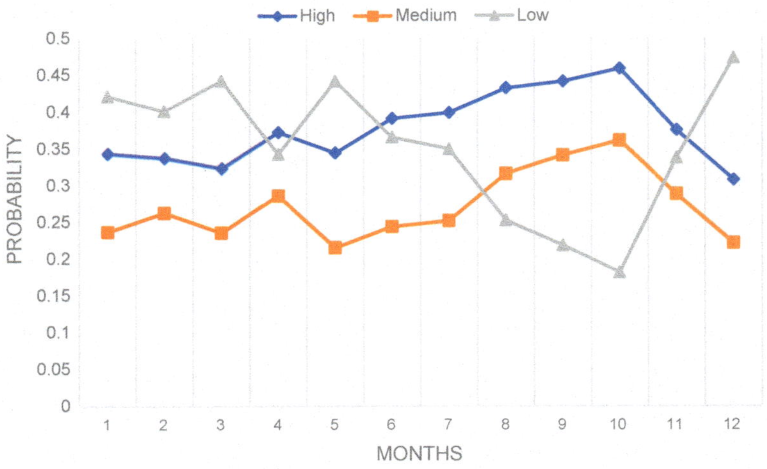

Fig. 4.10 The prediction result curves of the port P_2

4.6.3 Comparative Experiment and Results Analysis

In order to illustrate the advantages of the presented DHFBN method, we make a comprehensive comparison with the classical BN (Raftery et al., 2017) and fuzzy BN (FBN) (Eleyedatubo et al., 2010). If we only consider the membership degree of one expert, the HFS will be reduced to the Zadeh's fuzzy set (FS) (Zadeh, 1965). According to the above hesitant fuzzy evaluation matrixes, we can obtain the fuzzy probabilities in the BN when the membership function is taken into account only. Besides, it is convenient to take the mean of HFEs as the input source of probabilistic information in the classical BN. The data in the above case is transformed by the two data conversion methods. The possibilities of the most possible risks by BN are presented in Table 4.8. Besides, taking the port P_2 as an example, the comparison results by DHFBN, BN and FBN are also presented in Fig. 4.11 (Song et al., 2019).

Based on the comparison results, it is obvious that in the classical BN, the risk of port P_2 increases from July to September, and reaches the highest risk in September, after that, it decreases from September till December constantly. However, as to the FBN and DHFBN results, the risk increases from July to October and reaches the highest risk in October. For the medium risk, the comparison results of the three methods are very similar. In addition, for the low risk, the prediction results of the

Table 4.8 The possibilities of the most possible risks of the given ports by BN

Risk\Port	P1	P2	P3	P4
High	0.434	0.325	0.181	0.126
Medium	0.298	0.243	0.317	0.497
Low	0.268	0.432	0.502	0.377

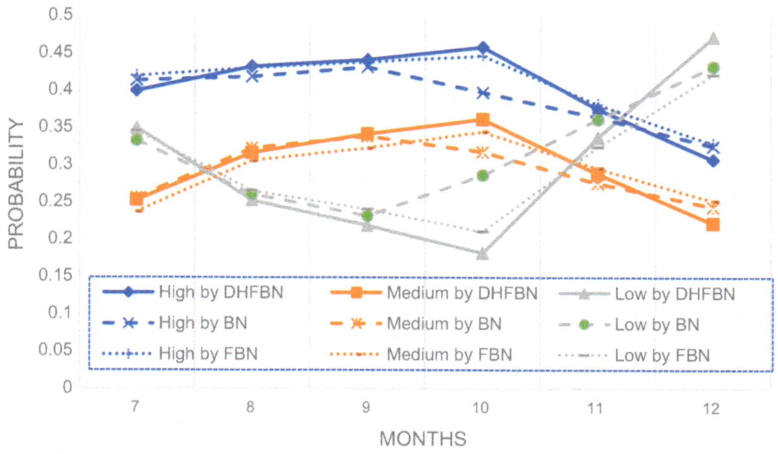

Fig. 4.11 The comparison results of the port P_2 by DHFBN, BN and FBN

three methods are almost same at the beginning three months. However, with the passage of time and the accumulation of uncertain information, the risk by DHFBN reaches the minimum at October.

In a word, the three methods are basically same in the trend of change, but the proposed DHFBN obtains more prominent and obvious prediction results with the accumulation of uncertain information over time. However, the trend changes of BN and FBN methods are relatively flat. The main reason for the differences is that the classical BN cannot depict the cognitive uncertainties and massive hesitant fuzzy data contained in the decision information. Though the FBN takes fuzzy uncertainties into account, it cannot make full use of uncertain information due to the rough granularity of fuzzy set. Compared with the classical BN and FBN, the proposed DHFBN not only makes full use of the massive original information with uncertainty as the sample increases, but also considers the influence of the time factor. It has certain advantages in characterization of uncertain information, especially in the hesitant fuzzy environment. The subtle difference in the original decision information can be better reflected in the final results. Besides, as time goes by, the risk of port investment is changing dynamically. The DHFBN combines the advantages of HFS in depicting massive uncertain information and the advantages of BN in probability reasoning. The main contribution of the proposed method is that it can not only make full use of the massive original information with uncertainty, but also save and accumulate the experience knowledge from previous reasoning and learning effectively. Different from other reasoning methods, it allocates dynamic uncertain information over time to iterate the decision making process. With the passage of time, more evidence and information are obtained, thus the DHFBN method can continuously improve the accuracy and reduce the uncertainty of reasoning effectively, i.e., the DHFBN can obtain a more reliable result for dynamic risk evaluation.

Table 4.9 Results comparison based on four methods

Methods	Alternative ranking
BN method with HFSs	$P_1 \succ P_2 \succ P_3 \succ P_4$
Aggregation method with HFSs	$P_1 \succ P_2 \succ P_3 \succ P_4$
Aggregation method with FSs	$P_3 \succ P_1 \succ P_4 \succ P_2$
Aggregation method with IFSs	$P_1 \succ P_4 \succ P_3 \succ P_2$

After that, in order to show superiority of the proposed methods with HFSs, we also prepare to compare and analyze some aggregation methods with different fuzzy sets. Since FSs and Intuitionistic Fuzzy Sets (IFSs) have been the most popular methods to deal with decision making problems, we make some comparisons with four methods, i.e., the BN method with HFSs, the aggregation method with HFSs, the aggregation method with FSs, and the aggregation method with IFSs. Table 4.9 presents the evaluation results of the four methods above (Song et al., 2019).

The results obtained by the proposed DHFBN method and the aggregation with HFSs are the same, and the optimal alternative are both P_1. However, if we adopt the aggregation methods with FSs and IFSs to solve the problem, the ranking results are a little different. The main reason is that the proposed method can make full use of the massive original preference information better, and is more delicate than FSs and IFSs. The comparative experiment validates the advantages and precision of the proposed DHFBN.

4.7 Remarks

The BN is an effective uncertain causal inference model in the field of uncertain reasoning. Different from other decision making models, it is a probabilistic knowledge representation and reasoning model that visualizes multi-knowledge graphically. Besides, the BN more appropriately contains causality and conditional correlation between network node variables. However, the increasing complexity and massive uncertain information of practical problems make it is difficult to obtain accurate information with sound reliability. In order to reserve original information as more as possible, this chapter considers the advantages of HFS in depicting massive uncertain data and presents the DHFBN model. Firstly, we introduce the concept of HFBN based on HF-event and the probability of the HF-event under the hesitant fuzzy environment. Then, to integrate the causality with uncertainty between different times, this chapter combines the time dimension with HFBN and gives a dynamic analysis and prediction method under the hesitant fuzzy environment (named as DHFBN). The structure with the most significant causality is learned by the improved PSO algorithm based on the HFIF. In addition, we introduce an improved EM algorithm to find the maximum likelihood estimation of parameters under the hesitant fuzzy environment. The whole reasoning process based on the DHFBN is also presented. Finally, a case study about the optimal investment port evaluation of "Twenty-First-Century Maritime Silk Road" illustrates the application and validity of the proposed DHFBN model.

References

Allahviranloo, M., & Afandizadeh, S. (2008). Investment optimization on port's development by fuzzy integer programming. *European Journal of Operational Research, 186*, 423–434.

Bailey, T. L., & Elkan, C. (1995). Unsupervised learning of multiple motifs in biopolymers using Expectation Maximization. *Machine Learning, 21*, 51–80.

Bielza, C., & Li, G. (2011). Multi-dimensional classification with Bayesian Networks. *International Journal of Approximate Reasoning, 52*, 705–727.

Borsuk, M. E., Stow, C., & Reckhow, K. H. (2004). A Bayesian Network of eutrophication models for synthesis, prediction and uncertainty analysis. *Ecological Modelling, 173*, 219–239.

Bradford, J., Bulpitt, A., Needham, C., et al. (2006). Insights into protein-protein interfaces using a Bayesian Network prediction method. *Journal of Molecular Biology, 362*, 365–386.

Chen, D., & Yang, Z. Z. (2017). Investment in container ports along the Maritime Silk Road in the context of international industry transfer: The case of the port of Colombo. *Maritime Economics & Logistics, 1*, 1–17.

Chen, M., & Han, L. (2016). Driving factors, areas of cooperation and mechanisms for International Cooperation in the Blue Economy of the 21st Century Maritime Silk Road. *Engineering Sciences, 18*, 98–102.

Chen, N., Xu, Z. S., & Xia, M. M. (2013). Correlation coefficients of hesitant fuzzy sets and their applications to clustering analysis. *Applied Mathematical Modelling, 37*, 2197–2211.

Cheng, J., & Druzdzel, M. J. (2011). AIS-BN: An adaptive importance sampling algorithm for evidential reasoning in large Bayesian Networks. *Journal of Artificial Intelligence Research, 13*, 158–188.

Cheng, J. W., & Liang, Y. U. (2007). Formation and evolution of world container ports system and coupling mechanism with international trade networks. *Geographical Research, 26*, 557–568.

Chickering, D. M. (1996). *Learning Bayesian Networks is NP-complete*. Springer.

Chou, C. C. (2007). A fuzzy MCDM method for solving marine transshipment container port selection problems. *Applied Mathematics & Computation, 186*, 435–444.

Christopher, L. (2015). China's 21st century maritime silk road initiative, energy security and SLOC Access. *Maritime Affairs Journal of the National Maritime Foundation of India, 11*, 1–18.

Commander, C. N., Wilson, P. S., & Hamilton, M. F. (2014). A brief history of the modeling of sound propagation in bubbly liquids. *Journal of the Acoustical Society of America, 135*, 22–32.

Duda, R. O., Hart, P. E., & Stork, D. G. (2001). *Pattern classification*. Wiley & Sons.

Eleyedatubo, A. G., Wall, A., & Wang, J. (2010). Marine and offshore safety assessment by incorporative risk modeling in a fuzzy Bayesian Network of an induced mass assignment paradigm. *Risk Analysis, 28*, 95–112.

Fei, L., & Deng, Y. (2019). Multi-criteria decision making in Pythagorean fuzzy environment. *Applied Intelligence*. https://doi.org/10.1007/s10489-019-01532-2

Friedman, N., Dan, G., & Moises, G. (1997). Bayesian Network Classifiers. *Machine Learning, 29*, 131–163.

Gheisari, S., & Meybodi, M. R. (2016). BNC-PSO: Structure learning of Bayesian Networks by Particle Swarm Optimization. *Information Sciences, 348*, 272–289.

Hao, Z. N., Xu, Z. S., Zhao, H., et al. (2018). A dynamic weight determination approach based on the intuitionistic fuzzy Bayesian Network and its application to emergency decision making. *IEEE Transactions on Fuzzy Systems, 26*, 1893–1907.

Hosack, G. R., Hayes, K. R., & Dambacher, J. (2008). Assessing model structure uncertainty through an analysis of system feedback and Bayesian Networks. *Ecological Applications A Publication of the Ecological Society of America, 18*, 1070–1082.

Jensen, F. V. (1997). *An introduction to Bayesian Networks*. Springer.

Karim, M. A. (2015). China's proposed Maritime Silk Road: Challenges and opportunities with special reference to the bay of Bengal Region. *Pacific Focus, 30*(2015), 297–319.

Len, C. (2015). China's 21st century maritime silk road initiative, energy security and SLOC Access. *Maritime Affairs Journal of the National Maritime Foundation of India, 11*, 1–18.

Liao, H. C., Xu, Z. S., & Zeng, X. J. (2015). Novel correlation coefficients between hesitant fuzzy sets and their application in decision making. *Knowledge-Based Systems, 82*, 115–127.

Liang, X. S. (2014). Unraveling the cause-effect relation between time series. *Physical Review E, 052201*. https://doi.org/10.1103/PhysRevE.90.052150.

Liu, Y., Ouyang, Li, C. P., et al. (2017). Ensemble method to joint inference for knowledge extraction. *Expert Systems with Applications, 83*, 114–121.

Liu, Y., Yin, X. B., & Xu, Y. P. (2017a). The analysis of gales over the "Maritime Silk Road" with remote sensing data. *Acta Oceanologica Sinica, 36*, 15–22.

Malone, B. (2015). Advanced methodologies for Bayesian Network. In *Advanced methodologies for Bayesian Networks*. Springer.

Meara, B. C. (2010). New heuristic methods for joint species delimitation and species tree inference. *Systematic Biology, 56*, 59–73.

Mokhtari, K., Ren, J., Roberts, C., et al. (2012). Decision support framework for risk management on sea ports and terminals using fuzzy set theory and evidential reasoning approach. *Expert Systems with Applications, 39*, 5087–5103.

Musso, E., Ferrari, C., & Benacchio, M. (2006). Port investment: Profitability, economic impact and financing. *Research in Transportation Economics, 16*, 171–218.

Pauplin, O., & Jiang, J. M. (2012). DBN-based structural learning and optimization for automated handwritten character recognition. *Pattern Recognition Letters, 33*, 685–692.

Pearl, J. (1988). *Probabilistic reasoning in intelligent systems: Networks of plausible inference*. Morgan Kaufmann.

Qiao, F. L., Guansuo, K., et al. (2019). China published ocean forecasting system for the 21st Century Maritime Silk Road on December 10, 2018. *Acta Oceanologics Sinica, 38*, 1–3.

Rafael, C., Andres, C., Manuel, G.-O., et al. (2016). Improvements to variable elimination and symbolic probabilistic inference for evaluating influence diagrams. *International Journal of Approximate Reasoning, 70*, 13–35.

Raftery, A. E., Gneiting, T., et al. (2017). Using Bayesian model averaging to calibrate forecast ensembles. *Monthly Weather Review, 133*, 1155-–1174.

Ross, B. J., & Eduardo, Z. (2007). Evolving dynamic Bayesian Networks with multi-objective genetic algorithms. *Applied Intelligence, 26*, 13–23.

Schwarz, G. (1978). Estimating the dimension of a model. *Annals of Statistics, 6*, 461–464.

Sharpe, F. W. (2012). Capital asset prices: A theory of market equilibrium under conditions of risk. *Journal of Finance, 19*, 425–442.

Song, C. Y., Zhang, Y. X., & Xu, Z. S. (2019). An improved structure learning algorithm of Bayesian Network Based on the hesitant fuzzy information flow. *Applied Soft Computing*. https://doi.org/10.1016/j.asoc.2019.105549

Song, C. Y., Zhang, Y. X., Xu, Z. S., et al. (2020). Dynamic hesitant fuzzy Bayesian Network and its application in the optimal investment port decision making problem of "twenty-first century maritime silk road." *Applied Intelligence*. https://doi.org/10.1007/s10489-020-01647-x

Stephane, H., Ranger, N., Mestre, O., et al. (2011). Assessing climate change impacts, sea level rise and storm surge risk in port cities: A case study on Copenhagen. *Climatic Change, 104*, 113–137.

Torra, V., & Narukawa, Y. (2009). On hesitant fuzzy sets and decision. In *The 18th IEEE International Conference on Fuzzy Systems* (pp., 1378–1381), Jeju Island, Korea.

Torra, V. (2010). Hesitant fuzzy sets. *International Journal of Intelligent Systems, 25*, 529–539.

Xia, M. M., & Xu, Z. S. (2011). Hesitant fuzzy information aggregation in decision making. *International Journal of Approximate Reasoning, 52*, 395–407.

Yang, L. Z., Zhang, R., Hou, T. P., et al. (2016). Hesitant cloud model and its application in the risk assessment of "The Twenty-First Century Maritime Silk Road." *Mathematical Problems in Engineering, 6*, 1–11.

Yang, Y., Tang, J., Wei, S., et al. (2013). Combining local search into-dominated sorting for multi-objective line-cell conversion problem. *International Journal of Computer Integrated Manufacturing, 26*, 316–326.

Zadeh, L. A. (1965). Fuzzy sets. *Information & Control, 8*, 338–353.

Zadeh, L. A. (1968). Probability measures of fuzzy events. *Journal of Mathematical Analysis & Applications, 23*, 421–427.

Zhang, D. (2016). Strengthening the rise of the 21st Century Maritime Silk Road strategic pivot. *Engineering Sciences, 18*, 105–110.

Zhang, X. D. (2018). Analysis of dynamic characteristics of the 21st Century Maritime Silk Road. *Journal of Ocean University of China, 17*(2018), 487–497.

Zhang, Y., Brady, M., & Smith, S. (2002). Segmentation of brain MR images through a hidden Markov random field model and the expectation-maximization algorithm. *IEEE Transactions on Medical Imaging, 20*, 45–57.

Chapter 5
Regression Analysis Models Under the Hesitant Fuzzy Environment

The complexity of practical problems generates lots of uncertain information, which brings great challenges to the study of regression analysis. Therefore, considering the advantages of HFS in depicting uncertain information, this chapter introduces the generalized regression neural network (GRNN) based on an improved fruit fly optimization algorithm and the optimal logistic regression model based on maximum entropy estimation under the hesitant fuzzy environment. We also apply them to the prediction of air quality index and emergency extreme air pollution event (EEAPE) respectively.

5.1 Motivations and Background

The neural network is one of the research hotspots in the field of artificial intelligence since the 1980s (Lavine, 2007). It simulates neurons from the perspective of information processing, which is the basic unit of information storage and processing in the human brain (Judd, 1991). The neural network is a mathematical algorithm model for Parallel Distributed Processing, consisting of a large number of neurons connected to each other based on different connection methods (Refenes et al., 1993). Each neuron represents a specific output function named as activation function. The connection between two neurons represents a weighting value for the signal passing through the connection. It is equivalent to the memory of neural network. The output of the network varies with different connection methods, weighting values and activation functions. The neural network has prominent advantages in nonlinear fitting, and it can map complex nonlinear relationships (Dillon, 1993; He & Liang, 2009). In addition, the learning rules of neural network are simple and easy to implement by machine. Owing to the strong robustness (Bechlioulis & Rovithakis, 2012; Hsiao et al., 2008), memory ability (Wayne et al., 2016), self-learning ability (Rubaai & Young, 2016) and non-linear mapping ability (Wang et al., 2017a) of neural network,

C. Song and Z. Xu, *Techniques of Decision Making, Uncertain Reasoning and Regression Analysis Under the Hesitant Fuzzy Environment and Their Applications*, Uncertainty and Operations Research, https://doi.org/10.1007/978-981-16-5800-6_5

it has been widely applied in the fields of pattern recognition (Addona et al., 2017), data prediction (Meng et al., 2017), intelligent robots (Saeedi et al., 2016; Wai & Muthusamy, 2013), automatic control (Jin et al., 2017; Lungu & Lungu, 2016), economy (Markellos et al., 2016; Singh & Dwivedi, 2018) and so on.

With the deepening of research work on neural network, scholars have proposed a variety of models, such as the Linear Neural Network (Hinton & Nowlan 1990), the Hopfield Neural Network (Hopfield, 1984), the Error Back Propagation Training Neural Network (BPNN) (Funahashi, 1989; Rumelhart et al., 1986), etc. By introducing the radial basis function (RBF) into the design of neural network, Broomhead and Lowe proposed the concept of the Radial Basis Function Neural Network (RBFNN) (Broomhead & Lowe, 1988). The RBFNN is a feed-forward neural network with the unique best approximation (Park & Sandberg, 2014), which avoids falling into the local minimum. It is an artificial neural network that uses the radial basis function as an activation function. The output of the RBFNN is a linear combination of the input radial basis function and the neuron parameters. As a special form of RBFNN, the generalized regression neural network (GRNN) (Specht, 1991) not only has the advantages of RBFNN, but also has a better stability than the traditional RBFNN. In addition, since the GRNN is derived from the radial basis function, there is only one free parameter in GRNN, i.e., the smooth parameter (Fernández-Gámez et al., 2016). In the process of constructing the GRNN, the prediction performance of the network only depends on the smooth factor. The most prominent advantage of the GRNN is the global convergence of its computational results (Wang et al. 2016a). Due to the GRNN's simple structure, ease of training, fast learning convergence and approximation to any non-linear functions, it has been widely applied in time series analysis (FiRat et al., 2010), pattern recognition (Alilou & Yaghmaee, 2015; Polat & Yildirim, 2008), information prediction (Bendu et al., 2017) and other fields.

In the classical GRNN, the input variables always consist of single membership degrees with sound reliability. However, due to the complexity and uncertainty of practical problems, it is hard to provide crisp values or certain consensuses. Besides, it is not easy to depict the ambiguity, imprecision and randomness of alternatives and preference information accurately. The uncertainty is not a transitional state caused by people's ignorance or limited knowledge, but an objective reflection of the essential characteristics of nature (Eddy et al., 1996). To depict the uncertainty comprehensively, Torra and Narukawa (2009) proposed the concept of hesitant fuzzy set (HFS) with the membership degree consisting of several possible values. It can depict massive uncertain information with more granularities and flexibility and avoid the loss of information. Due to the excellent characteristics of HFSs in uncertain information description, it has been widely applied in the fields of data analysis (Chen et al., 2013), medical diagnosis (Choi & Han, 2016), classification (Li et al., 2017) and so on. However, few researches on the GRNN consider the intensive data with uncertainty in practical problems. By depicting the massive data with the HFSs, we can expand the potential of the HFS in depicting massive data. It is also important for solving the practical problems in the era of big data.

In order to deal with the massive data with uncertainty and the dynamic characteristics of the application of GRNN, we introduce the GRNN model under hesitant fuzzy environment, which combines HFS with the GRNN. To determine the most appropriate smooth factor of GRNN, this chapter provides an improved fruit fly optimization algorithm with fast decreasing step (FDS-FOA) based on a dynamic step size function (Song et al.,2021a, 2021b). The FDS-FOA can balance the ability in global search and local search and allocate time to the two different search periods reasonably. It also improves the accuracy and efficiency of global optimization. Furthermore, the implementation process of the optimized GRNN based on FDS-FOA under hesitant fuzzy environment is presented. The advantages of the optimized GRNN model are summarized as follows (Song et al.,2021a, 2021b):

(a) The optimized GRNN algorithm can make full use of the massive original data and the experts' preferences with uncertainty effectively and avoid the loss of information.
(b) The optimized GRNN algorithm determines the most appropriate smooth factor by the FDS-FOA more quickly and accurately by a dynamic step size function.
(c) The optimized GRNN algorithm is more effective and reasonable in solving the complicated nonlinear problems under hesitant fuzzy environment, and it obtains better prediction results with higher accuracy and efficiency than traditional neural networks.

What's more, few researches on the logistic regression model consider samples with massive uncertain information in practical situations. This chapter also introduces the concept of hesitant fuzzy information flow (HFIF) to depict the causal relationship between two hesitant fuzzy variable sequences and select the main factors. It combines the advantages of the HFS in depicting uncertain information and advantages of the information flow (IF) in the causal analysis of nonlinear systems. To ensure the mutual independence of variables, the correlation coefficient between two HFSs is also introduced. Then we can screen out the core factors of the logistic regression model based on the HFIF and correlation coefficient. In actual problems, it is usually difficult to obtain sufficient samples and accurate information due to complexity and limitations of objective conditions. To infer the evolution of events from a small number of samples with uncertain information, this section presents the logistic regression model under hesitant fuzzy environment and introduces a new parameter estimation method based on the maximum entropy principle. It could deal with situations with only a few observed variables and no information about occurrence results of events. The Levenberg–Marquardt Algorithm (LMA) (More, 1977) under the hesitant fuzzy environment is provided to solve the parameter estimation problem with small samples and uncertain information in the logistic regression model. By combining the gradient descent method (Tseng & Yun, 2009) which is implementable and the Newton method (Battiti, 2014) which is fast convergent, the LMA greatly improves the accuracy and efficiency of global optimization. A Kolmogorov–Smirnov (K-S) test (Brown, 1982) is introduced to determine whether the optimized logistic regression model is applicable. An implementation process for the optimized logistic regression model based on the maximum entropy estimation under the hesitant fuzzy environment is also presented. The advantages of the optimized logistic regression model are summarized as follows (Song et al., 2021b):

a. The optimized logistic regression model can effectively use a small number of samples with massive uncertain information and avoid the loss of information as much as possible.
b. The optimized model determines main factors by the HFIF and most appropriate parameters by the LMA more accurately and rapidly.
c. The optimized model is more accurate and effective in managing complicated problems with small samples under hesitant fuzzy environment. Compared with the traditional logistic regression model, this model has better prediction effect and higher prediction accuracy.

5.2 Preliminaries

The GRNN is an improved RBFNN, which is built based on mathematical statistics and non-linear regression analysis. It has prominent advantages in non-linear mapping and approximation. Due to the flexible network structure and high fault tolerance of the GRNN, it is ideally suited to solve complex nonlinear problems. When the sample data are scarce, the prediction effect is still satisfying. Different from other feed-forward neural networks, the weight of GRNN is determined by the training samples. This may avoid the local minimum in the training process. In addition, it only needs to set a smoother factor. Compared with other traditional neural networks, the GRNN has faster learning speed and higher learning accuracy.

The structure of GRNN consists of four layers, including input layer, patter layer, summation layer and output layer. The number of neurons in the input layer is equal to the dimension of the input vector in the learning sample. Each neuron in the input layer is a simple distribution unit and passes the input variables to the patter layer directly. The number of neurons in patter layer is equal to the number of learning samples, and each neuron corresponds to a sample. Besides, there are two kinds of neurons in the summation layer. The number of neurons in the output layer is equal to the dimension of the output vector in the learning sample.

As a new notion to measure the causal relationship between variables by the time rate of information from a variable sequence to the other one, the IF and the normalized information flow (NIF) were first proposed by Liang (2014) respectively as:

$$T_{2\to 1} = \frac{C_{11}C_{12}C_{2,d1} - C_{12}^2 C_{1,d1}}{C_{11}^2 C_{22} - C_{11}C_{12}^2} \tag{5.1}$$

$$\tau_{2\to 1} = \frac{T_{2\to 1}}{Z_{2\to 1}} \tag{5.2}$$

where X_i and X_j are two series, C_{ij} denotes the covariance between X_i and X_j, $C_{i,dj}$ denotes the covariance between X_i and $\dot{X}_j$, and $Z_{2\to 1} \equiv |T_{2\to 1}| + \left|\frac{dH_1^*}{dt}\right| + \left|\frac{dH_1^{noise}}{dt}\right|$, in which H_1^* and H_1^{noise} are the marginal entropy and the stochastic effect respectively.

In addition, $\dot{X}_j$ is the difference approximation of $\frac{dX_j}{dt}$ by the Euler forward scheme, then $\dot{X}_{j,n} = \frac{X_{j,n+k}-X_{j,n}}{k\Delta t}$, where Δt denotes the time step, $k = 1$ for general time series, and $k = 2$ for extreme intensive sampled series. If $\tau_{2\to1} = 0$, then X_2 is not the cause of X_1; if $\tau_{2\to1} > 0$, then X_2 tends to make X_1 more uncertain and this also means that X_2 is the cause of X_1.

The logistic regression is a generalized linear regression analysis model and is widely applied in data mining, automatic disease diagnosis, economic prediction, etc. The logistic function is defined as:

$$\sigma(z) = \frac{1}{1+e^{-\lambda z}} \begin{cases} \to 1 \ \ if\, z \to +\infty \\ = 0.5 \ \ if\, z = 0 \\ \to 0 \ \ if\, z \to -\infty \end{cases} \quad (\lambda > 0) \tag{5.3}$$

Its geometric shape is a S-shaped curve as shown in Fig. 5.1 (Song et al., 2021b).

For a given training set $T = \{(x_1, y_1), (x_2, y_2), \ldots, (x_m, y_m)\}$, x_i consists of n independent variables, and $y_i = 1\ or\ 0$ means that the event occurs or does not occur, $i = 1, 2, \ldots, m$. Let $P(y = 1|x) = p$ be the conditional probability that the event y occurs under the condition of x, then the logistic regression model is

$$P(y = 1|x) = \frac{1}{1 + e^{-g(x)}} \tag{5.4}$$

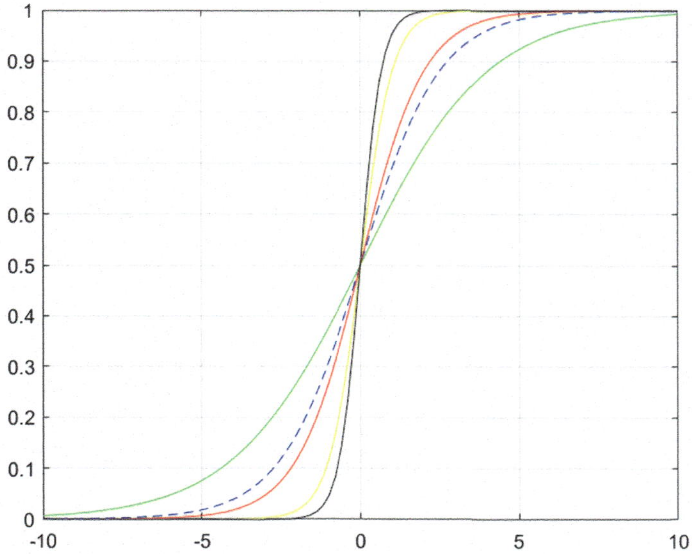

Fig. 5.1 The logistic regression curves with different λ

where $g(x) = \alpha + w_1 \cdot x_1 + w_2 \cdot x_2 + \cdots + w_n \cdot x_n$. In addition, the estimated weight parameters $\alpha, w_1, w_2, \ldots, w_n$ can be determined by the maximum likelihood estimation (Greenland & Drescher, 1993). The output result of the logistic function $y_i = 1\left(if\ P \geq 0.5\right)$ denotes that the event occurs and $y_i = 0\left(if\ P < 0.5\right)$ denotes the event does not occur. So the logistic regression model can also be regarded as a kind of probability estimation.

5.3 Optimized GRNN Based on FDS-FOA Under the Hesitant Fuzzy Environment

Considering the advantages of the HFS in depicting uncertain information, this section introduces a GRNN under the hesitant fuzzy environment, which integrates the HFS into GRNN. Then, we adopt the FDS-FOA with a dynamic step size function to optimize the smooth factor of GRNN. A specific implementation process of the optimized GRNN based on FDS-FOA is also presented (Song et al.,2021a, 2021b).

5.3.1 Generalized Regression Neural Network Under the Hesitant Fuzzy Environment

Considering the uncertainty in the application of GRNN, we introduce a new GRNN under the hesitant fuzzy environment. Different from the traditional GRNN, the input of GRNN under the hesitant fuzzy environment is expressed by HFSs. The detailed structure is illustrated in Fig. 5.2 (Song et al.,2021a, 2021b).

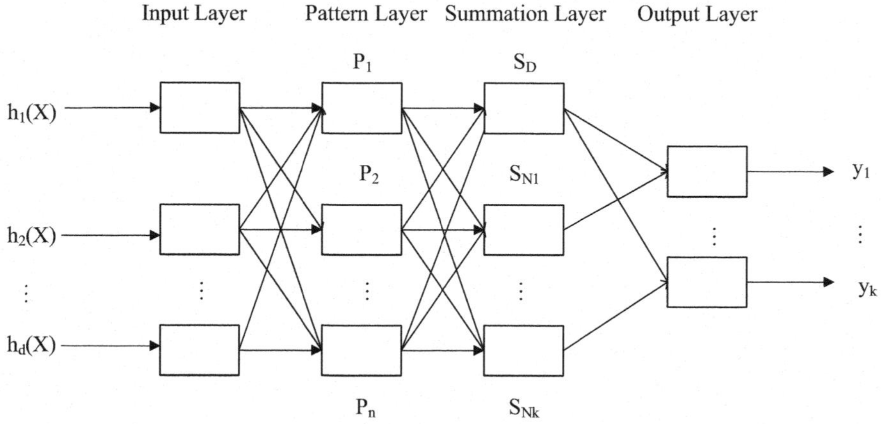

Fig. 5.2 The structure of GRNN under the hesitant fuzzy environment

(1) Input layer

The number of neurons in the input layer is equal to the number of the entered HFEs $h_i(X)(i = 1, 2, \ldots, n)$ in the learning samples. Each neuron passes the input hesitant fuzzy variable to the patter layer directly.

(2) Pattern layer

Same as the classical GRNN, the number of neurons in the patter layer equals to the number of the learning samples, and each neuron corresponds to a sample. The transfer function of the neurons in the patter layer is defined as follows:

$$p_i = \exp\left[-\frac{d(H(X), H_i(X))^T * d(H(X), H_i(X))}{2\sigma^2}\right] \tag{5.5}$$

where $i = 1, 2, \ldots, n$, $H(X)$ refers to the input hesitant fuzzy variable of the network, $H_i(X)$ refers to the learning sample corresponding to the i th neuron in the patter layer, $d(H(X), H_i(X))$ refers to the normalized hesitant fuzzy Euclidean distance between $H(X)$ and $H_i(X)$, and σ (named as smooth factor in this chapter) is the standard deviation of Gauss function.

(3) Summation layer

There are two kinds of neurons in the summation layer to sum the output of the neurons in the pattern layer respectively. In the summation layer, the outputs of neurons in the pattern layer is arithmetically summed and the connection weight between the pattern layer and each neuron is 1. The transfer function is defined as:

$$S_D = \sum_{i=1}^{n} p_i = \sum_{i=1}^{n} \exp\left[-\frac{d(H(X), H_i(X))^T * d(H(X), H_i(X))}{2\sigma^2}\right] \tag{5.6}$$

What's more, the summation layer performs weighted summation of the outputs of neurons in the pattern layer, and the connection weight between the ith neuron in the pattern layer and the jth neuron in the summation layer is the jth element in the ith output sample Y_i. The transfer function is defined as:

$$S_{Nj} = \sum_{i=1}^{n} y_{ij} p_i = \sum_{i=1}^{n} y_{ij} \exp\left[-\frac{d(H(X), H_i(X))^T * d(H(X), H_i(X))}{2\sigma^2}\right] \tag{5.7}$$

where $j = 1, 2, \ldots, k$, σ is the smooth factor.

(4) Output layer

The number of neurons in the output layer equals to the dimension of the output vector in the learning sample. The jth element of the predicted values corresponding to the jth neuron in the output layer is defined as:

$$y_j = \frac{S_{Nj}}{S_D} \tag{5.8}$$

where $j = 1, 2, \ldots, k$.

The GRNN is based on the nonlinear regression analysis. The regression analysis of the dependent variable Y with respect to the independent hesitant fuzzy variable $H(X)$ is actually to calculate Y with the maximum probability. Suppose that $f(H(X), Y)$ is the joint density of the random variables $H(X)$ and Y, then the conditional mean of Y refers to the regression of Y with respect to the hesitant fuzzy variable $H(X)$. According to the Parzen non-parametric estimation (Hastie et al., 2004), the predicted output of the network can be presented as follows:

$$\widehat{Y} = \frac{\sum_{i=1}^{n} Y_i \exp\left[-\frac{d(H(X),H_i(X))^T * d(H(X),H_i(X))}{2\sigma^2}\right]}{\sum_{i=1}^{n} \exp\left[-\frac{d(H(X),H_i(X))^T * d(H(X),H_i(X))}{2\sigma^2}\right]} \tag{5.9}$$

where $H(X)$ refers to the input hesitant fuzzy variable of the network, $H_i(X)$ and Y_i refer to the ith input and ith output of the training samples respectively, σ is the smooth factor and $i = 1, 2, \ldots, n$.

Actually, the predicted output $\widehat{Y}$ is the weighted average of the outputs Y_i ($i = 1, 2, \ldots, n$) in training samples, and the weighting factor of each output is the exponent of squared normalized hesitant fuzzy Euclidean distance between the corresponding training sample $H_i(X)$ and the input $H(X)$. In addition, the root mean square error (RMSE) between the predicted values of the GRNN and the actual values is introduced to evaluate the performance of the GRNN model (Noori et al., 2010):

$$RMSE\left(Y, \widehat{Y}\right) = \sqrt{\frac{\sum_{i=1}^{n}\left(Y_i - \widehat{Y}_i\right)^2}{n}} \tag{5.10}$$

where $i = 1, 2, \ldots, n$, $Y = \{y_1, y_2, \cdots, y_n\}$ is the set of actual values, and $\widehat{Y} = \{\widehat{y}_1, \widehat{y}_2, \ldots, \widehat{y}_n\}$ is the set of predicted values. It measures the degree that the predicted values deviate from the actual values. The smaller the RMSE value is, the higher the prediction accuracy of the GRNN model will be.

Compared with other neural network algorithms, the GRNN only needs to adjust the smooth factor σ, which is easier to implement. The smooth factor σ determines the prediction accuracy and generalization ability of the GRNN. Many scholars have studied how to determine the value of the smooth factor (Wang et al., 2016b; Wu et al., 2015), and they often choose the smoother factor based on the prior knowledge and personal experience. It will bring great randomness and errors in the regression analysis. Therefore, it is necessary to develop an efficient and automatic method to determine an appropriate value of the smooth factor σ. To achieve this, we adopt an improved fruit fly optimization algorithm to optimize the value of the smoother factor in the GRNN, which will be explained in detail in the next section.

5.3.2 *Fruit Fly Optimization Algorithm with Fast Decreasing Step*

Inspired by the foraging behavior of fruit fly, Pan (2016) proposed a new global optimization swarm intelligence algorithm named as the fruit fly optimization algorithm (FOA). The fruit fly swarm starts from their own positions and move within a certain range randomly. After that, the position with the highest taste concentration in the fruit fly swarm is selected, and other fruit flies move to the position. Taste concentration is the only information based on which the fruit flies judge the distance to food, the farther the distance is, the lower the taste concentration will be. Therefore, the value of the taste concentration can be obtained according to the distance. Through the iterative search, the fruit fly swarm approaches the final position of the food step by step. The detailed search process is presented in Fig. 5.3 (Song et al.,2021a, 2021b).

Compared with other intelligent algorithms, the FOA needs to adjust fewer parameters and avoids the interaction between parameters. Besides, the FOA converges to global optimization faster, and it is more efficient and easier to implement. Since the excellent properties of FOA, it has been widely applied in data mining (Lin, 2013), functional optimization (Du et al., 2018), power forecasting (Hu et al., 2017) and other fields. However, there are still some shortcomings that need to be improved. The iterative step size of the standard FOA is generated by a random function and

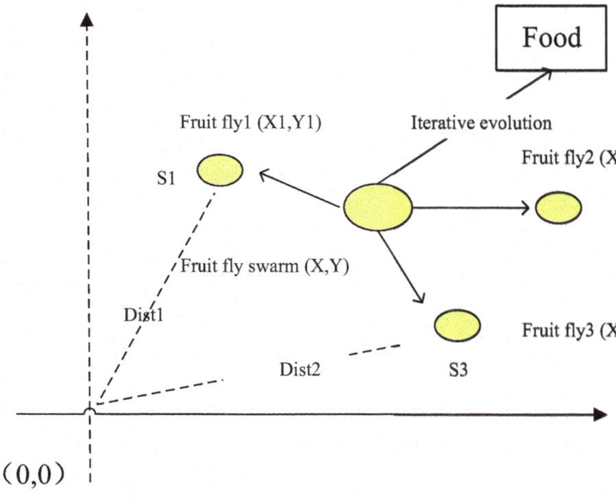

Fig. 5.3 The food finding iterative process of fruit fly swarm

remains constant through the whole optimization process. This will result in a low efficiency with a small step size in the prophase of the search optimization process, and it will be easy to fall into local optimum. In the later period of the search process, the step size may be too large to conduct a deep and precise search and the optimal solution may be missed. The step size determines the search ability and accuracy of the FOA and thus how to optimize the step size is crucial for the FOA.

In this section, we present an improved FOA with fast decreasing step (FDS-FOA) by a dynamic step size function (Song et al.,2021a, 2021b). It considers the characteristics of two periods in the search process and provides a more accurate result with high efficiency. The dynamic step size function can achieve a dynamic step size which adapts to different optimization periods. At the earlier stage of the search process, it has the largest search step with high global optimization ability, which avoids obtaining the local optimal solution. With the deepening of search process, the step size decreases fast with a higher local optimization ability, and it can make up for the deficiency of the traditional FOA in accuracy to some extent. The decreasing process of the step size is presented in Fig. 5.4 (Song et al.,2021a, 2021b).

The detailed steps of the FDS-FOA are listed as follows (Song et al.,2021a, 2021b):

Step 1: Set the basic parameters of the FDS-FOA, such as the initial step size, the maximum number of iterations and the scale of the fruit flies. The initial location of the fruit fly swarm is generated by the following formulas:

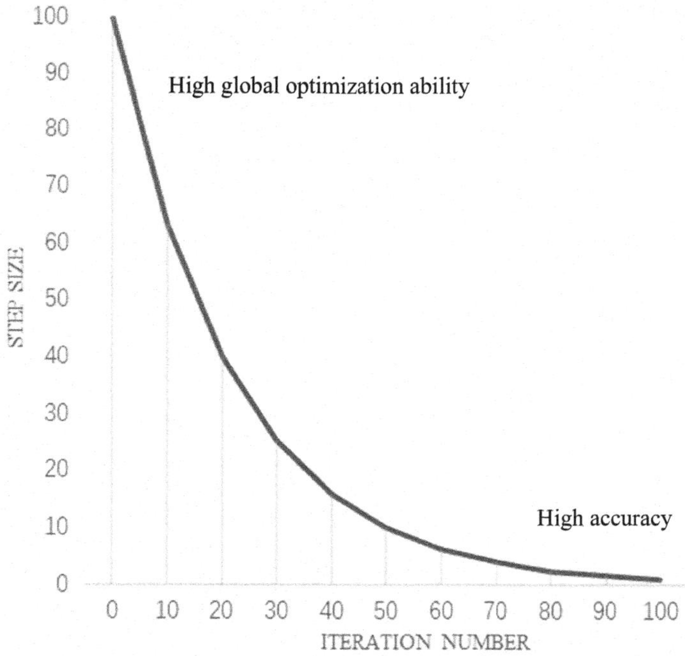

Fig. 5.4 Fast decreasing step size

$$x_0 = random \quad () \tag{5.11}$$

$$y_0 = random \quad () \tag{5.12}$$

Step 2: Search for food by the sense of smell, and determine the direction and distance of the fruit flies by the dynamic step size function:

$$L_i = L_0 \cdot \left(\frac{1}{100}\right)^{\frac{G_i}{G\max}} \tag{5.13}$$

where L_0 is the initial step size, $G_{\max}$ and G_i refer to the maximum number and current number of iterations, respectively. The location of the fruit fly swarm can be updated: $x_i = x_0 + L_i$ and $y_i = y_0 + L_i$.

Step 3: Calculate the distance between the location of the fruit fly and the origin and deduce the value of smell concentration:

$$Dist_i = \sqrt{x_i^2 + y_i^2} \tag{5.14}$$

$$S_i = \frac{1}{Dist_i} \tag{5.15}$$

Step 4: Calculate the smell concentration of the location of each fruit fly by the smell concentration function. By comparing the smell concentrations of different fruit flies, we identify the position with the highest smell concentration:

$$Smell_i = Function(S_i) \tag{5.16}$$

$$[bestSmell] = \max(Smell_i) \tag{5.17}$$

Step 5: Record and remain the position with the highest smell concentration (x_b, y_b), and then other fruit flies fly towards the position and gather together again:

$$Smellbest = bestSmell \tag{5.18}$$

$$x_b = x(bestSmell) \text{ and } y_b = y(bestSmell) \tag{5.19}$$

Step 6: Search for food by the sense of smell again, and update the position of each fruit fly by the dynamic step size function. Recalculate the values of smell concentration, and check whether the highest smell concentration in this iteration is better than the one in the previous iteration. If it is, then we replace the highest smell concentration with the former one; otherwise, go to the next step.

Step 7: Check whether the termination condition is satisfied. If it is satisfied, then we end the run and output the global optimal solution. Otherwise, return to Step 2.

The FDS-FOA can search for the global optimal solution more quickly and accurately by the dynamic step size. At the earlier stage of the search optimization process, the improved algorithm can achieve global search by a fast decreasing step, and it converges rapidly. In the later period of the search optimization process, the range of step size is gradually decreased, and the FDS-FOA conducts a local high-precision search to improve convergence accuracy. Through a dynamic step size and the reasonable allocation of time in two search periods, the improved FDS-FOA can balance the capability of global search and local search. It improves the accuracy and efficiency of global optimization.

5.3.3 Optimized GRNN Based on FDS-FOA

Since the smooth factor σ is the most important element that determines the performance of GRNN, we adopt the FDS-FOA to determine the most appropriate smooth factor σ to optimize and improve the GRNN. First, we adopt the RMSE between the predicted values of the GRNN and the actual values as the function of smell concentration. Then we identify the position with the highest smell concentration through the random foraging of fruit flies and the iterative optimization, which ensures the RMSE between the predicted values of the GRNN and the actual values is minimized. Furthermore, we record the position with the highest smell concentration and obtain the most appropriate value of the smooth factor σ. Finally, we can construct an optimal GRNN model with the most appropriate smooth factor based on the FDS-FOA under hesitant fuzzy environment. A specific implementation process of the optimized GRNN based on FDS-FOA is illustrated in Fig. 5.5 (Song et al., 2021b).

The HFS makes full use of the uncertain knowledge and fuzzy information. Besides, the FDS-FOA makes up for the deficiency of the GRNN in determining the most appropriate smooth factor, which influences the prediction results fundamentally. The optimized GRNN based on FDS-FOA under hesitant fuzzy environment combines the advantages of the HFSs in depicting uncertain information and the advantages of the FDS-FOA in global optimization. It provides more accurate and reliable prediction results.

5.4 Application of the Optimized GRNN Model to the Prediction of Air Quality Index

To illustrate the practicability of the optimized GRNN based on FDS-FOA under the hesitant fuzzy environment, we provide an air quality index (AQI) prediction model based on the optimized GRNN. After that, a practical AQI prediction problem of

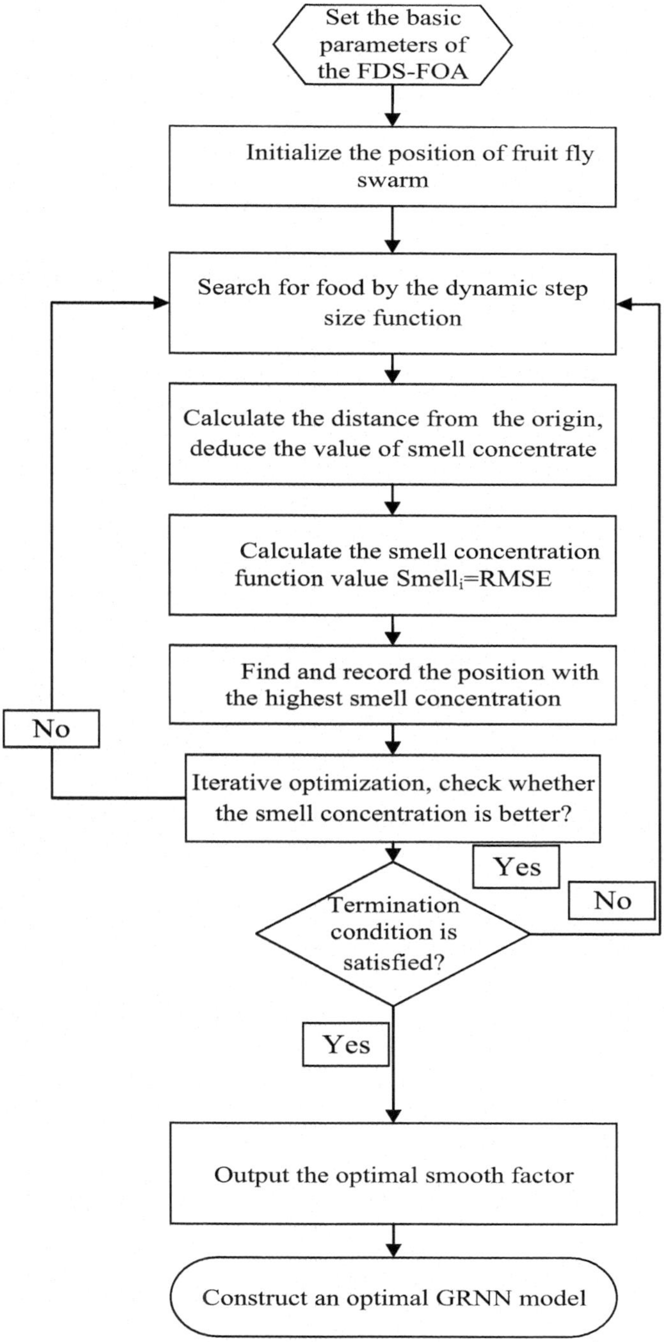

Fig. 5.5 The specific implementation process of the optimized GRNN based on FDS-FOA

Beijing is presented to evaluate the performance of the proposed model. Besides, we conduct some comparative analysis and sensitivity analysis to illustrate the advantages of the optimized GRNN.

5.4.1 AQI Prediction Model Based on the Optimized GRNN

The quality of air reflects the degree of air pollution, which is measured by the concentration of pollutants in the air. To evaluate the quality of air quantitatively, the AQI (Wang et al., 2017b) was introduced. It simplifies the concentration of several major air pollutants into a single conceptual index number and can classify the degree of air pollution and air quality status, as presented in Table 5.1 (Song et al., 2021b).

In recent years, the serious air pollution problem has caused widespread concern. It not only damages people's health, but also inhibits the development of economy. The air pollution is a complicated phenomenon, which is influenced by many factors. Complex mechanisms and other uncertainties also increase the difficulty in predicting the AQI. Therefore, the prediction of AQI is particularly important. To achieve this goal, we first identify and determine the main indicators that influence the AQI prediction. This section mainly focuses on the concentration of pollutants in the air and the dynamically changing meteorological factors. The main pollutants involved in AQI prediction are: $PM_{2.5}$, PM_{10}, SO_2, NO_2, CO and O_3. Besides, the meteorological conditions also affect the air quality, mainly including temperature (T), maximum wind speed (MWS) and average relative humidity (ARH). However, the data of the main pollutants in the air and meteorological conditions are dynamically changing. The large amounts of the data collected from the bureau of meteorology and department of environment (National Meteorological Information Center) may be intensive and contain more uncertainty.

To depict the uncertainty and dynamic changes of the main pollutants and meteorological conditions, we adopt the HFSs to depict the data with uncertainty. To predict the AQI accurately and efficiently, we construct a prediction model by the optimized GRNN based on FDS-FOA under the hesitant fuzzy environment. As shown in Fig. 5.6, the main idea of the AQI prediction model is to train the network by the training samples first and then obtain the most appropriate smooth factor of the GRNN by FDS-FOA. After that, we construct the optimized GRNN model based on the FDS-FOA. At last, the model is tested by the testing samples (Song et al.,2021a, 2021b).

Table 5.1 The classification of air quality degree

Air quality degree	Excellent	Good	Light polluted	Moderate polluted	Heavy polluted	Serious polluted
AQI	0–50	51–100	101–150	151–200	201–300	>300

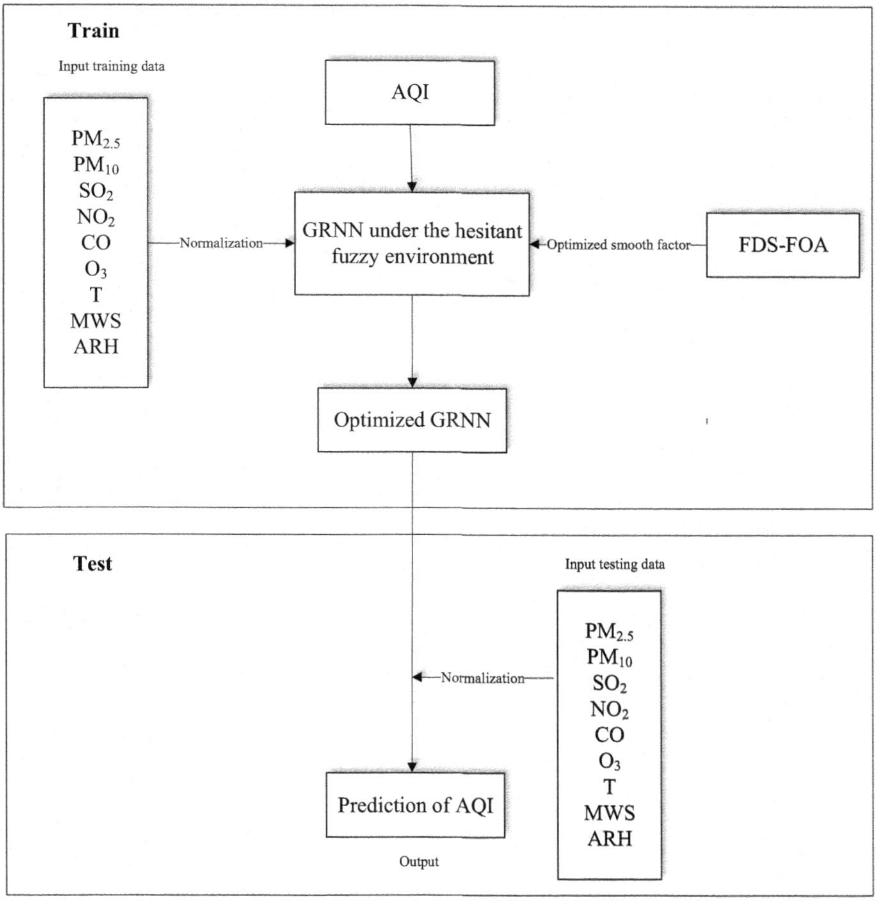

Fig. 5.6 The process of the AQI prediction model based on the optimized GRNN by the FDS-FOA

5.4.2 Case Study and Data Processing

In order to illustrate the validity of the proposed AQI prediction model based on the optimized GRNN by FDS-FOA, we present a practical AQI prediction problem in Beijing, China. In recent decades, Beijing has been trapped in air pollution, which has damaged the health of people. Therefore, relevant departments have taken drastic measures to remediate pollution sources, as well as adjusting energy structure and increasing the use of clean energy. According to the numbers of days for each level of AQI in the past five years (see Fig. 5.7), we can see that, since 2014, the concentration of major pollutants in the atmosphere of Beijing has generally declined, and the number of days with good AQI increase significantly.

However, in autumn and winter, heavy pollution is still prone to occur due to the unfavorable meteorological conditions and increased pollutant emissions in heating

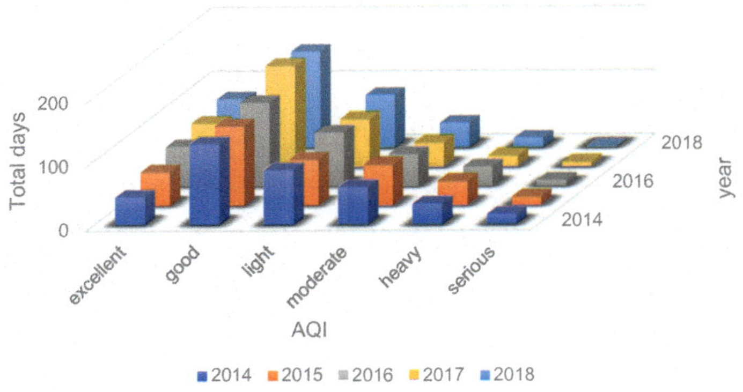

Fig. 5.7 The number of days for each level of air quality

seasons. Therefore, the prediction of AQI in Beijing is a matter of cardinal significance. We utilize the HFEs to depict their daily minimum, average and maximum values at the same time. The daily minimum and maximum values of temperature are also expressed by the HFEs. Besides, we adopt the average values to depict ARH and AQI and the maximum values to depict the MWS, which are not changing so prominently. To unify different kinds of data, we transform the original data into the hesitant fuzzy information by the following linear transformation:

$$\gamma_i = \frac{x_i - \min(x)}{\max(x) - \min(x)} \tag{5.20}$$

where x_i $(i = 1, 2, \cdots, n)$ are the original data of each attribute. The normalization of temperature is presented in Table 5.2 as an example to understand the above equation (Song et al.,2021a, 2021b).

Then, the original data of the concentration of pollutants in the air and meteorological factors can be transformed into HFSs. They are normalized and provided for the proposed AQI model based on the optimized GRNN under the hesitant fuzzy environment.

Table 5.2 The process of normalizing the temperature

Value	Date				
	10/1	10/2	…	12/31	All
Minimum	15	16	…	−6	−9
Maximum	26	26	…	3	28
Normalized	0.65	0.68	…	0.08	0
	0.95	0.95	…	0.32	1

5.4.3 Experiment and Comparative Analysis

Based on the data of concentration of pollutants and meteorological conditions from 2014 to 2018, we construct the model of AQI prediction based on the optimized GRNN. Those data are normalized and divided in two sections: 1796 datasets for training and 30 datasets for testing. The normalized data are input into to the AQI prediction model based on the optimized GRNN. Through training, we can obtain the model with the most appropriate value of smooth factor $\sigma = 0.0476$. Then, we test the trained prediction model by the 30 datasets, and the AQI curves of the actual value and the predicted value by the optimized GRNN are presented in Fig. 5.8. Besides, the value of RMSE is 5.087, which demonstrates the good performance of the model in accuracy.

In addition, we make a comparison with the Back Propagation Neural Network (BPNN) to highlight the effectiveness and advantages of the proposed model. It is a multi-layer feed-forward neural network based on the error back propagation algorithm. The BPNN is a flexible multi-layer feed-forward neural network. The numbers of middle layers and the neurons in each layer can be set according to different conditions and determine the performance of the BPNN. The AQI curves of the actual and predicted value by the BPNN are presented in Fig. 5.9 (Song et al.,2021a, 2021b). Besides, the value of RMSE is 9.786, which is larger than 5.087. It is obvious that the accuracy of the optimized GRNN is higher.

The experimental results indicate that the convergence speed of the optimized GRNN is much faster than that of the traditional BPNN under the same conditions. The optimized GRNN improves the effectiveness of the prediction and is ideal for dynamic and real-time prediction of AQI. Moreover, the structure of the optimized GRNN is simple to determine according to the specific problem. There is only one parameter that needs to be determined by the FDS-FOA. Besides, the prediction accuracy of the optimized GRNN is much better than that of the traditional neural networks. When the sample data are small, the prediction result of the proposed

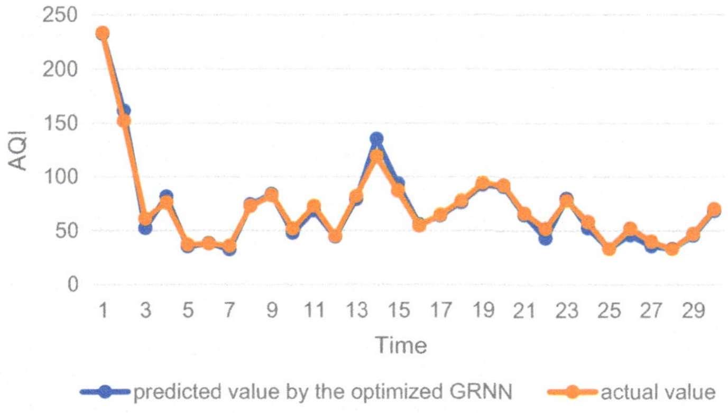

Fig. 5.8 The AQI curves of actual and predicted value by the optimized GRNN

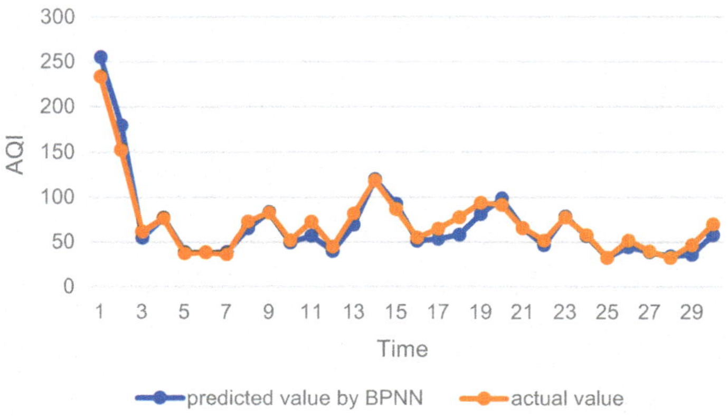

Fig. 5.9 The AQI curves of actual and predicted value by BPNN

model is also good. However, the structure of BPNN is much complicated, and there is no valid method to determine the most appropriate number of hidden layer nodes, learning rate and so on. In addition, the stability of prediction results by BPNN is very poor, which is inconsistent with reality.

The optimized GRNN under the hesitant fuzzy environment not only can make full use of the massive original data effectively, but also can depict the uncertain information more delicately. However, the traditional neural networks cannot depict the uncertain information and are insensitive to little change of data. The relevant parameters of the optimized GRNN are determined based on the samples in the training set by certain rules. Besides, we determine the most appropriate smooth factor of the GRNN by the FDS-FOA. However, the initial weights of traditional BPNN are generated randomly. This leads to the shortcoming that the BPNN model converges slowly and is easy to fall into the local minimum in the training process. Then, the prediction results derived by the traditional BPNN may not meet the expected requirements. Our model can simulate the learning process of the neural network and determine the most appropriate smooth factor of GRNN through the FDS-FOA. The optimized GRNN is a better forward network with the best approximation and it overcomes the limitation of falling into the local minimum. The prediction results derived by our model are more precise and reliable.

5.4.4 Sensitivity Analysis

As mentioned above, the value of the smooth factor determines the performance of the GRNN. In practical applications, it is difficult to determine an appropriate smooth factor. The smaller the value of the smooth factor is, the better the approximation of the model to the sample will be; while it may lead to over-fitting. The larger the value of smooth factor is, the smoother the approximation process of the model

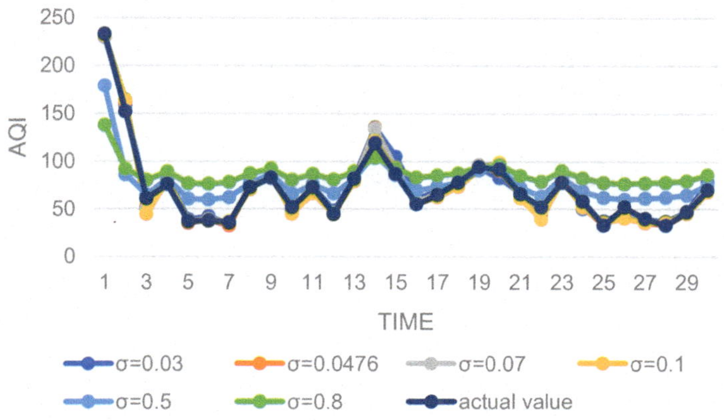

Fig. 5.10 The AQI curves of GRNN with different smooth factors

Table 5.3 The calculation results of RMSE based on different values of smooth factor

Smooth factors	0.03	0.0476	0.07	0.1	0.5	0.8
RMSE	6.104	5.087	5.624	6.018	20.856	32.357

to the sample data will be; while the RMSE increases accordingly. Therefore, we introduce the FDS-FOA to determine the most appropriate smooth factor of the GRNN. To illustrate the influence of the smooth factor in GRNN on the prediction results, five groups of values of the smooth factor σ are set to make a sensitivity analysis of the smooth factor in the GRNN: (1)$\sigma = 0.03$; (2)$\sigma = 0.07$; (3)$\sigma = 0.1$; (4)$\sigma = 0.5$; (5)$\sigma = 0.8$. The convergence curves of prediction results based on the different values of σ are shown in Fig. 5.10. In addition, we calculate the values of RMSE between the prediction results with different smooth factors and the actual data (see Table 5.3) (Song et al.,2021a, 2021b).

From Fig. 5.10, we can see that the GRNN model fits better. In addition, Table 5.3 indicates that, when $\sigma = 0.0476$, the prediction result is the best. It means that we can obtain the most appropriate value of smooth factor by the FDS-FOA algorithm quickly, which optimizes the GRNN and improves the accuracy of prediction.

In general, it is difficult to determine the smooth factor of GRNN. The traditional FOA algorithm is easy to fall into the local optimum in determining the smooth factor. Therefore, we improve the traditional FOA algorithm by a dynamic step size function, which can make up for this deficiency. The optimized GRNN based on the FDS-FOA under the hesitant fuzzy environment can not only make full use of uncertain information, but also determine the most appropriate smooth factor of GRNN. It has prominent advantages in dealing with prediction problems with uncertain information.

5.5 Optimized Logistic Regression Model Based on the Maximum Entropy Estimation Under the Hesitant Fuzzy Environment

Considering the complexity and uncertainty in the application of the logistic regression, this section first introduces the concept of HFIF to select main factors. The correlation coefficient between two HFSs is also introduced to ensure that all the factors are mutually independent. After that, a new logistic regression model under the hesitant fuzzy environment is presented. Then, a new optimized method based on the maximum entropy estimation is also provided to determine the parameters. At last, the LMA under the hesitant fuzzy environment is given to solve the parameter estimation problem with small samples and uncertain information. A K-S test is also carried out to judge whether the optimized logistic regression model is applicable. A brief implementation process for the optimized logistic regression model is illustrated in Fig. 5.11 (Song et al., 2021b).

5.5.1 *Hesitant Fuzzy Information Flow*

With the nonlinearity of the evolution and the complexity of practical problems, massive data with uncertainty brings more challenges to the application of the logistic regression. To begin with, a new notion named HFIF is introduced to determine main factors that affect the results of events.

Definition 5.1 (Song et al., 2019). For two hesitant fuzzy series $H_1 = \{\langle x, h_1(x_i)\rangle | x_i \in X\}$ and $H_2 = \{\langle x, h_2(x_i)\rangle | x_i \in X\}$ $(i = 1, 2, \ldots, n)$, the rate of information flowing from H_2 to H_1 is:

$$T(h)_{2\to 1} = \frac{Cov(H_1, H_1)Cov(H_1, H_2)Cov\big(H_2, \dot{H}_1\big) - Cov^2(H_1, H_2)Cov\big(H_1, \dot{H}_1\big)}{Cov^2(H_1, H_1)Cov(H_2, H_2) - Cov(H_1, H_1)Cov^2(H_1, H_2)} \tag{5.21}$$

where Cov denotes the covariance between two hesitant fuzzy series, and $\dot{H}$ denotes the difference approximation of $\frac{dH}{dt}$ by the Euler forward scheme. For a two-dimensional dynamic system $\frac{dH}{dt} = U(H, t) + V(H, t)\dot{W}$, the change rate of the marginal entropy H_1^* of the hesitant fuzzy series H_1 is $\frac{dH_1^*}{dt} = -S\Big(U_{H_1}\frac{\partial \log \rho_{H_1}}{\partial \bar{h}_{H_1}(x)}\Big) - \frac{1}{2}S\Bigg(g_{11}\frac{\partial^2 \log \rho_{H_1}}{\partial \bar{h}^2_{H_1}(x)}\Bigg)$, where U and V denote arbitrary nonlinear functions of H, $\dot{W}$ denotes a two-dimensional vector of white noise, S denotes the expectation function, ρ_H denotes the marginal density of H, and $g_{ij} = \sum_k b_{ik}b_{jk}$. Furthermore, it can be conducted that:

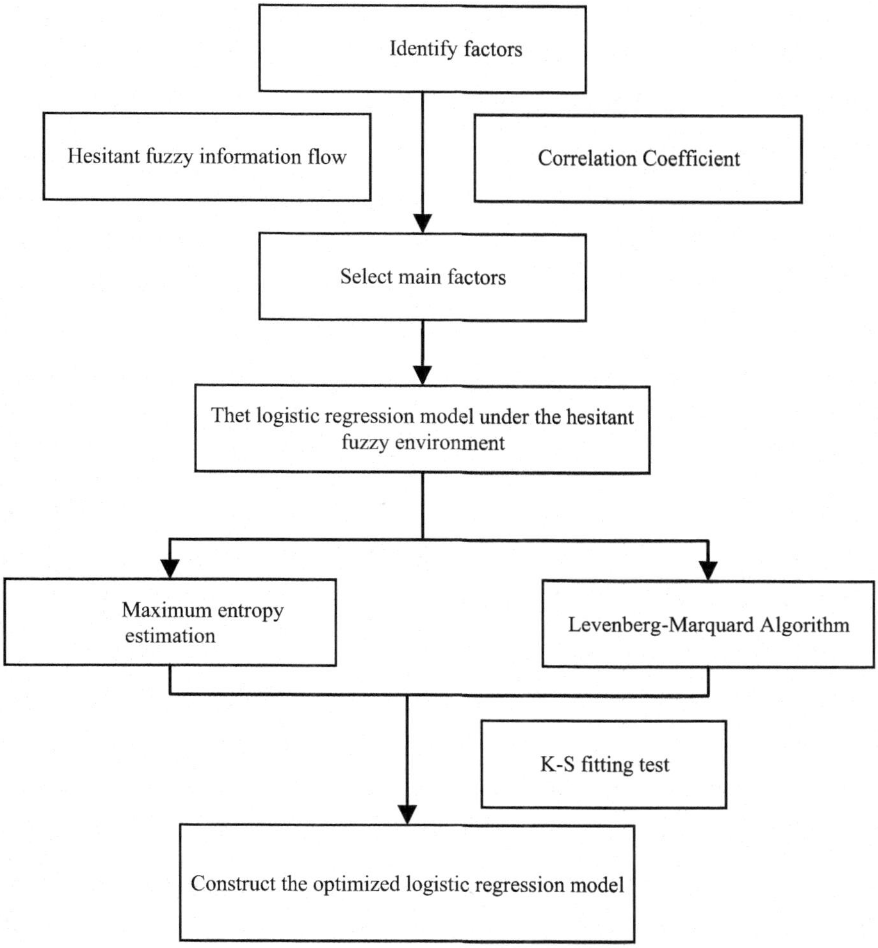

Fig. 5.11 The brief implementation process of the optimized logistic regression model

$$-S\left(U_{H_1}\frac{\partial \log \rho_{H_1}}{\partial \overline{h}_{H_1}(x)}\right) = -S\left[\frac{1}{\rho_{H_1}}\frac{\partial\left(F_{H_1}\rho_1\right)}{\partial \overline{h}_{H_1}(x)} - \frac{\partial U_{H_1}}{\partial \overline{h}_{H_1}(x)}\right] = S\left(\frac{\partial U_{H_1}}{\partial \overline{h}_{H_1}(x)}\right) - S\left[\frac{1}{\rho_{H_1}}\frac{\partial\left(U_{H_1}\rho_{H_1}\right)}{\partial \overline{h}_{H_1}(x)}\right] \tag{5.22}$$

The equation of $\frac{dH_1^*}{dt}$ is:

$$\frac{dH_1^*}{dt} = S\left(\frac{\partial F_{H_1}}{\partial \overline{h}_{H_1}(x)}\right) + T(h)_{2\to 1} + \left[-\frac{1}{2}S\left(\frac{1}{\rho_{H_1}}\frac{\partial^2 g_{11}\rho_{H_1}}{\partial \overline{h}^2_{H_1}(x)}\right) - \frac{1}{2}S\left(g_{11}\frac{\partial^2 \log \rho_{H_1}}{\partial \overline{h}^2_{H_1}(x)}\right)\right] \tag{5.23}$$

where $T(h)_{2\to1} = -S\left[\frac{1}{\rho_{H_1}}\frac{\partial(U_{H_1}\rho_{H_1})}{\partial \bar{h}_{H_1}(x)}\right] + \frac{1}{2}S\left(\frac{1}{\rho_{H_1}}\frac{\partial^2 g_{11}\rho_{H_1}}{\partial \bar{h}^2_{H_1}(x)}\right)$ is the rate of hesitant fuzzy information flowing, and $-\frac{1}{2}S\left(\frac{1}{\rho_{H_1}}\frac{\partial^2 g_{11}\rho_{H_1}}{\partial \bar{h}^2_{H_1}(x)}\right) - \frac{1}{2}S\left(g_{11}\frac{\partial^2 \log \rho_{H_1}}{\partial \bar{h}^2_{H_1}(x)}\right) = \frac{dH_1^{*noise}}{dt}$ denotes the stochastic effect.

Assume that all variables are subject to the original Gaussian distribution (Liang, 2015) and $\mathrm{U} = u + AN + BB^T$, $u = (u_1, u_2)^T$, $A = (a_{ij})_{i,j=1,2}$ and $B = (b_{ij})_{i,j=1,2}$ are three constant matrices. Then

$$\rho_{H_1} = \frac{1}{\sqrt{2\pi}\sigma_{H_1}}\exp\left[-\frac{\left(\bar{h}_{H_1}(x) - \mu_{H_1}\right)^2}{2\sigma^2_{H_1}}\right] \tag{5.24}$$

Therefore, it is easy to infer that

$$\frac{dH_1^{*noise}}{dt} = \frac{1}{2}\frac{g_{11}}{\sigma_{H_1}} \tag{5.25}$$

Based on the above analysis, the normalized HFIF (NHFIF) is defined as:

$$\tau(h)_{2\to1} = \frac{abs T(h)_{2\to1}}{abs(T(h)_{2\to1}) + abs\left(\frac{dH_1^{*noise}}{dt}\right)} \tag{5.26}$$

where abs is the absolute value function and $\tau(h)_{2\to1} \in [0, 1]$.

Comparing the above definition with the traditional normalization formula, it is obvious that we omit the term $\left|S\left(\frac{\partial U_{H_1}}{\partial \bar{h}_{H_1}(x)}\right)\right|$. It measures the contribution itself and results in a relatively small value of causality that can lead to errors. The value of $\tau(h)_{2\to1}$ measures the effect of H_2 on H_1. If $\tau(h)_{2\to1} \to 1$, then the series H_2 does completely cause the series H_1; if $\tau(h)_{2\to1} \to 0$, then the series H_2 is not an important factor in the occurrence and development of the series H_1. This means that the causal relationship between the two series is extremely weak. Therefore, we can determine the cause-effect relationship and main factors that affect the results of events by calculating the NHFIF $\tau(h)_{1\to2}$.

After that, we introduce the concept of correlation coefficient between to HFSs to ensure that all the factors are mutually independent. Given two HFSs H_1 and H_2, the correlation coefficient between two HFSs $M = \{x, h_M(x)|x \in X\}$ and $N = \{x, h_N(x)|x \in X\}$ is (Li et al., 2017):

$$\rho(M,N)=\frac{\frac{1}{n}\sum_{i=1}^{n}\left[\frac{1}{l_{Mi}}\sum_{k=1}^{l_{Mi}}\gamma_{Mik}-\frac{1}{n}\sum_{i=1}^{n}\left(\frac{1}{l_{Mi}}\sum_{k=1}^{l_{Mi}}\gamma_{Mik}\right)\right]\cdot\left[\frac{1}{l_{Ni}}\sum_{k=1}^{l_{Ni}}\gamma_{Nik}-\frac{1}{n}\sum_{i=1}^{n}\left(\frac{1}{l_{Ni}}\sum_{k=1}^{l_{Ni}}\gamma_{Nik}\right)\right]}{\left[\frac{1}{n}\sum_{i=1}^{n}\left(\frac{1}{l_{Mi}}\sum_{k=1}^{l_{Mi}}\gamma_{Mik}-\frac{1}{n}\sum_{i=1}^{n}\left(\frac{1}{l_{Mi}}\sum_{k=1}^{l_{Mi}}\gamma_{Mik}\right)\right)^2\cdot\frac{1}{n}\sum_{i=1}^{n}\left(\frac{1}{l_{Ni}}\sum_{k=1}^{l_{Ni}}\gamma_{Nik}-\frac{1}{n}\sum_{i=1}^{n}\left(\frac{1}{l_{Ni}}\sum_{k=1}^{l_{Ni}}\gamma_{Nik}\right)\right)^2\right]^{\frac{1}{2}}} \tag{5.27}$$

where $h_M(x_i) = \{\gamma_{Mi1}, \gamma_{Mi2}, \ldots, \gamma_{Mil_{Mi}}\}$ and $h_N(x_i) = \{\gamma_{Ni1}, \gamma_{Ni2}, \ldots, \gamma_{Nil_{Ni}}\}$ $(i = 1, 2, \ldots, n)$. The value of $\rho(M, N)$ measures the relationship between two factors. If $\rho(M, N)$ is greater than 0.5, then there is a significant correlation between them.

5.5.2 Logistic Regression Model Under the Hesitant Fuzzy Environment

In this subsection, we introduce a new logistic regression model under the hesitant fuzzy environment, which combines HFS with the logistic regression. Different from the traditional logistic regression model, variables under the hesitant fuzzy environment are expressed by HFSs (Song et al., 2021b). Then we adjust the traditional logistic regression model according to the operation laws of HFSs. The definition of the logistic regression model under hesitant fuzzy environment is presented as follows:

Definition 5.2 (Song et al., 2021b). Let $H_i = \{\langle x, h(x)\rangle | x \in X\}$ be an n-dimensional independent random hesitant fuzzy variable consisting of n HFEs, i.e., $H_i = \{\overline{h}_{i1}, \overline{h}_{i2}, \ldots, \overline{h}_{in}\}$. $y_i = 1$ *or* 0 denotes that the event occurs or does not occur, $i = 1, 2, \ldots, m$, and $P(y = 1|H) = p$ is the conditional probability that the event y occurs under the condition of H. The logistic regression model under the hesitant fuzzy environment is:

$$P(y = 1|H) = \frac{1}{1 + \mathrm{e}^{-g(H)}} \tag{5.28}$$

where $g(H) = \alpha + w_1 \cdot \overline{h}_1(x) + \cdots + w_n \cdot \overline{h}_n(x)$, in which $\alpha, w_1, \ldots, w_n$ are the estimated weight parameters.

Similarly, we can determine the conditional probability that y does not occur under the condition of H: $P(y = 0|H) = 1 - P(y = 1|H) = 1 - \frac{1}{1+\mathrm{e}^{-g(H)}} = \frac{1}{1+\mathrm{e}^{g(H)}}$. For convenience, the conditional probability that y occurs under the condition of H could be presented as $P(y = 1|H) = \frac{1}{1+\mathrm{e}^{-g(H)}} = \frac{\mathrm{e}^{g(H)}}{1+\mathrm{e}^{g(H)}}$. Then, the odds of the probability of occurrence to the probability of nonoccurrence is $odds = \frac{P(y=1|H)}{P(y=0|H)} = \frac{p}{1-p} = \mathrm{e}^{g(H)}$ (called the odds of experiencing an event). The logarithm of $odds$ is

$\ln \frac{p}{1-p} = g(H) = \alpha + w_1 \cdot \overline{h}_1(x) + \ldots + w_n \cdot \overline{h}_n(x)$. After that, we determine the estimated weight parameters by the traditional maximum likelihood estimation.

Definition 5.3 (Song et al., 2021b). Suppose that the observed values of m samples are $y_1, y_2, \ldots, y_m$ respectively. The conditional probabilities that y_i occurs and that y_i does not occur under the condition of H_i are $P(y_i = 1|H_i) = p_i$ and $P(y_i = 0|H_i) = 1 - p_i$ respectively, then the probability of y_i is defined as:

$$P(y_i) = p_i^{y_i} \cdot (1 - p_i)^{1-y_i} \quad i = 1, 2, \ldots, m \tag{5.29}$$

Since each sample is independent of each other, their joint distribution is the product of each marginal distribution. Then the likelihood function of the estimated weight parameters under the hesitant fuzzy environment is defined.

Definition 5.4 (Song et al., 2021b). Suppose that conditional probabilities that the event y occurs and that y does not occur under the condition of H are $P(y = 1|H) = p = \pi(H)$ and $P(y = 0|H) = 1 - p = 1 - \pi(H)$ respectively. The likelihood function of the estimated weight parameters under the hesitant fuzzy environment is.

$$L(w) = \prod_{i=1}^{m} (\pi(H_i))^{y_i} \cdot (1 - \pi(H_i))^{1-y_i} \quad i = 1, 2, \ldots, m \tag{5.30}$$

After that, we determine the estimated weight parameters that maximize the value of the likelihood function $L(w)$ by the maximum likelihood estimation. The logarithm of $L(w)$ is $\ln L(w) = \prod_{i=1}^{m} (y_i \cdot \ln[\pi(H_i)] + (1 - y_i)\ln[1 - \pi(H_i)])$, which is a higher-order continuous differentiable convex function of w. In this way, the problem is transformed into an optimization problem with the logarithmic likelihood function $\ln L(w)$ as the objective function. According to the Convex Optimization Theory, classical numerical optimization algorithms such as gradient descent method and Newton method can be used to derive the optimal solution.

The traditional maximum likelihood estimation method needs a great quantity of observed samples, which is difficult to obtain in some situations. In view of insufficient samples, the traditional maximum likelihood estimation method is not suitable for the parameter estimation. Therefore, it is necessary to develop an efficient method to determine appropriate values of the estimated weight parameters $\alpha, w_1, \ldots, w_n$. To achieve this, a novel parameter estimation method is proposed to optimize the value of the estimated weight parameters in the logistic regression model under the hesitant fuzzy environment, and it will be explained in detail in the next subsection.

5.5.3 Maximum Entropy Estimation

The entropy is a parameter that characterizes the state of matter in thermodynamics and it measures the disorder degree of things (Jones & Jones, 2000). A greater entropy corresponds to a higher degree of disorder. Similarly, in information theory, the entropy denotes the uncertainty degree of random variables. Given a random variable X, if its values are $x_1, x_2, \ldots, x_m$, then the information entropy of X is $E(X) = \sum_{i=1}^{m} p(x_i) \cdot \ln\left(\frac{1}{p(x_i)}\right) = -\sum_{i=1}^{m} p(x_i) \cdot \ln p(x_i)$. The concept of entropy is very important in the study of statistical learning and machine learning. In addition, the maximum entropy is a criterion of probabilistic model learning. Based on the idea of maximum entropy, the model with maximum entropy in all possible models is the best one. If there are some constraints in the probability model, then the maximum entropy principle is to select the model with the maximum entropy from the set of possible models satisfying the constraints. The maximum entropy principle states that when predicting the probability distribution of a random event, the prediction should satisfy all know constraints and makes no subjective assumptions about unknown conditions. In this case, the probability distribution is the most uniform and the risk of prediction is the least, therefore the entropy of the obtained probability distribution is the largest. In other words, the principle of maximum entropy means selecting the model with maximum entropy in the set of models satisfying the constraints.

Accurate and sufficient data information is an important prerequisite for decision making. However, in the actual decision-making process, it is difficult to obtain accurate information and sufficient samples. So it is too difficult to meet the basic requirements of traditional logistic regression analysis in most situations. This section tries to infer the intrinsic law of event evolution from a small number of samples with uncertain information. We take advantages of HFSs in depicting uncertain information and introduce a new logistic regression model. After that, we present a new parameter estimation method based on the maximum entropy principle. This method can deal with the situations with only few observed samples and no information about the outcome of events, and it is explained in detail as follows (Song et al., 2021b):

Inspire by the information and coding theory, the entropy of the event y_i is defined as:

$$\begin{aligned} E(P(H_i)) &= -C\left[P_i \ln P_i + (1-P_i)\ln(1-P_i)\right] \\ &= -C\left[P_i \ln\left(\frac{P_i}{1-P_i}\right) + \ln(1-P_i)\right] \\ &= -C\left\{\frac{\left(\alpha + \sum_{j=1}^{n} w_j \cdot \overline{h}_{ij}(x)\right)}{1+\exp\left[-\left(\alpha + \sum_{j=1}^{n} w_j \cdot \overline{h}_{ij}(x)\right)\right]} - \ln\left(1+\exp\left(\alpha + \sum_{j=1}^{n} w_j \cdot \overline{h}_{ij}(x)\right)\right)\right\} \end{aligned} \tag{5.31}$$

where C is a positive value, $P_i = P(y_i = 1|H_{ij})(j = 1, 2, \ldots, n)$ is the conditional probability of $y_i = 1$ under the hesitant fuzzy conditions of $H_{ij}(i = 1, 2, \ldots, m; j = 1, 2, \ldots, n)$, $\alpha, w_1, w_2, \ldots, w_n$ denote the estimated weight parameters, and $\overline{h}_{ij}(x)$ denotes the mean of the jth HFE for the ith sample. According to the maximum entropy principle, we can obtain the optimal parameters with the maximum value of $E(P(H_i))$. It follows the principle that the entropy of an isolated system tends to the maximum. Then we can construct an optimization model as follows (Song et al., 2021b):

Model 1

$$\max E(P(H_i))$$
$$= -C\left\{\frac{\left(\alpha + \sum\limits_{j=1}^{n} w_j \cdot \overline{h}_{ij}(x)\right)}{1 + \exp\left[-\left(\alpha + \sum\limits_{j=1}^{n} w_j \cdot \overline{h}_{ij}(x)\right)\right]} - \ln\left(1 + \exp\left(\alpha + \sum_{j=1}^{n} w_j \cdot \overline{h}_{ij}(x)\right)\right)\right\}$$

There are m samples (H_i, y_i) and $H_i = \{\overline{h}_{i1}, \overline{h}_{i2}, \ldots, \overline{h}_{in}\}$. It is difficult to find the weight parameters to make $E(P(H_i))$ for $i = 1, 2, \ldots, m$ reach the maximum value at the same time. So we take the maximum value of the sequence $\{E(P(H_i)), i = 1, 2, \ldots, m\}$ as the objective function and build an optimization model based on the maximum entropy principle. Let $\beta = (\alpha, w_1, w_2, \ldots, w_n)$ and we define the objective function based on the maximum value of $\{E(P(H_i)), i = 1, 2, \ldots, m\}$ as:

$$F(\beta) = \max \sum_{i=1}^{m} E(P(H_i))$$
$$= \min \sum_{i=1}^{m} C\left\{\frac{\left(\alpha + \sum_{j=1}^{n} w_j \cdot \overline{h}_{ij}(x)\right)}{1 + \exp\left[-\left(\alpha + \sum_{j=1}^{n} w_j \cdot \overline{h}_{ij}(x)\right)\right]} - \ln\left(1 + \exp\left(\alpha + \sum_{j=1}^{n} w_j \cdot \overline{h}_{ij}(x)\right)\right)\right\}$$

It is a higher-order differentiable continuous convex function of β and is equivalent to finding the minimum value of the objective function. According to the Convex Optimization Theory (Ameluxen et al., 2013) and classical numerical optimization algorithms such as the gradient descent method and the Newton method, the optimal estimated weight parameters α, w_j $(j = 1, 2, \ldots, n)$ can be obtained and will be introduced in the next subsection.

5.5.4 Levenberg-Marquardt Algorithm

The optimization algorithm is a mathematical method to study how to determine some factors under the given constraints to make a certain objective function reach the optimum. Common optimization methods include the gradient descent method and Newton method. The gradient descent method updates parameters according to a certain step size along the opposite direction of the gradient to minimize the objective function. However, it ignores the second derivative term and the convergence rate is slowed down when it approaches the target value. So the gradient descent method is usually used as the initial stage of optimization. On the other hand, Newton method makes full use of the second derivative and is faster. It has good convergence in the last period but is not suitable for the initial period. It is often combined with the fastest gradient descent method.

Inspired by the gradient descent method and Newton method, Levenberg and Marquardt proposed a new damped Gauss–Newton method called the LMA. The LMA combines the advantages of the gradient descent method in easy implementing and advantages of the Newton method in fast convergence. It divides the search process into two periods. The LMA proceeds with the gradient descent method until it gets close to the solution. With the deepening of search process, the Newton method automatically takes over the process with a faster convergence, and it can make up for the deficiency of the traditional gradient descent method in convergence to some extent. The introduction of the damping factor λ determines the automatic switching of the algorithm and it is adjusted in each iteration. In this section, we introduce the LMA under the hesitant fuzzy environment to solve the parameter estimation problem with few samples and uncertain information in the logistic regression model (Song et al., 2021b).

Let $\beta = (\alpha, w_1, w_2, \ldots, w_n)$, then according to the Taylor expansion, we have

$$F^{'}(\beta + h) = F^{'}(\beta) + F^{''}(\beta) \cdot h + O\left(\|h\|^2\right) \simeq F^{'}(\beta) + F^{''}(\beta) \cdot h \tag{5.32}$$

where $\|h\|$ is sufficiently small. If the objective function is minimum at $\beta + h$, then $F^{'}(\beta + h) = 0$. Thus, $Lh_n = -F^{'}(\beta)$, $L = F^{''}(\beta)$, and h_n is the downward direction of Newton method. Then let $\beta := \beta + h_n$ and we compute the next iteration. It should be noted that $L = F^{''}(\beta)$ is a positive definite matrix and h_n is the downward direction.

Calculating the second derivative information $L = F^{''}(\beta)$ is a must but has so much trouble. The main idea of LMA is to replace the calculation of L with the Jacobian matrix, which is easier to calculate and improves the optimization efficiency. Then we provide the derivation of the above equation by the Jacobian matrix: $F(\beta) = \frac{1}{2} \cdot \sum_{i=1}^{m} (f(\beta))^2 = \frac{1}{2} \cdot \|f(\beta)\|^2 = \frac{1}{2} \cdot f^T(\beta) \cdot f(\beta)$. The Taylor expansion of f is $f(\beta + h) = f(\beta) + J(\beta) \cdot h + o\left(\|h\|^2\right)$, where $(J(\beta))_{ij} = \frac{\partial f_i}{\partial \beta_j}(\beta)$ denotes the Jacobian matrix. Since $\frac{\partial F}{\partial \beta_j}(\beta) = \sum_{i=1}^{m} f_i(\beta) \cdot \frac{\partial f_i(\beta)}{\partial \beta_j}$ and $\frac{\partial^2 F}{\partial \beta_j \partial \beta_k}(\beta) = \sum_{i=1}^{m} \left(\frac{\partial f_i}{\partial \beta_j}(\beta) \cdot \frac{\partial f_i}{\partial \beta_k}(\beta) + f_i(\beta) \frac{\partial^2 f}{\partial \beta_j \cdot \partial \beta_k}(\beta) \right)$, it can be conducted that $F^{'}(\beta) = J^T(\beta) \cdot f(\beta)$ and $F^{''}(\beta) = J(\beta)^T \cdot J(\beta) + \sum_{i=1}^{m} f_i(\beta) \cdot f_i^{''}(\beta)$. Because $\frac{\partial^2 F}{\partial \beta_j \partial \beta_k}(\beta) = \sum_{i=1}^{m} \left(\frac{\partial f_i}{\partial \beta_j}(\beta) \cdot \frac{\partial f_i}{\partial \beta_k}(\beta) + f_i(\beta) \frac{\partial^2 f}{\partial \beta_j \cdot \partial \beta_k}(\beta) \right)$, it is obvious that $F^{''}(\beta) = J(\beta)^T \cdot J(\beta) + \sum_{i=1}^{m} f_i(\beta) \cdot f_i^{''}(\beta)$. In addition, $F^{'}(\beta^*) = f(\beta^*) = 0$ when t reaches the extreme point.

Later on, we illustrate the derivation of Gauss–Newton Method, based on which the LMA is developed by adding a variable factor. On account of $f(\beta+h)\approx l(h)=f(\beta)+J(\beta)\cdot h$ and $F(\beta+h)\approx L(h)=\frac{1}{2}l(h)^T\cdot l(h)=\frac{1}{2}f^T(\beta)\cdot f(\beta)+h^T\cdot J^T\cdot f+\frac{1}{2}h^T\cdot J^T\cdot J\cdot h$, the problem of finding the minimum value of $F(\beta+h)$ is transformed as follows:

$$h_{gn}=\arg\min_h\{L(h)\} \tag{5.33}$$

$$L^{'}(h)=J^T\cdot f(\beta)+J^T\cdot J\cdot h \tag{5.34}$$

$$L^{''}(h)=J^T\cdot J \tag{5.35}$$

Let $L^{'}(h)=0$, then it can be obtained that $\left(J^T\cdot J\right)h_{gn}=-J^T\cdot f(\beta)$, where J is full rank matrix. Then $h_{gn}^T\cdot F^{'}(\beta)=h_{gn}^T\cdot\left(J^T\cdot f(\beta)\right)=-h_{gn}^T\cdot\left(J^T\cdot J\right)\cdot h_{gn}<0$, which denotes that h_{gn} is the descent direction of F. Therefore, the problem of finding the minimum value of $F(\beta)$ can be simplified and reduced to find the minimum value of $L(h)$. Then Gauss–Newton method with $L^{''}(h)h_{gn}=-L^{'}(0)$ is similar to the Newton method with $F^{''}(h)h_n=-F^{'}(\beta)$. This transformation makes it unnecessary to calculate the second derivative of $F(\beta)$. The LMA, similar to the Gauss–Newton method, is depicted as $\left(J^T\cdot J+\mu\cdot I\right)h_{lm}=-g$ ($g=J^T\cdot f(\beta)$ and $\mu\geq 0$). What's more, the LMA degenerates to Gauss–Newton method when $\mu=0$, when the value of μ is large, then $h_{lm}=-\frac{F^{'}(\beta)}{\mu}$, and the LMA degenerates to a gradient descent method with smaller steps. On the basis of Gauss–Newton method, the focus of LMA is how to determine the value of μ properly. Then, an evaluation index $\zeta=\frac{F(\beta)-F(\beta+h_{lm})}{L(0)-L(h_{lm})}$ is introduced. It depicts the approximation degree of the descent of F with the descent of L. If the value of ζ is larger, then the approximation effect is better, and μ could be reduced to make LMA closer to Gauss–Newton method. If the value of ζ is small, then the approximation effect is poor, and the value of μ could be increased to make LMA closer to the gradient descent method. In addition, the conditions for the end of the iteration are specified as follows (Song et al., 2021b):

(1) The descent gradient is less than a certain threshold; or
(2) The difference between the values of two β is less than a certain threshold; or
(3) The number of iterations reaches the maximum $K_{\max}$.

The detailed algorithm process is provided in the Appendix. By continuously adjusting and updating parameters of the logistic regression model based on the maximum entropy estimation with LMA, the objective function is minimized with the most approximate parameters. After that, the optimized logistic regression model under the hesitant fuzzy environment is constructed.

5.5.5 K-S Fitting Test

In order to test and verify the effectiveness the of the optimized logistic regression model, this section introduces the K-S test as a fitting test (Song et al., 2021b). It is a commonly used method to test the fitness of the optimized model and the ability to distinguish event occurrence from non-event occurrence. The value of $K - S$ is between 0 and 1, and it indicates the prediction effect of the optimized model.

Definition 5.5 (Song et al., 2021b). Suppose that $H_0 : F_{m1}(\beta) = F_{m2}(\beta)$ is the null hypothesis and $H_1 : F_{m1}(\beta) \neq F_{m2}(\beta)$ is the alternative hypothesis, then the value of $K - S$ is

$$K - S = \max|F_{m1}(\beta) - F_{m2}(\beta)| \tag{5.36}$$

where $F_{m1}(\beta)$ and $F_{m2}(\beta)$ are the cumulative probability distributions of samples that the event does not occur and occur respectively.

In addition, the curves of the cumulative distribution and probability density are obtained with $N \to \infty$. The maximum value of the cumulative distribution function is the $K - S$. If $K - S \geq 0.35$, then the effect of the optimized model is acceptable. The detailed classification standard is also provided in Table 5.4 (Brown, 1982).

The optimized logistic regression model combines the advantages of the HFIF and the correlation coefficient between HFSs to ensure the factors mutually independent. It can simplify the problems and optimize main factors. Due to the complexity of practical problems, the introduction of the HFIF and the correlation coefficient can repair deficiencies of traditional models in determining main factors. In order to deal with the situations with only a few observed variables and no information about the outcome of events, a new parameter estimation method based on the maximum entropy principle is also introduced. What's more, the LMA determines the most approximate parameters with easy implementation and fast convergence. In conclusion, the optimized logistic regression model under the hesitant fuzzy environment can manage the situations with small samples and massive uncertain information more efficiently and accurately.

Table 5.4 The classification standard of the logistic model

K-S	The effect of the optimized logistic model
<0.2	Bad
0.2–0.4	General
0.4–0.5	Good
0.5–0.6	Better
0.6–0.75	Very good
0.75–1	Perfect

5.6 Application of the Optimized Logistic Regression Model to the Prediction of Emergency Extreme Air Pollution Event

5.6.1 Factors Identification of the Emergency Extreme Air Pollution Event

As one of the most dangerous weather events, the EEAPE will seriously destroy and threaten peoples' production and life. In recent years, many large cities in Asia have been plagued by EEAPE (Gordon et al., 2014). It is reported that the Indian city of New Delhi has been rated as the most polluted city in the world by many publications due to the extreme air pollution level of PM 2.5. Therefore, it is very meaningful to make objective assessment and accurate risk analysis of the EEAPE, which will surely be helpful to develop emergency response plans and avoid harm to human health.

The mechanism of the EEAPE is pretty complicated and with many uncertainties. It is difficult to predict the accurate time and the degree of air pollution in advance. This chapter tries to construct factors from the perspective of pollutants and meteorological conditions. These factors may include: the concentrations of main pollutants ($PM_{2.5}$, PM_{10}, SO_2, NO_2, CO and O_3) in the air, precipitation (P), temperature (T), wind speed (WS), atmosphere pressure (AP), and relative humidity (RH). However, the values of the above factors are changing dynamically, which contain great uncertainty. This section uses 30 sets of simulation samples (see Appendix) to illustrate the proposed model. In order to depict dynamic changes of uncertain information accurately and efficiently, this section introduces the concept of HFS. The HFEs can depict the daily minimum, average and maximum values of those factors at the same time. In addition, the linear transformation is presented to unify different kinds of raw data into hesitant fuzzy information:

$$\gamma_i = \frac{x_i - \min(x)}{\max(x) - \min(x)} \tag{5.37}$$

where x_i $(i = 1, 2, \cdots, n)$ are the original data of each factor. After that, the original data of the factors can be transformed into HFSs. Since EEAPE is a continuous dynamic event with strong suddenness and small sample data, it is difficult to meet with the basic requirements of traditional statistical analysis. According to hesitant fuzzy sequences and occurrence results of EEAPE, we can calculate NHFIF to measure the causal relationship (see Table 5.5). Due to that the values of NHFIF from CO, O_3 and T to EEAPE are too small, the causal relationship is extremely weak. Therefore, the above three factors are not considered in the next section. Then, we also calculate the correlation coefficients between the remaining factors to ensure that all the factors are mutually independent. The calculation results are presented in Table 5.6 (Song et al., 2021b).

Table 5.5 The values of NHFIF from the factors to the EEAPE

Factors	NHFIF
$PM_{2.5}$	0.7623
PM_{10}	0.6108
SO_2	0.6860
NO	0.6735
CO	0.6166
O_3	0.3428
P	0.1022
T	0.2064
WS	0.6362
AP	0.3675
RH	0.1558

Table 5.6 The correlation coefficients between the factors

Correlation coefficients	$PM_{2.5}$	PM_{10}	SO_2	NO	P	WS	AP	RH
$PM_{2.5}$	–	0.612	0.038	−0.075	0.348	−0.568	−0.729	0.056
PM_{10}	0.612	–	−0.465	0.582	0.646	−0.675	−0.782	0.704
SO_2	0.038	−0.465	–	−0.731	0.025	−0.258	−0.156	−0.885
NO	−0.075	0.582	−0.731	–	0.228	−0.092	−0.068	−0.805
P	0.348	0.646	0.025	0.228	–	−0.808	0.906	−0.096
WS	−0.568	−0.675	−0.258	−0.092	−0.808	–	−0.693	0.362
AP	−0.729	−0.782	−0.156	−0.068	0.906	−0.693	–	−0.009
RH	0.056	0.704	−0.885	−0.805	−0.096	0.362	−0.009	–

By analyzing the results of NHFIF and correlation coefficients between factors, we can identify and determine the main factors of the EEAPE from a large amount of uncertain information: $PM_{2.5}$, PM_{10}, SO_2, NO and WS. Those selected factors are the foundation for the construction of the optimized logistic regression model.

5.6.2 *Construction and Prediction Results of the Optimized Logistic Regression Model*

After determining the main factors of EEAPE by HFIF and the correlation coefficient, we can construct the optimized logistic predication probability model based on the maximum entropy estimation under the hesitant fuzzy environment. Since there are only few samples with massive uncertain information, it is difficult to determine parameters by traditional maximum likelihood estimation. Hence, the parameter estimation method based on the maximum entropy principle and LMA is conducted. Based on the data of samples and hesitant fuzzy sequences of the determined five main factors, we can define the objection function and build an optimization model based on the maximum entropy principle. By adjusting and updating parameters of the logistic regression model based on the maximum entropy estimation with LMA, we can obtain the most approximate parameters $\beta = (\alpha, w_1, w_2, \ldots, w_5)$ when the objective function is minimized. Therefore, we can construct the optimized logistic regression model under the hesitant fuzzy environment as follows (Song et al., 2021b):

$$P = \frac{1}{1+e^{-(\alpha+w_1\cdot\overline{h}_{PM_{2.5}}(x)+w_2\cdot\overline{h}_{PM_{10}}(x)+w_3\cdot\overline{h}_{SO_2}(x)+w_4\cdot\overline{h}_{NO}(x)+w_5\cdot\overline{h}_{WS}(x))}} \tag{5.38}$$

where $\overline{h}_{PM_{2.5}}(x), \overline{h}_{PM_{10}}(x), \overline{h}_{SO_2}(x), \overline{h}_{NO}(x)$ and $\overline{h}_{WS}(x)$ are the corresponding hesitant fuzzy information of the five main factors, and the most approximate parameters $\beta = (\alpha, w_1, w_2, \ldots, w_5) = (57.638, 0.006, -0.1304, -12.387, -0.013, -28.892)$.

The probability threshold P_D has different values in different situations, thus it is usually difficult to determine a reasonable probability threshold to judge whether the EEAPE occurs. For convenience and better understanding, the probability threshold is set as $P_D = 0.6$ in this chapter. If the predicted probability $P \geq P_D = 0.6$, then the EEAPE occurs. Otherwise, it does not occur. After that, the normalized data are input into to the optimized prediction model based on the maximum entropy estimation. Then we test the optimized prediction model, and the predicted probabilities and results of the EEAPE are presented in Fig. 5.12 and Table 5.7 (Song et al., 2021b). For the predicted probability of the EEAPE, T (True) indicates that the predicted result is correct and F (False) denotes that the predicted result is wrong.

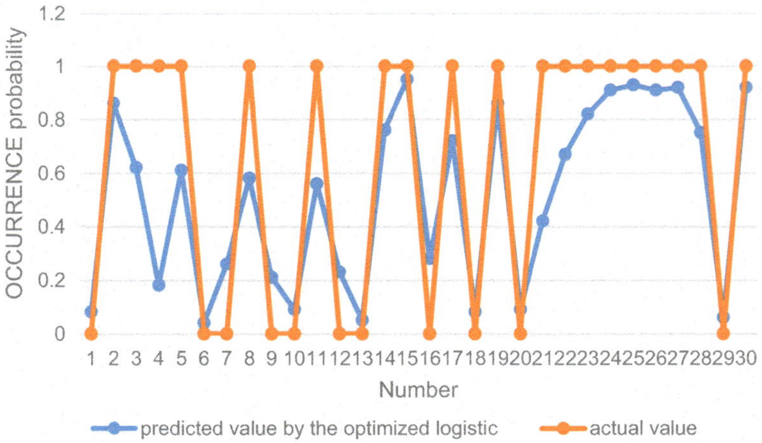

Fig. 5.12 The curves of the actual value and the predicted probability

Table 5.7 The predicted results of the EEAPE by the optimized logistic model

Number	Actual value	Predicted value	Result	Number	Actual value	Predicted value	Result
1	0	0.08	T	16	0	0.28	T
2	1	0.86	T	17	1	0.72	T
3	1	0.62	T	18	0	0.08	T
4	1	0.18	F	19	1	0.86	T
5	1	0.61	T	20	0	0.09	T
6	0	0.04	T	21	1	0.42	F
7	0	0.26	T	22	1	0.67	T
8	1	0.58	F	23	1	0.82	T
9	0	0.21	T	24	1	0.91	T
10	0	0.09	T	25	1	0.93	T
11	1	0.56	F	26	1	0.91	T
12	0	0.23	T	27	1	0.92	T
13	0	0.05	T	28	1	0.75	T
14	1	0.76	T	29	0	0.06	T
15	1	0.95	T	30	1	0.92	T

By analyzing the predicted results above, it is obvious that the prediction accuracy of the optimized logistic model is 86.7%, which demonstrates the good performance of the optimized logistic regression model in accuracy. In addition, the value of K-S is 0.815, indicates that the optimized logistic regression model is acceptable. Then the null hypothesis is refused, and the ability of the optimized model to distinguish event occurrence from non-event occurrence is strong.

5.6.3 Comparative Analysis and Sensitivity Analysis

In order to highlight the advantages of the optimized logistic regression model, a comparative study between the traditional logistic regression model (model 1), the fuzzy logistic regression model (Pradhan, 2010) (model 2) and the proposed optimized logistic regression model (model 3) is conducted. In order to avoid the contingency and randomness of the algorithms, each simulation experiment is conducted ten times and the average of ten simulation experiments is regarded as the final result. The comparative results by different models are presented in Table 5.8 (Song et al., 2021b).

The prediction results indicate that the optimized logistic model in this section are more accurate and objective than the traditional methods under the same conditions. It is obvious that the stability of the optimized logistic model is also higher. The optimized logistic also improves the effectiveness and is more suitable for the prediction

Table 5.8 The predicted results of EEAPE by different models

Number	True value	Model 1	Result	Model 2	Result	Model 3	Result
1	0	0.17	T	0.12	T	0.08	T
2	1	0.68	T	0.64	T	0.86	T
3	1	0.44	F	0.71	T	0.62	T
4	1	0.31	F	0.43	F	0.18	F
5	1	0.65	T	0.82	T	0.61	T
6	0	0.06	T	0.22	T	0.04	T
7	0	0.21	T	0.28	T	0.26	T
8	1	0.42	F	0.35	F	0.58	F
9	0	0.16	T	0.32	T	0.21	T
10	0	0.08	T	0.14	T	0.09	T
11	1	0.29	F	0.63	T	0.56	F
12	0	0.63	F	0.72	F	0.23	T
13	0	0.12	T	0.26	T	0.05	T
14	1	0.81	T	0.65	T	0.76	T
15	1	0.72	T	0.56	F	0.95	T
16	0	0.36	T	0.41	T	0.28	T
17	1	0.69	T	0.76	T	0.72	T
18	0	0.42	T	0.39	T	0.08	T
19	1	0.47	F	0.63	T	0.86	T
20	0	0.24	T	0.42	T	0.09	T
21	1	0.39	F	0.51	F	0.42	F
22	1	0.88	T	0.70	T	0.67	T
23	1	0.86	T	0.73	T	0.82	T
24	1	0.54	F	0.52	F	0.91	T
25	1	0.78	T	0.66	T	0.93	T
26	1	0.49	F	0.52	F	0.91	T
27	1	0.62	T	0.68	T	0.92	T
28	1	0.55	F	0.65	T	0.75	T
29	0	0.31	T	0.22	T	0.06	T
30	1	0.70	T	0.81	T	0.92	T

problems with few samples and massive uncertain information. Moreover, different decision makers with pessimistic principle or optimistic principle may adopt different values of probability threshold. In order to illustrate the influence of the probability threshold on the prediction results, four groups of values of the probability threshold P_D are set to make a sensitivity analysis of the optimized model: (1) $P_D = 0.5$; (2) $P_D = 0.6$; (3)$P_D = 0.7$; (4)$P_D = 0.8$. The prediction results with different values of the probability threshold P_D are shown in Table 5.9 (Song et al., 2021b).

Table 5.9 The predicted results of EEAPE with different probability threshold

Number	True Value	Predicted probability	$P_D = 0.5$	$P_D = 0.6$	$P_D = 0.7$	$P_D = 0.8$
1	0	0.08	T	T	T	T
2	1	0.86	T	T	T	T
3	1	0.62	T	T	F	F
4	1	0.18	F	F	F	F
5	1	0.61	T	T	F	F
6	0	0.04	T	T	T	T
7	0	0.26	T	T	T	T
8	1	0.58	T	F	F	F
9	0	0.21	T	T	T	T
10	0	0.09	T	T	T	T
11	1	0.56	T	F	F	F
12	0	0.23	T	T	T	T
13	0	0.05	T	T	T	T
14	1	0.76	T	T	T	F
15	1	0.95	T	T	T	T
16	0	0.28	T	T	T	T
17	1	0.72	T	T	T	F
18	0	0.08	T	T	T	T
19	1	0.86	T	T	T	T
20	0	0.09	T	T	T	T
21	1	0.42	F	F	F	F
22	1	0.67	T	T	F	F
23	1	0.82	T	T	T	T
24	1	0.91	T	T	T	T
25	1	0.93	T	T	T	T
26	1	0.91	T	T	T	T
27	1	0.92	T	T	T	T
28	1	0.75	T	T	T	T
29	0	0.06	T	T	T	T
30	1	0.92	T	T	T	T

Comparing the results above, it is obvious that the accuracy of prediction of the optimized model is dynamically changing when the probability threshold varies from 0.5 to 0.8. So a reasonable value of probability threshold is important. If the probability threshold is too small, which indicates that the decision makers are too optimistic and confident about the prediction results of the optimized model. It may result in some risk or even wrong solutions. If the probability threshold is too large, then the decision makers are too conservative and pessimistic about the model. It is likely to result in a waste of resources and affect the efficiency of emergency scheme selection. To determine a reasonable probability threshold is very difficult but important for different problems and situations.

The optimized logistic model under the hesitant fuzzy environment not only can make full use of the few samples effectively, but also can depict the massive uncertain information more delicately. Traditional logistic models cannot manage the situations with few samples and uncertain formation clearly. In order to determine the most appropriate values of the estimated weight parameters, this chapter introduces a objective function based on the maximum entropy principle, which could manage the situations with only few samples and no information about the occurrence results of the events. After that, the LMA under the hesitant fuzzy environment is introduced to optimize the value of the estimated weight parameters. It combines the advantages of the gradient descent method in easy implement and the advantages of the Newton method in fast convergence. The optimized logistic model can determine the most appropriate parameters of logistic through the LMA. It is a better regression model with the best approximation and overcomes the limitations of traditional maximum likelihood estimation that needs a large number of observed values. In a word, the optimized logistic regression model under the hesitant fuzzy environment has prominent advantages in managing the situations of few samples with uncertain information, and the prediction results are more reliable with better accuracy.

5.7 Remarks

This chapter mainly studies the regression analysis models under the hesitant fuzzy environment. We introduce the optimized GRNN model based on FDS-FOA and the optimized logistic regression model based on the maximum entropy estimation under the hesitant fuzzy environment. The applications in the prediction of AQI and EEAPE demonstrate the advantages of the two optimized regression analysis models presented in this chapter. The prediction results also provide an effective decision-making basis for experts to make policies and emergency response plans.

Appendix

This appendix provides the pseudo codes of the Levenberg–Marquardt method and 30 sets of simulation samples.

(1) **Algorithm 1 Levenberg–Marquardt method**

begin:

$k := 0;\; v := 2;\; x := x_0$

$A := J(x)^T J(x);\; g := J(x)^T f(x)$

$found := (\|g\|_\infty \le \varepsilon_1);\; \mu := \tau * \max\{a_{ii}\}$

while (not found) **and** ($k < k_{\max}$)

$k := k+1;$ Solve $(A + \mu I) h_{lm} = -g$

if $\|h_{lm}\| \le \varepsilon_2 (\|x\| + \varepsilon_2)$

$found := true$

else

$x_{new} := x + h_{lm}$

$\rho := (F(x) - F(x_{new})) / (L(0) - L(h_{lm}))$

if $\rho > 0$ {step acceptable}

$x := x_{new}$

$A := J(x)^T J(x);\; g := J(x)^T f(x)$

$found := (\|g\|_\infty \le \varepsilon_1)$

$\mu := \tau * \max\left\{\frac{1}{3}, 1 - (2\rho - 1)^3\right\};\; v := 2$

else

$\mu := \mu * v;\; v := 2 * v$

End

(2) **Simulation samples**
See Table 5.10.

Table 5.10 The values of factors and risk occurrence

Samples	$PM_{2.5}$	PM_{10}	SO_2	NO	CO	O_3
1	242–261	258–266	6–9	93–95	2	73–76
2	265–276	361–374	22–25	117–120	3.5	13–15
3	209–219	272–280	24–26	113–114	3.4	10–13
4	252–265	284–292	18–19	104–105	3.6	17–21
5	221–233	240–253	39–41	103–106	3	15–16
6	129–142	169–177	23–26	100–103	2.7	15–18
7	84–99	128–136	21–22	92–95	2.4	11–16
8	223–246	253–262	22–25	111–114	4.1	14–17
9	58–65	57–66	6–8	35–38	1.3	59–61
10	34–39	65–71	9–13	49–52	0.8	39–40
11	212–220	255–263	19–22	100–104	3.3	8–10
12	41–52	45–58	15–18	47–51	0.9	50–52
13	42–55	63–72	9–13	45–48	0.9	51–55
14	301–322	336–348	21–23	129–131	4.6	8–11
15	217–240	213–225	12–15	105–106	2.4	15–16
16	45–51	48–55	2–5	28–32	0.9	157–161
17	153–166	123–135	3–5	69–73	1.6	25–28
18	98–112	79–86	2–4	48–50	1.5	59–62
19	159–165	168–177	10–13	65–67	1.4	185–191
20	96–112	165–172	7–9	58–61	0.9	124–128
21	184–197	166–181	26–28	43–45	2.3	236–241
22	212–220	255–269	19–22	100–102	3.3	8–11
23	301–324	356–370	21–23	129–133	4.6	8–12
24	454–482	412–436	8–12	141–144	6.8	6–9
25	198–205	190–204	13–15	102–105	3.8	38–43
26	311–322	339–363	17–20	153–157	6	17–19
27	364–372	389–396	19–21	153–155	7.5	13–16
28	223–245	222–230	16–17	115–116	5.3	11–12
29	167–177	128–139	18–20	83–85	3.3	11–15
30	34–46	20–35	10–13	34–37	1	54–59

(continued)

Table 5.10 (continued)

Samples	$PM_{2.5}$	PM_{10}	SO_2	*NO*	*CO*	O_3
Samples	*P*	*T*	*WS*	*AP*	*RH*	*Risk*
1	0	(1, 14)	1–2	1001–1011	0.17–0.2	1
2	0	(2, 14)	1–2	1004–1018	0.13–0.15	1
3	0	(4, 13)	1–2	1004–1013	0.16–0.31	1
4	0	(5, 11)	1–2	1013–1020	0.18–0.25	1
5	0	(0, 10)	3–4	1022–1026	0.23–0.26	1
6	0	(−2, 8)	1–2	1000–1013	0.21–0.24	0
7	0	(−2, 9)	1–2	1001–1010	0.34–0.38	0
8	0	(−3, 11)	3–4	1004–1012	0.17–0.25	1
9	0	(−2, 10)	1–2	1004–1014	0.22–0.27	0
10	1–3	(−1, 9)	1–2	1013–1021	0.13–0.21	0
11	0	(−3, 9)	3–4	1022–1033	0.15–0.22	1
12	0	(−3, 8)	1–2	1000–1015	0.23–0.27	0
13	0	(0, 7)	1–2	1001–1013	0.22–0.31	0
14	5–22	(−3, 10)	1–2	1004–1011	0.24–0.35	1
15	0	(−3, 10)	1–2	1004–1013	0.11–0.22	1
16	0	(0, 10)	1–2	1016–1022	0.08–0.17	0
17	1–2	(−3, 9)	3–4	1013–1018	0.12–0.21	1
18	0	(−3, 8)	1–2	1022–1029	0.15–0.24	0
19	6–13	(−4, 7)	1–2	1025–1033	0.18–0.26	1
20	0	(−3, 8)	1–2	1021–1030	0.21–0.25	0
21	0	(1, 7)	1–2	1020–1032	0.23–0.31	1
22	0	(2, 8)	1–2	1016–1027	0.25–0.32	1
23	0	(−2, 8)	3–4	1015–1022	0.19–0.27	1
24	0	(−6, 4)	3–4	1018–1026	0.16–0.24	1
25	0	(−3, 0)	1–2	1020–1028	0.22–0.27	1
26	0	(−9, −2)	4–5	1022–1027	0.20–0.26	1
27	0	(−10, −5)	4–5	1025–1033	0.15–0.21	1
28	0	(−10, −2)	3–4	1023–1030	0.23–0.29	1
29	0	(−10, −1)	1–2	1022–1031	0.22–0.28	1
30	0	(−7, 0)	1–2	1018–1026	0.09–0.21	0

References

Addona, D., Doriana, M., & Matarazzo, D. (2017). Tool-wear prediction and pattern-recognition using artificial neural network and DNA-based computing. *Journal of Intelligent Manufacturing, 28*, 1–17.

Alilou, V. K., & Yaghmaee, F. (2015). Application of GRNN in non-texture image inpainting and restoration. *Pattern Recognition Letters, 62*, 24–31.

Ameluxen, D., Lotz, M., Mccoy, M. B., et al. (2013). Living on the edge: A geometric theory of phase transitions in convex optimization. *Physical Review Letters, 111*, 3929–3940.

Battiti, R. (2014). First- and second-order methods for learning: Between steepest descent and Newton's method. *Neural Computation, 4*, 141–166.

Bechlioulis, C. P., & Rovithakis, G. A. (2012). A prior guaranteed evolution within the neural network approximation set and robustness expansion via prescribed performance control. *IEEE Transactions on Neural Network and Learning Systems, 23*(2012), 669–675.

Bendu, H., Deepak, B. B., & Murugan, S. (2017). Multi-objective optimization of ethanol fueled HCCI engine performance using hybrid GRNN-PSO. *Applied Energy, 187*, 601–611.

Broomhead, D. S., & Lowe, D. (1988). Multivariable functional interpolation and adaptive networks. *Complex Systems, 2*, 321–355.

Brown, C. C. (1982). On a goodness-of-fit for the logistic model based on statistics. *Communications in Statistics, 11*, 1087–1105.

Chen, N., Xu, Z. S., & Xia, M. M. (2013). Correlation coefficients of hesitant fuzzy sets and their applications to clustering analysis. *Applied Mathematical Modelling, 37*, 2197–2211.

Choi, H., Han, K., Choi, K., et al. (2016). A fuzzy medical diagnosis based on quantiles of diagnostic measures. *Journal of Intelligent and Fuzzy Systems, 31*, 3197–3202.

Dillon, T. S. (1993). Artificial neural network applications to power systems and their relationship to symbolic methods. *International Journal of Electrical Power & Energy Systems, 13*, 66–72.

Du, T. S., Ke, X. T., Liao, J. G., et al. (2018). DSLC-FOA: An improved fruit fly optimization algorithm application to structural engineering design optimization problems. *Applied Mathematical Modelling, 55*, 314–339.

Eddy, E. M., Washburn, T. F., Bunch, D. O., et al. (1996). Targeted disruption of the estrogen receptor gene in male mice causes alternation of spermatogenesis and infertility. *Endocrinology, 137*, 4796–4805.

Fernández-Gámez, M. A., Gil-Corral, G.-V., & F. . (2016). Corporate reputation and market value: Evidence with generalized regression neural networks. *Expert Systems with Applications, 46*, 69–76.

FiRat, M., Turan, M. E., & Yurdusev, M. A. (2010). Comparative analysis of neural network techniques for predicting water consumption time series. *Journal of Hydrology, 384*, 46–51.

Funahashi, K. (1989). On the approximate realization of continuous mappings by neural networks. *Neural Networks, 2*, 183–192.

Gordon, P. S. B., Bruce, P. N. G., Grigg, P. J., et al. (2014). Respiratory risks from household air pollution in low and middle income countries. *Lancet Respiratory Medicine, 2*, 823–860.

Greenland, S., & Drescher, K. (1993). Maximum likelihood estimation of the attributable fraction from logistic models. *Biometrics, 49*, 865–872.

Hastie, T., Rosset, S., Tibshirani, R., et al. (2004). The entire regularization path for the support vector machine. *Journal of Machine Learning Research, 5*, 1391–1415.

He, S., & Jiang, L. (2009). Modeling nonlinear elastic behavior of reinforced soil using artificial neural networks. *Applied Soft Computing, 9*, 954–961.

Hinton, G. E., & Nowlan, S. J. (1990). The bootstrap Widrow-Hoff rule as a cluster-formation algorithm. *Neural Computation, 2*, 355–362.

Hopfield, J. (1984). Neurons with graded response have collective computational properties like those of two state neurons. *Proceeding of the National Academy of Sciences, 81*, 3088–3092.

Hsiao, F. H., Xu, S. D., & Tsai, Z. R. (2008). Robustness design of fuzzy control for nonlinear multiple time-delay large-scale systems vie neural-network-based approach. *IEEE Transactions on Systems Man & Cybernetics Part B, 38*, 244–251.

Hu, R., Wen, S. P., Zeng, Z. G., et al. (2017). A short-term power load forecasting model based on the generalized regression neural network with decreasing step fruit fly optimization algorithm. *Neurocomputing, 22*, 24–31.

Jin, L., Zhang, Y., Li, S., et al. (2017). Noise-tolerant ZNN models for solving time-varying zero-finding problems: A control-theoretic approach. *IEEE Transactions on Automatic Control, 62*, 992–997.

Jones, G. A., & Jones, J. M. (2000). *Information and coding theory*. Springer-Verlag Ltd.
Judd, J. S. (1991). Neural network design and the complexity of learning. *Neurocomputing, 3*, 197–200.
Lavine, D. S. (2007). Neural network modeling of emotion. *Physics of Life Reviews, 4*, 37–63.
Li, C. Q., Zhao, H., & Xu, Z. X. (2017). Kernel C-means clustering algorithms for hesitant fuzzy information in decision making. *International Journal of Fuzzy Systems, 20*, 1–14.
Liang, X. S. (2015). Normalizing the causality between time series. *Physical Review E, 92*, 022126.
Lin, S. M. (2013). Analysis of service satisfaction in web auction logistics service using a combination of fruit fly optimization algorithm and general regression neural network. *Neural Computing & Applications, 22*, 783–791.
Lungu, M., & Lungu, R. (2016). Automatic control of aircraft lateral-directional motion during landing using neural networks and radio-technical subsystems. *Neurocomputing, 171*, 471–471.
Markellos, R. N., Psychoyios, D., & Schneider, F. (2016). Sovereign debt markets in light of the shadow economy. *European Journal of Operational Research, 252*, 220–231.
Meng, H., Bianchi-Berthouze, N., Deng, Y., et al. (2017). Time-delay neural network for continuous emotional dimension prediction from facial expression sequences. *IEEE Transactions on Cybernetics, 46*, 916–929.
More, J. J. (1977). The Levenberg-Marquardt Algorithm: Implementation and theory in numerical analysis. *Lecture Notes in Mathematics* (Vol. 630).
National Meteorological Information Center (NMIC). http://data.cma.cn/
Noori, R., Hoshyaripour, G., Ashrafi, K., et al. (2010). Uncertainty analysis of developed ANN and ANFIS model in prediction of carbon monoxide daily concentration. *Atmospheric Environment, 44*, 476–482.
Pan, W. C. (2016). A new fruit fly optimization algorithm: Taking the financial distress model as an example. *Knowledge-Based Systems, 26*, 69–74.
Park, J., & Sandberg, I. W. (2014). Universal approximation using radial-basis-function networks. *Neural Computation, 3*, 246–257.
Polat, Ö., & Yıldırım, T. (2008). Genetic optimization of GRNN for pattern recognition without feature extraction. *Expert Systems with Applications, 34*(4), 2444–2448.
Pradhan, B. (2010). Landslide susceptibility mapping of a catchment area using frequency ratio, fuzzy logic and multivariate logistic regression approaches. *Journal of the Indian Society of Remote Sensing, 38*, 301–320.
Refenes, A. N., Azema Barac, M., Chen, L., et al. (1993). Currency exchange rate prediction and neural network design strategies. *Neural Computing & Applications, 1*, 46–58.
Rubaai, A., & Young, P. (2016). Hardware/software implementation of fuzzy-neural-network self-learning control methods for Brushless DC motor drives. *IEEE Transactions on Industry Applications, 52*, 414–424.
Rumelhart, D. E., Hinton, G. E., & Williams, R. J. (1986). Learning representations by back-propagating errors. *Nature, 323*, 533–536.
Saeedi, S., Paull, L., Trentini, M., et al. (2016). Neural network-based multiple robot simultaneous localization and mapping. *IEEE Transactions on Neural Networks & Learning Systems, 33*, 3–46.
Singh, P., & Dwivedi, P. (2018). Integration of new evolutionary approach with artificial neural network for solving short term load forecast problem. *Applied Energy, 217*, 537–549.
Song, C. Y., Wang, L. G., Hou, J., et al. (2021a). The optimized GRNN based on the FDS-FOA undet the hesitant fuzzy environment and its application in air quality index prediction. *Applied Intelligence*. https://doi.org/10.1007/s10489-021-02350-1
Song, C. Y., Wang, L. G., & Xu, Z. S. (2021b). An optimized logistic regression model based on the maximum entropy estimation under the hesitant fuzzy environment. *International Journal of Information Technology & Decision Making*. https://doi.org/10.1142/S0219622021500371
Specht, D. F. (1991). A general regression neural network. *IEEE Transactions on Neural Networks, 2*, 568–576.
Torra, V., & Narukawa, Y. (2009). On hesitant fuzzy sets and decision. In *The 18th IEEE International Conference on Fuzzy Systems* (pp. 1378–1382), Jeju Island, Korea.

Tseng, P., & Yun, S. (2009). A coordinate gradient descent method for non-smooth separable minimization. *Mathematical Programming, 117*, 387–423.

Wai, R. J., & Muthusamy, R. (2013). Fuzzy-neural-network inherited sliding-mode control for robot manipulator including actuator dynamics. *IEEE Transactions on Neural Networks & Learning Systems, 24*, 274–287.

Wang, D., Wei, S., Luo, H., et al. (2017b). A novel hybrid model for air quality index forecasting based on two-phase decomposition technique and modified extreme learning machine. *Science of the Total Environment, 580*, 719–733.

Wang, F., Shen, B., & Sun, S. (2016b). Improved GA and Pareto optimization-based facial expression recognition. *Assembly Automation, 36*, 192–199.

Wang, L., Kisi, O., Zounemat-Kermani, M., et al. (2016a). Solar radiation prediction using different techniques: Model evaluation and comparison. *Renewable & Sustainable Energy Review, 61*, 384–397.

Wang, T., Gao, H., & Qiu, J. (2017a). A combined adaptive neural network and nonlinear model predictive control for multi-rate network industrial process control. *IEEE Transactions on Neural Networks & Learning Systems, 27*, 416–425.

Wayne, G., Harley, T., Danihelka, I., et al. (2016). Hybrid computing using a neural network with dynamic external memory. *Nature, 538*, 471–476.

Wu, J. F., Peng, D. H., Li, Z. P., et al. (2015). Network intrusion detection based on a general regression neural network optimized by an improved artificial immune algorithm. *PLoS ONE, 10*, 1–13.

Xia, M. M., & Xu, Z. S. (2011). Hesitant fuzzy information aggregation in decision making. *International Journal of Approximate Reasoning, 52*, 395–407.

Xu, Z. S., & Xia, M. M. (2011). Distance and similarity measures for hesitant fuzzy sets. *Information Sciences, 181*(2011), 2128–2138.

Chapter 6
Decision Making Methods Based on Probabilistic and Interval-Valued Probabilistic Hesitant Fuzzy Sets

In the previous chapters, we have discussed the advantages of hesitant fuzzy sets (HFSs). Traditional HFS can depict the cognitive uncertainty better, but there are also some limitations in depicting probabilistic and statistical information. The probabilistic hesitant fuzzy set (PHFS) combines the advantages of probability theory and HFS, which can better retain and depict preference information of experts. In this section, we introduce a probabilistic hesitant fuzzy correlation coefficient and clustering algorithm. After that, we further present the concept of interval-valued probabilistic hesitant fuzzy set (IVPHFS), and discuss the properties, ranking and comparison methods, basic operation rules, operators and decision making method. At last, we apply the presented methods to the human environment risk assessment of "twenty-first century Maritime Silk Road" and the geopolitical risk assessment of the Arctic region.

6.1 Motivations and Background

Facing the actual multi-criteria decision making (MCDM) problems, the experts may prefer to use the hesitant fuzzy sets (HFSs) (Torra, 2010) to express their preferences by several numerical values between 0 and 1, which can depict the decision makers' (DMs) information more delicately. However, along with the deepening of the study, a serious deficiency of the hesitant fuzzy element (HFE) (Xia & Xu, 2011) has been gradually found: there is information loss in its application. For the sake of solving the problem of the hesitant fuzzy information loss in the decision-making process, Zhu and Xu (2016) combined the probabilistic information with the HFS and proposed the probabilistic hesitant fuzzy set (PHFS), which can make up for the deficiency of the HFS to a certain extent. As the excellent properties of the P-HFS, many scholars have carried on deeper researches (Jiang & Ma, 2017; Li & Wang, 2017). Zhang and

C. Song and Z. Xu, *Techniques of Decision Making, Uncertain Reasoning and Regression Analysis Under the Hesitant Fuzzy Environment and Their Applications*, Uncertainty and Operations Research, https://doi.org/10.1007/978-981-16-5800-6_6

Wu (2014a, 2014b) studied some basic operations of the PHFSs, and Zhang et al. (2017) further developed the operations and integrations of the PHFSs.

Because correlation is a significant measure in decision making, data analysis, classification and pattern recognition (Wei et al., 2011), many researchers have extended the concept of correlation to different uncertain environments, such as fuzzy environment (Chiang & Lin, 1999; Liu & Kao, 2002; Hong, 2006) and intuitionistic fuzzy environment (Huang & Wu, 2002; Park et al., 2009), etc. Researchers have put forward different forms of correlation coefficients to characterize the correlations, for example, the fuzzy correlation coefficient (Yu, 1993), the intuitionistic fuzzy correlation coefficient (Ye,) and the hesitant fuzzy correlation coefficient (Xu & Xia, 2011). Since the excellent characters of the HFS in depicting the DMs' preferences and hesitant information, Chen and Xu (2013) also proposed some correlation coefficients for HFSs. As the HFSs may lose information which is detrimental to the final decision results, the P-HFSs can better depict the probabilistic information in the HFSs and avoid the loss of information. Actually, the existing correlation coefficients for HFSs are unsuitable for the P-HFSs. To properly and truly measure the correlation between the PHFSs and avoid the information loss, it is necessary to propose new correlation coefficients for the PHFSs. In this section, by the concept of mean for a probabilistic hesitant fuzzy element (PHFE) and a PHFS, we introduce a correlation coefficient and its weighted form between the P-HFSs to deal with the probabilistic hesitant fuzzy information. Based on the correlation coefficients, we present a clustering algorithm for PHFSs. At last, we take a practical example to illustrate the new correlation coefficients between the PHFSs in cluster analysis and risk assessment of human environment for the Twenty-First Century Maritime Silk Road.

Because of its excellent characters, many scholars have concentrated on the HFS theory (Torra et al., 2014; Xu, 2014), and developed extensive extensions and applications of the HFSs. For the sake of expressing both the positive preferences and negative preferences at the same time, Zhu et al. (2012) proposed the concept of dual hesitant fuzzy set (DHFS), which contains both the membership and non-membership degrees. Furthermore, Yu et al. (2014) and Wang et al. (2013) defined some basic aggregation operators and correlation measures of DHFSs, which have been applied in the MCGDM problems widely (Zhang, 2015). Due to the lack or deficiency of the information, Chen et al. (2013) extended the HFS to interval-valued hesitant fuzzy set (IVHFS), in which the experts are difficult to provide their preferences exactly by crisp numbers, but interval values within [0,1] (Wei et al., 2013; Zhu et al., 2014). However, with regard to the group decision making problems, it is not appropriate and reasonable that each possible value is equally important. Hence it is necessary to consider the probabilistic information, otherwise it may lead to errors. Therefore, Zhu (2014) tried to overcome the defect of HFS by associating the probability with the HFS, and introduced the probabilistic hesitant fuzzy set (PHFS), which depicted both the preferences and probabilistic information better. Later, Hao et al. (2017) combined the probability distribution information with the DHFS, and proposed the concept of probabilistic dual hesitant fuzzy set (PDHFS), which contains both the membership and non-membership degrees with the corresponding probability.

Table 6.1 A summary on the HFS and its extensions

Different models	Characteristic of the elements	Probabilistic information
HFS	A set of several possible crisp values	Completely known, crisp value
DHFS	A set of several possible and impossible crisp values	Completely known, crisp value
IVHFS	A set of several possible interval values	Completely known, crisp value
PHFS	A probabilistic distribution of several possible crisp values	Completely known, crisp value
PDHFS	A probabilistic distribution of several possible and impossible crisp values	Completely known, crisp value
IVPHFS (given in this chapter)	A probabilistic distribution of several possible crisp values	Partially known, interval/crisp value

For convenience to understand better, we provide a summary of their characteristics and differences discussed above, which is listed in Table 6.1 (Song et al., 2019b).

However, owing to the ever-increasing complexity of the actual problems and uncertainty of the decision makers' cognitions, in some situations there are many difficulties for the decision makers to quantify their preferences by crisp values exactly and properly. One possible approach is to quantify the preference degrees by a set of several possible values and describe the probabilistic information by interval values. What's more, how to compare the probabilistic hesitant fuzzy element (PHFE) is still a basic consideration in the MCGDM problems. The score function and the deviation degree of PHFE was proposed to compare and rank the alternatives (Zhang et al., 2017). Analyzing the principle and calculation process of the method, it is obvious that there are two main shortcomings. One is that the method ranks the elements with absolute priorities, which is not reasonable and logical. Another defect is that the calculation process is too complex.

Therefore, according to the analysis discussed above and for the sake of overcoming the weaknesses, we also introduce a set named interval-valued probabilistic hesitant fuzzy set (IVPHFS). The major excellence of IVPHFS is that it could depict two different attributes of a target in a single framework: possible HFS and its corresponding interval probability. The former one provides the preference degrees consisting of several possible values between 0 and 1, and the latter depicts the hesitancy and uncertainty by the interval-valued probabilistic distribution. Moreover, we provide some basic operation laws and aggregation operators of IVPHFSs. After that, we give a comparison approach according to the possibility degree by the score function and standard deviation degree of interval-valued probabilistic hesitant fuzzy elements (IVPHFEs), which are expressed by interval values. Our approach is more precise and contains more probabilistic information. At last but not least, we introduce an efficient and reliable approach to deal with practical MCGDM problems under interval-valued probabilistic hesitant fuzzy environment.

6.2 Preliminaries

6.2.1 Probabilistic Hesitant Fuzzy Set

Zhu and Xu (2016) defined the concept of the PHFSs by using the probability distribution to represent the DMs' preferences, which is described as follows:

Definition 6.1 (Song et al., 2019b). A PHFS is depicted as $H = \{x, h_x(p_x)|x \in X\}$, where h_x denotes the possible membership degrees of the element and p_x is a set of the corresponding probabilities, which satisfies $\sum p_x = 1$.

What is more, $h(p) = \{h^l(p^l)|l = 1, 2, \ldots, |h(p)|\}$ is depicted as the probabilistic hesitant fuzzy element (PHFE), where p^l is the probability of the hesitant fuzzy element h^l, which satisfies $\sum_{l=1}^{|h(p)|} p^l = 1$.

Apparently, we can see that the PHFE can reserve much more assessment information than the former HFE, so that the PHFE is more reliable and rational to express the DMs' preferences.

6.2.2 Correlation Coefficients of HFSs

Many scholars have studied the characteristics of the correlation coefficients for the HFSs. Starting from the HFEs, Xu and Xia (2011) put forward several correlation coefficient formulas. They first supposed that the HFEs had the same length and the values in them were arranged in ascending order. If the HFEs do not have the same length, then there are several common ways to expand the shorter HFE to the same length as the longer one. As a matter of fact, the DMs usually expand the shorter HFE by increasing the minimum value until two HFEs have the same length based on the pessimistic principle; while increasing the maximum value of the shorter HFE based on the optimistic principle. According to the pessimistic principle, Chen et al. (2013) put forward a new method to calculate the correlation coefficient between two HFSs.

Definition 6.2 (Song et al., 2019b). For two HFEs $h_A = \{\gamma_{A1}, \gamma_{A2}, \ldots, \gamma_{Al}\}$ and $h_B = \{\gamma_{B1}, \gamma_{B2}, \ldots, \gamma_{Bl}\}$, the correlation coefficient of h_A and h_B is denoted as $\rho(h_A, h_B)$, which has the following characteristics:

(1) $|\rho(h_A, h_B)| \leq 1$;

(2) $\rho(h_A, h_B) = 1$, if $h_A = h_B$;
(3) $\rho(h_A, h_B) = \rho(h_B, h_A)$.

Definition 6.3 (Song et al., 2019b). If $A = \{\langle x_i, h_A(x_i)\rangle | x_i \in X, i = 1, 2, \ldots, n\}$ is a HFS, then the definition of informational energy for A is:

$$E_{HFS} = \sum_{k=1}^{n} \left(\frac{1}{l_k} \sum_{i=1}^{l_k} h_{A\sigma(k)}^2(x_i) \right) \tag{6.1}$$

Definition 6.4 (Song et al., 2019b). For two HFSs $A = \{\langle x_i, h_A(x_i)\rangle | x_i \in X, i = 1, 2, \ldots, n\}$ and $B = \{\langle x_i, h_B(x_i)\rangle | x_i \in X, i = 1, 2, \ldots, n\}$, their correlation is defined as follows:

$$C_{HFS} = \sum_{k=1}^{n} \left(\frac{1}{l_k} \sum_{i=1}^{l_k} h_{A\sigma(k)}(x_i) \cdot h_{B\sigma(k)}(x_i) \right) \tag{6.2}$$

Definition 6.5 (Song et al., 2019b). For two HFSs $A = \{\langle x_i, h_A(x_i)\rangle | x_i \in X, i = 1, 2, \ldots, n\}$ and $B = \{\langle x_i, h_B(x_i)\rangle | x_i \in X, i = 1, 2, \ldots, n\}$, their correlation coefficient is defined as:

$$\begin{aligned} \rho_{HFS}(A, B) &= \frac{C_{HFS}(A, B)}{[C_{HFS}(A, A)]^{\frac{1}{2}} \cdot [C_{HFS}(B, B)]^{\frac{1}{2}}} \\ &= \frac{\sum_{k=1}^{n} \left(\frac{1}{l_k} \sum_{i=1}^{l_k} h_{A\sigma(k)}(x_i) \cdot h_{B\sigma(k)}(x_i) \right)}{\left[\sum_{k=1}^{n} \left(\frac{1}{l_k} \right) h_{A\sigma(k)}^2(x_i) \right]^{1/2} \cdot \left[\sum_{k=1}^{n} \left(\frac{1}{l_k} \right) h_{B\sigma(k)}^2(x_i) \right]^{1/2}} \end{aligned}$$

Definition 6.6 (Song et al., 2019b). For two HFSs $A = \{\langle x_i, h_A(x_i)\rangle | x_i \in X, i = 1, 2, \ldots, n\}$ and $B = \{\langle x_i, h_B(x_i)\rangle | x_i \in X, i = 1, 2, \ldots, n\}$ on a reference set X. Let $\omega = (\omega_1, \omega_2, \ldots, \omega_n)^T$ be the weighting vector of $x_i \in X (i = 1, 2, \ldots, n)$ with $\omega_i \in [0, 1]$, $i = 1, 2, \ldots, n$ and $\sum_{i=1}^{n} \omega_i = 1$. Then the weighted correlation coefficient between the HFSs A and B can be constructed as:

$$\begin{aligned} \rho_{\omega HFS}(A, B) &= \frac{C_{\omega HFS}(A, B)}{[C_{\omega HFS}(A, A)]^{1/2} \cdot [C_{\omega HFS}(B, B)]^{1/2}} \\ &= \frac{\sum_{k=1}^{n} \omega_i \left(\frac{1}{l_k} \sum_{i=1}^{l_k} h_{A\sigma(k)}(x_i) \cdot h_{B\sigma(k)}(x_i) \right)}{\left[\sum_{k=1}^{n} \omega_i \left(\frac{1}{l_k} \right) h_{A\sigma(k)}^2(x_i) \right]^{1/2} \cdot \left[\sum_{k=1}^{n} \omega_i \left(\frac{1}{l_k} \right) h_{B\sigma(k)}^2(x_i) \right]^{1/2}} \end{aligned}$$

Example 1 (Song et al., 2019b). Let A and B be two HFSs in $X = \{x_1, x_2, x_3\}$, and

$$A = \{\langle x_1, \{0.4, 0.5\}\rangle, \langle x_2, \{0.3, 0.5, 0.6\}\rangle, \langle x_3, \{0.2, 0.5\}\rangle\},$$

$$B = \{\langle x_1, \{0.2, 0.5, 0.6\}\rangle, \langle x_2, \{0.5, 0.8\}\rangle, \langle x_3, \{0.4\}\rangle\}.$$

Since the HFEs have not the same length, we usually extend the shorter HFE by adding the minimum value until they have the same length as to the pessimistic principle. After that, we can get:

$$A = \{\langle x_1, \{0.4, 0.4, 0.5\}\rangle, \langle x_2, \{0.3, 0.5, 0.6\}\rangle, \langle x_3, \{0.2, 0.5\}\rangle\},$$

$$B = \{\langle x_1, \{0.2, 0.5, 0.6\}\rangle, \langle x_2, \{0.5, 0.5, 0.8\}\rangle, \langle x_3, \{0.4, 0.4\}\rangle\}.$$

According to Definition 6.5, we get:

$$\begin{aligned} C_{HFS}(A, A) &= \sum_{k=1}^{3}\left(\frac{1}{l_k}\sum_{i=1}^{l_k} h^2_{A\sigma(i)}(x_i)\right) \\ &= \frac{1}{3}\sum_{j=1}^{3} h^2_{A\sigma(j)}(x_1) + \frac{1}{3}\sum_{j=1}^{3} h^2_{A\sigma(j)}(x_2) + \frac{1}{2}\sum_{j=1}^{2} h^2_{A\sigma(j)}(x_3) \\ &= \frac{1}{3}(0.4^2 + 0.4^2 + 0.5^2) + \frac{1}{3}(0.3^2 + 0.5^2 + 0.6^2) + \frac{1}{2}(0.2^2 + 0.5^2) \\ &= 0.648 \end{aligned}$$

$$\begin{aligned} C_{HFS}(B, B) &= \sum_{k=1}^{3}\left(\frac{1}{l_k}\sum_{i=1}^{l_k} h^2_{B\sigma(i)}(x_i)\right) \\ &= \frac{1}{3}\sum_{j=1}^{3} h^2_{B\sigma(j)}(x_1) + \frac{1}{3}\sum_{j=1}^{3} h^2_{B\sigma(j)}(x_2) + \frac{1}{2}\sum_{j=1}^{2} h^2_{B\sigma(j)}(x_3) \\ &= \frac{1}{3}(0.2^2 + 0.5^2 + 0.6^2) + \frac{1}{3}(0.5^2 + 0.5^2 + 0.8^2) + \frac{1}{2}(0.4^2 + 0.4^2) \\ &= 0.757 \end{aligned}$$

Then, based on Definition 6.6, we have:

$$\begin{aligned} C_{HFS}(A, B) &= \sum\nolimits_{k=1}^{3}\left(\frac{1}{l_k}\sum\nolimits_{i=1}^{l_k} h_{A\sigma(k)}(x_i)\cdot h_{B\sigma(k)}(x_i)\right) \\ &= \frac{1}{3}\sum\nolimits_{i=1}^{3} h_{A\sigma(k)}(x_1)\cdot h_{B\sigma(k)}(x_1) + \frac{1}{3}\sum\nolimits_{i=1}^{3} h_{A\sigma(k)}(x_2)\cdot h_{B\sigma(k)}(x_2) \\ &\quad + \frac{1}{2}\sum\nolimits_{i=1}^{2} h_{A\sigma(k)}(x_2)\cdot h_{B\sigma(k)}(x_2) \\ &= \frac{1}{3}(0.4\times 0.2 + 0.4\times 0.5 + 0.5\times 0.6) \end{aligned}$$

$$+\frac{1}{3}(0.3\times 0.5+0.5\times 0.5+0.6\times 0.8)$$
$$+\frac{1}{2}(0.2\times 0.4+0.5\times 0.4)=0.627$$

At last, we use the above Definition to calculate the correlation coefficient:

$$\rho_{HFS}(A,B)=\frac{C_{HFS}(A,B)}{[C_{HFS}(A,A)]^{\frac{1}{2}}\cdot[C_{HFS}(B,B)]^{\frac{1}{2}}}=\frac{0.627}{\sqrt{0.648}\cdot\sqrt{0.757}}=0.895$$

It is obvious that $0<\rho_{HFS}(A,B)<1$.

According to the analysis, the correlation coefficients defined above can measure the relationship between two HFSs, and are pretty significant in diverse fields. However, there are some weaknesses in the existing correlation coefficients between the HFSs. For example, it is impractical to ensure that all the HFEs are in the same length, and some adding values may change the original information. To overcome such shortcomings, we will reconsider the correlation coefficients from the angle of PHFSs.

6.2.3 Concept of Interval Value

Definition 6.7 (Xu & Da, 2002). Let $\widetilde{a}$ be an interval value, and $\widetilde{a}=\left[a^L,a^U\right]=\left\{x\middle|a^L\le x\le a^U\right\}$. For any two interval values $\widetilde{a}=\left[a^L,a^U\right]$ and $\widetilde{b}=\left[b^L,b^U\right]$, if $a^L\ge 0$ and $b^L\ge 0$, $\lambda\in[0,1]$, then

(1) $\widetilde{a}+\widetilde{b}=\left[a^L+b^L,a^U+b^U\right]$;
(2) $\widetilde{a}^{\lambda}=\left[\left(a^L\right)^{\lambda},\left(a^U\right)^{\lambda}\right]$;
(3) $\lambda\widetilde{a}=\left[\lambda a^L,\lambda a^U\right]$;
(4) $\widetilde{a}\cdot\widetilde{b}=\left[a^L\cdot b^L,a^U\cdot b^U\right]$.

6.2.4 PHFSs and Their Basic Operations

Definition 6.8 (Zhang et al., 2017). Let $H=\{x,h_x(p_x)|x\in X\}$ be a probabilistic hesitant fuzzy set, where h_x denotes the possible membership degree named probabilistic hesitant fuzzy element (PHFE) and p_x is the associated possibility. Also there is

$$h(p)=\{\gamma_l(p_l)|l=1,2,\ldots,|h(p)|\},\quad\sum_{l=1}^{h(p)}p_l\le 1\tag{6.3}$$

If $\sum_{l=1}^{|h(p)|} p_l < 1$, then we could define a normalized PHFE as $\dot{h}(p) = \{\gamma_l(\dot{p}_l)|l = 1, 2, \ldots, |h(p)|\}$, $\dot{p}_l = p_l / \sum_{l=1}^{|p_l|} p_l$, $l = 1, 2, \ldots, |h(p)|$. In order to understand easily, the values of γ_l discussed in this section are assumed in ascending order, and all the PHFEs discussed in this section are normalized and denoted as $h(p)$.

Definition 6.9 (Zhang et al., 2017). Let $h(p)$, $h_1(p)$ and $h_2(p)$ be three PHFEs, $\lambda > 0$, then

(1) $\lambda h(p) = \underset{\gamma_l \in h}{\cup} \{[1 - (1 - \gamma_l)^\lambda](p_l)\}$;

(2) $h^\lambda(p) = \underset{\gamma_l \in h}{\cup} \{[\gamma_l^\lambda](p_l)\}$;

(3) $h_1(p) \oplus h_2(p) = \underset{\gamma_{1_l} \in h_1, \gamma_{2_k} \in h_2}{\cup} \{[\gamma_{1_l} + \gamma_{2_k} - \gamma_{1_l}\gamma_{2_k}](p_{1_l} \cdot p_{2_k})\}$;

(4) $h_1(p) \otimes h_2(p) = \underset{\gamma_{1_l} \in h_1, \gamma_{2_k} \in h_2}{\cup} \{[\gamma_{1_l}\gamma_{2_k}](p_{1_l} \cdot p_{2_k})\}$.

6.2.5 *Ranking Method of PHFEs*

Definition 6.10 (Zhang et al., 2017). For a PHFE $h(p) = \{\gamma_l(p_l)|l = 1, 2, \ldots, |h(p)|\}$, the score of $h(p)$ is $s(h(p)) = \sum_{l=1}^{|h_l(p)|} \gamma_l \cdot p_l$. If we denote the score of $h(p)$ as $\overline{\gamma}$, then the deviation degree is $d(h(p)) = \sum_{l=1}^{|h(p)|} (p_l(\gamma_l - \overline{\gamma}))^2$.

According to the score and deviation functions, Zhang et al. (2017) established a ranking method for two PHFEs $h_1(p)$ and $h_2(p)$:

(1) If $s(h_1(p)) > s(h_2(p))$, then $h_1(p) > h_2(p)$;
(2) If $s(h_1(p)) < s(h_2(p))$, then $h_1(p) < h_2(p)$;
(3) If $s(h_1(p)) = s(h_2(p))$ and $d(h_1(p)) < d(h_2(p))$, then $h_1(p) > h_2(p)$;
(4) If $s(h_1(p)) = s(h_2(p))$ and $d(h_1(p)) > d(h_2(p))$, then $h_1(p) < h_2(p)$;
(5) If $s(h_1(p)) = s(h_2(p))$ and $d(h_1(p)) = d(h_2(p))$, then we define that $h_1(p)$ is equivalent to $h_2(p)$, denoted as $h_1(p) \sim h_2(p)$.

6.3 Correlation Coefficients of PHFSs

In this section, we will introduce the concept of correlation coefficient for PHFSs and present the correlation coefficient formulas, and then we will discuss their properties.

6.3.1 *Some Concepts Related to PHFEs*

For the sake of better understanding the concept of correlation coefficient of P-HFSs, we first give some basic definitions for PHFEs.

Let $h_{x_i}(p_x) = \{\gamma_{i1}(p_{i1}), \gamma_{i2}(p_{i2}), \ldots, \gamma_{il_i}(p_{il_i})\}$ be a P-HFE on X, γ_{ik} $(k = 1, 2, \ldots, l_i)$ are the possible values associated with the corresponding probability p_{ik}, and as well l_i is the number of the values in $h_{x_i}(p_x)$, $\sum_{k=1}^{l_i} p_{ik} = 1$. Then we give the following definitions:

Definition 6.11 (Xu & Zhou, 2016). The mean of the PHFE $h_{x_i}(p_x)$ is defined as:

$$\overline{h}_{x_i}(p_x) = \sum\nolimits_{k=1}^{l_i} (\gamma_{ik} \cdot p_{ik}) \tag{6.4}$$

Definition 6.12. The hesitant degree of the PHFE $h_{x_i}(p_x)$ is:

$$\varphi_{h_{x_i}(p_x)} = \sqrt{\frac{1}{l_i}\sum_{k=1}^{l_i}\left[\gamma_{ik} - \overline{h}_{x_i}(p_x)\right]^2} = \sqrt{\frac{1}{l_i}\sum_{k=1}^{l_i}\left[\gamma_{ik} - \sum\nolimits_{k=1}^{l_i}(\gamma_{ik} \cdot p_{ik})\right]^2} \tag{6.5}$$

Example 2 Let $h_1(p_1)$ and $h_2(p_2)$ be two PHFEs, and $h_1(p_1) = \{0.6(0.4), 0.7(0.3), 0.8(0.3)\}$, $h_2(p_2) = \{0.6(0.6), 0.7(0.4)\}$. Based on the above Definitions, we can get $\overline{h}_1(p_1) = 0.71$, $\overline{h}_2(p_2) = 0.66$, $\varphi_{h_1(p_1)} = 0.084$, and $\varphi_{h_2(p_2)} = 0.055$. As a result, we can see that the PHFE h_1 is better and more hesitant than the PHFE h_2.

6.3.2 Correlation Coefficient of PHFSs

In this part, we will give some definitions first, and then introduce a correlation coefficient of PHFSs.

Definition 6.13 (Song et al., 2019b). Let $A = \{\langle x, h_{Ax_i}(p_x)\rangle | x_i \in X\}$ be a PHFS on the reference set X with $h_{Ax_i}(p_x) = \{\gamma_{Ai1}(p_{Ai1}), \gamma_{Ai2}(p_{Ai2}), \ldots, \gamma_{Ail_{Ai}}(p_{Ail_i})\}$, $i = 1, 2, \ldots, n$. Since the mean of the PHFE is $\overline{h}_{Ax_i}(p_x)$, then we can define the mean of the PHFS A as follows:

$$\overline{A} = E(A) = \frac{1}{n}\sum_{i=1}^{n}\overline{h}_{Ax_i}(p_x) = \frac{1}{n}\sum_{i=1}^{n}\left[\sum_{k=1}^{l_i}(\gamma_{ik} \cdot p_{ik})\right] \tag{6.6}$$

Furthermore, in the following, we give the variance of the PHFS A:

Definition 6.14 (Song et al., 2019b). If the mean of the P-HFE is $\overline{h}_{Ax_i}(p_x)$ and the mean of the PHFS A is $\overline{A}$, then we give the variance of the PHFS A as:

$$Var(A) = \frac{1}{n}\sum_{i=1}^{n}\left[\overline{h}_{Ax_i}(p_x) - \overline{A}\right]^2 \tag{6.7}$$

Definition 6.15 (Song et al., 2019b). Let $A = \{\langle x, h_{Ax_i}(p_x)\rangle | x_i \in X\}$ and $B = \{\langle x, h_{Bx_i}(p_x)\rangle | x_i \in X\}$ be two P-HFSs on the reference set X, where $h_{Ax_i}(p_x) = \{\gamma_{Ai1}(p_{Ai1}), \gamma_{Ai2}(p_{Ai2}), \ldots, \gamma_{Ail_{Ai}}(p_{Ail_i})\}$, $h_{Bx_i}(p_x) = \{\gamma_{Bi1}(p_{Bi1}), \gamma_{Bi2}(p_{Bi2}), \ldots, \gamma_{Bil_{Ai}}(p_{Bil_i}), i = 1, 2, \ldots, n$. If the mean of the PHFEs are $\overline{h}_{Ax_i}(p_x)$ and $\overline{h}_{Bx_i}(p_x)$, then the mean of the two P-HFSs are $\overline{A}$ and $\overline{B}$, respectively. Thus, the correlation between the PHFSs A and B is defined as follows:

$$C(A, B) = \frac{1}{n}\sum_{i=1}^{n}\left[\overline{h}_{Ax_i}(p_{Ax}) - \overline{A}\right] \cdot \left[\overline{h}_{Bx_i}(p_{Bx}) - \overline{B}\right] \tag{6.8}$$

where $\overline{h}_{Ax_i}(p_{Ax}) = \sum_{k=1}^{l_{Ai}}(\gamma_{Aik} \cdot p_{Aik})$, $\overline{h}_{Bx_i}(p_{Bx}) = \sum_{k=1}^{l_{Bi}}(\gamma_{Bik} \cdot p_{Bik})$, and $\overline{A} = E(A) = \frac{1}{n}\sum_{i=1}^{n}\overline{h}_{Ax_i}(p_x) = \frac{1}{n}\sum_{i=1}^{n}\left[\sum_{k=1}^{l_i}(\gamma_{Aik} \cdot p_{Aik})\right]$, $\overline{B} = E(B) = \frac{1}{n}\sum_{i=1}^{n}\overline{h}_{Bx_i}(p_x) = \frac{1}{n}\sum_{i=1}^{n}\left[\sum_{k=1}^{l_i}(\gamma_{Bik} \cdot p_{Bik})\right]$, $i = 1, 2, \ldots, n$.

Remark 1 For the two PHFSs A and B, it is easy to prove the following theorem:

Theorem 1 (Song et al., 2019b). For a reference set X, let $A = \{\langle x, h_{Ax_i}(p_{Ax})\rangle | x_i \in X\}$ be a PHFS on X, with $h_{Ax_i}(p_{Ax}) = \{\gamma_{Ai1}(p_{Ai1}), \gamma_{Ai2}(p_{Ai2}), \ldots, \gamma_{Ail_{Ai}}(p_{Ail_i})\}$, $i = 1, 2, \ldots, n$, then

$$C(A, A) = Var(A) \tag{6.9}$$

After we have given some basic definitions about PHFSs, inspired by Liao et al. (2015), below we introduce the correlation coefficient for the PHFSs:

Definition 6.16 (Song et al., 2019b). For a reference set X, let $A = \{\langle x, h_{Ax_i}(p_{Ax})\rangle | x_i \in X\}$ and $B = \{\langle x, h_{Bx_i}(p_{Bx})\rangle | x_i \in X\}$ be two PHFSs on X, with $h_{Ax_i}(p_{Ax}) = \{\gamma_{Ai1}(p_{Ai1}), \gamma_{Ai2}(p_{Ai2}), \ldots, \gamma_{Ail_{Ai}}(p_{Ail_i})\}$ and $h_{Bx_i}(p_{Bx}) = \{\gamma_{Bi1}(p_{Bi1}), \gamma_{Bi2}(p_{Bi2}), \ldots \gamma_{Bil_{Ai}}(p_{Bil_i}), i = 1, 2, \ldots, n$. Then the correlation coefficient between PHFSs A and B is:

$$\begin{aligned}\rho(A, B) &= \frac{C(A, B)}{[C(A, A) \cdot C(B, B)]^{\frac{1}{2}}} \\ &= \frac{\frac{1}{n}\sum_{i=1}^{n}\left[\bar{h}_{Ax_i}(p_{Ax}) - \bar{A}\right] \cdot \left[\bar{h}_{Bx_i}(p_{Bx}) - \bar{B}\right]}{\left[\frac{1}{n}\sum_{i=1}^{n}\left(\bar{h}_{Ax_i}(p_x) - \bar{A}\right)^2 \cdot \frac{1}{n}\sum_{i=1}^{n}\left(\bar{h}_{Bx_i}(p_x) - \bar{B}\right)^2\right]^{\frac{1}{2}}}\end{aligned} \tag{6.10}$$

Remark 2 This chapter introduces the correlation coefficient formula to reveal the relationship between PHFSs. Our interest here is to develop an easy way to excavate the relationship between the PHFSs. In fact, the correlation coefficient formula satisfies the following conditions:

(1) $\rho(A, B) = \rho(B, A)$;

(2) $\rho(A, A) = 1$;
(3) $\rho(A, A^c) = -1$, where $A^c = \{\langle x, h^c_{Ax_i}(p_{Ax})\rangle | x_i \in X\}$ with $h^c_{Ax_i}(p_{Ax}) = \{1 - \gamma_{Ai1}(p_{Ai1}), 1 - \gamma_{Ai2}(p_{Ai2}), \ldots, 1 - \gamma_{Ail_{Ai}}(p_{Ail_i})\}$, $i = 1, 2, \ldots, n$;
(4) $-1 \leq \rho(A, B) \leq 1$.

Proof According to the above Definition, it is easy for us to prove (1), (2) and (3). As to (4), it can be proven that:

$$|C(A, B)| = \left| \frac{1}{n} \sum_{i=1}^{n} \left[\overline{h}_{Ax_i}(p_x) - \overline{A} \right] \cdot \left[\overline{h}_{Bx_i}(p_x) - \overline{B} \right] \right|$$
$$\leq \frac{1}{n} \sum_{i=1}^{n} \left| \left[\overline{h}_{Ax_i}(p_x) - \overline{A} \right] \right| \cdot \left| \left[\overline{h}_{Bx_i}(p_x) - \overline{B} \right] \right|$$

As we all know, the Cauchy–Schwarz inequality is:

$$(a_1 b_1 + a_2 b_2 + \ldots + a_n b_n) \leq \left(a_1^2 + a_2^2 + \ldots + a_n^2\right) \cdot \left(b_1^2 + b_2^2 + \ldots + b_n^2\right)$$

where $a_i, b_i \in R$, $i = 1, 2, \ldots, n$, so we can get:

$$|C(A, B)| \leq \sqrt{\frac{1}{n} \sum_{i=1}^{n} \left| \left[\overline{h}_{Ax_i}(p_x) - \overline{A} \right] \right|^2} \cdot \sqrt{\frac{1}{n} \sum_{i=1}^{n} \left| \left[\overline{h}_{Bx_i}(p_x) - \overline{B} \right] \right|^2}$$
$$= |C(A, A)|^{1/2} \cdot |C(B, B)|^{1/2}$$

As a result, we have $|\rho(A, B)| = \frac{|C(A,B)|}{[C(A,A)]^{1/2} \cdot [C(B,B)]^{1/2}} \leq 1$.

Example 3 (Song et al., 2019b). Let A and B be two PHFSs on $X = \{x_1, x_2, x_3\}$,

$$A = \left\{ \begin{array}{l} \langle x_1, \{0.5(0.3), 0.7(0.7)\}\rangle, \\ \langle x_2, \{0.6(0.4), 0.8(0.3), 0.9(0.3)\}\rangle, \\ \langle x_3, \{0.4(0.6), 0.5(0.4)\}\rangle \end{array} \right\}.$$

$$B = \left\{ \begin{array}{l} \langle x_1, \{0.2(0.6), 0.4(0.4)\}\rangle, \\ \langle x_2, \{0.5(0.7), 0.8(0.3)\}\rangle, \\ \langle x_3, \{0.3(0.5), 0.6(0.3), 0.7(0.2)\}\rangle \end{array} \right\}$$

We can obtain:

$$\overline{A} = E(A) = \frac{1}{n} \sum_{i=1}^{n} \overline{h}_{Ax_i}(p_x) = \frac{1}{n} \sum_{i=1}^{n} \left[\sum_{k=1}^{l_i} (\gamma_{Aik} \cdot p_{Aik}) \right]$$

$$= \frac{1}{3}\left[\begin{array}{l}(0.7 \times 0.3 + 0.5 \times 0.7) + (0.9 \times 0.4 + 0.8 \times 0.3 + 0.6 \times 0.3) \\ +(0.5 \times 0.6 + 0.4 \times 0.4)\end{array}\right]$$

$$= 0.6$$

$$\overline{B} = E(B) = \frac{1}{n}\sum_{i=1}^{n}\overline{h}_{Bx_i}(p_x) = \frac{1}{n}\sum_{i=1}^{n}\left[\sum\nolimits_{k=1}^{l_i}(\gamma_{Bik} \cdot p_{Bik})\right]$$

$$= \frac{1}{3}\left[\begin{array}{l}(0.4 \times 0.6 + 0.2 \times 0.4) + (0.8 \times 0.7 + 0.5 \times 0.3) \\ +(0.7 \times 0.5 + 0.6 \times 0.3 + 0.3 \times 0.2)\end{array}\right]$$

$$= 0.54$$

$$C(A, A) = \frac{1}{n}\sum_{i=1}^{n}\left[\overline{h}_{Ax_i}(p_x) - \overline{A}\right]^2$$

$$= \frac{1}{3}\left[(0.56 - 0.6)^2 + (0.78 - 0.6)^2 + (0.59 - 0.6)^2\right] = 0.011$$

$$C(B, B) = \frac{1}{n}\sum_{i=1}^{n}\left[\overline{h}_{Bx_i}(p_x) - \overline{B}\right]^2$$

$$= \frac{1}{3}\left[(0.32 - 0.54)^2 + (0.71 - 0.54)^2 + (0.59 - 0.54)^2\right] = 0.027 \quad \ldots$$

$$C(A, B) = \frac{1}{n}\sum_{i=1}^{n}\left[\overline{h}_{Ax_i}(p_{Ax}) - \overline{A}\right] \cdot \left[\overline{h}_{Bx_i}(p_{Ax}) - \overline{B}\right]$$

$$= \frac{1}{3}\left[\begin{array}{l}(0.56 - 0.6) \times (0.32 - 0.54) + (0.78 - 0.6) \times (0.71 - 0.54) \\ +\ (0.59 - 0.6) \times (0.59 - 0.54)\end{array}\right]$$

$$= 0.013 \quad \ldots$$

Then we can calculate the correlation coefficient as:

$$\rho(A, B)\frac{C(A, B)}{[C(A, A) \cdot C(B, B)]^{1/2}} = \frac{0.013}{\sqrt{0.011} \cdot \sqrt{0.027}} = 0.754$$

It is obvious that $0 < \rho(A, B) < 1$.

6.3.3 Weighted Correlation Coefficient Between PHFSs

As to the actual problems, each element may have different meanings and influences, so we should assign the objects $x_i \in X\ (i = 1, 2, \ldots, n)$ different weights. Therefore, in this part, we will provide the weighted form of the correlation coefficient for PHFSs.

Definition 6.17 (Song et al., 2019b). Suppose $A = \left\{\left\langle x, h_{Ax_i}(p_x)\right\rangle | x_i \in X\right\}$ is a PHFS on the reference set X, $h_{Ax_i}(p_x) = \left\{\gamma_{Ai1}(p_{Ai1}), \gamma_{Ai2}(p_{Ai2}), \ldots, \gamma_{Ail_{Ai}}\left(p_{Ail_i}\right)\right\}$, $i = 1, 2, \ldots, n$. Let $\omega = (\omega_1, \omega_2, \ldots, \omega_n)^T$ be the weighting vector of $x_i \in X (i = 1, 2, \ldots, n)$ with $\omega_i \in [0, 1]$, $\sum_{i=1}^{n} \omega_i = 1, i = 1, 2, \ldots, n$.

Then, the weighted mean of the PHFS A is define as follows:

$$\overline{A}_\omega = \frac{1}{n}\sum_{i=1}^{n} \omega_i \overline{h}_{Ax_i}(p_x) = \frac{1}{n}\sum_{i=1}^{n}\left[\omega_i \sum_{k=1}^{l_{Ai}} (\gamma_{Aik} \cdot p_{Aik})\right] \tag{6.11}$$

Also, we can give the following weighted variance of the PHFS A as follows:

Definition 6.18 (Song et al., 2019b). The weighted variance of the PHFS A is defined as:

$$Var_\omega(A) = \frac{1}{n}\sum_{i=1}^{n}\left[\omega_i \overline{h}_{Ax_i}(p_x) - \overline{A}_\omega\right]^2 \tag{6.12}$$

Next, we can give the weighted correlation between two PHFSs:

Definition 6.19 (Song et al., 2019b). For a reference set X, let $A = \left\{\left\langle x, h_{Ax_i}(p_x)\right\rangle | x_i \in X\right\}$ and $B = \left\{\left\langle x, h_{Bx_i}(p_x)\right\rangle | x_i \in X\right\}$ be two PHFSs on X with $h_{Ax_i}(p_x) = \left\{\gamma_{Ai1}(p_{Ai1}), \gamma_{Ai2}(p_{Ai2}), \ldots, \gamma_{Ail_{Ai}}\left(p_{Ail_i}\right)\right\}$, $h_{Bx_i}(p_x) = \left\{\gamma_{Bi1}(p_{Bi1}), \gamma_{Bi2}(p_{Bi2}), \ldots, \gamma_{Bil_{Ai}}\left(p_{Bil_i}\right)\right\}$, $i = 1, 2, \ldots, n$ and let $\omega = (\omega_1, \omega_2, \ldots, \omega_n)^T$ be the weighting vector of $x_i \in X (i = 1, 2, \ldots, n)$ with $\omega_i \in [0, 1], i = 1, 2, \ldots, n$ satisfying $\sum_{i=1}^{n} \omega_i = 1$. Then the weighted correlation between PHFSs A and B is:

$$\begin{aligned} C_\omega(A, B) &= \frac{1}{n}\sum_{i=1}^{n}\left[\omega_i \overline{h}_{Ax_i}(p_{Ax}) - \bar{A}_\omega\right] \cdot \left[\omega_i \overline{h}_{Bx_i}(p_{Bx}) - \bar{B}_\omega\right] \\ &= \frac{1}{n}\sum_{i=1}^{n}\left[\omega_i \overline{h}_{Ax_i}(p_{Ax}) - \omega_i \sum_{k=1}^{l_i}(\gamma_{Aik} \cdot p_{Aik})\right] \\ &\quad \cdot \left[\omega_i \overline{h}_{Bx_i}(p_{Bx}) - \omega_i \sum_{k=1}^{l_i}(\gamma_{Bik} \cdot p_{Bik})\right] \end{aligned} \tag{6.13}$$

where $\overline{h}_{Ax_i}(p_{Ax}) = \sum_{k=1}^{l_{Ai}} (\gamma_{Aik} \cdot p_{Aik})$, $\overline{h}_{Bx_i}(p_{Bx}) = \sum_{k=1}^{l_{Bi}} (\gamma_{Bik} \cdot p_{Bik})$, $i = 1, 2, \ldots, n$.

Definition 6.20 (Song et al., 2019b). Assume that $A = \left\{\left\langle x, h_{Ax_i}(p_{Ax})\right\rangle | x_i \in X\right\}$ and $B = \left\{\left\langle x, h_{Bx_i}(p_{Bx})\right\rangle | x_i \in X\right\}$ are two PHFSs on a reference set

X, where $h_{Ax_i}(p_{Ax}) = \{\gamma_{Ai1}(p_{Ai1}), \gamma_{Ai2}(p_{Ai2}), \ldots, \gamma_{Ail_{Ai}}(p_{Ail_i})\}$, $h_{Bx_i}(p_{Bx}) = \{\gamma_{Bi1}(p_{Bi1}), \gamma_{Bi2}(p_{Bi2}), \ldots, \gamma_{Bil_{Ai}}(p_{Bil_i})\}, i = 1, 2, \ldots, n$. Let $\omega = (\omega_1, \omega_2, \ldots, \omega_n)^T$ be the weighting vector of $x_i \in X\,(i = 1, 2, \ldots, n)$ with $\omega_i \in [0, 1],\ \ i = 1, 2, \ldots, n$ and $\sum_{i=1}^{n} \omega_i = 1$. Then the weighted correlation coefficient between the PHFSs A and B can be defined as:

$$\begin{aligned}\rho_\omega(A, B) &= \frac{C_\omega(A, B)}{[C_\omega(A, A) \cdot C_\omega(B, B)]^{1/2}} \\ &= \frac{\sum_{i=1}^{n}\left[\omega_i \bar{h}_{Ax_i}(p_{Ax}) - \bar{A}_\omega\right] \cdot \left[\omega_i \bar{h}_{Bx_i}(p_{Bx}) - \bar{B}_\omega\right]}{\sqrt{\sum_{i=1}^{n}\left[\omega_i \bar{h}_{Ax_i}(p_{Ax}) - \bar{A}_\omega\right]^2} \cdot \sqrt{\sum_{i=1}^{n}\left[\omega_i \bar{h}_{Bx_i}(p_{Bx}) - \bar{B}_\omega\right]^2}}\end{aligned} \tag{6.14}$$

In a similar way, we can easily prove that the weighted correlation coefficient $\rho_\omega(A, B)$ between the PHFSs A and B also satisfies the four conditions of the correlation coefficient.

In this section, we have proposed two correlation coefficient formulas. From the construction process, we can see that the new formulas can preserve the original information provided by the DMs to the greatest extent as we do not need to add any value in the HFEs.

6.3.4 Clustering Algorithm for PHFSs

Inspired by the clustering algorithm (Xu et al., 2008) and the above correlation coefficient formula for PHFSs, we will provide an efficient clustering algorithm for the PHFSs in this part. For the sake of better understanding, we first introduce some basic concepts:

Definition 6.21 (Song et al., 2019b). Given a reference set X, let $A_j (j = 1, 2, \ldots, n)$ be n PHFSs over X. We denote the correlation matrix for PHFSs as $C = (\rho_{ij})_{m\times m}$, where $\rho_{ij} = \rho(A_i, A_j)$ is the correlation coefficient between the two PHFSs A_i and A_j, and $\rho_{ij} = \rho(A_i, A_j)$ has the following characteristics:

(1) $0 \le \rho_{ij} \le 1, \ \ i, j = 1, 2, \ldots, n;$
(2) $\rho_{ii} = 1, \ \ i = 1, 2, \ldots, n;$
(3) $\rho_{ij} = \rho_{ji}, \ \ i, j = 1, 2, \ldots, n.$

Definition 6.22 (Song et al., 2019b). Let $C = (\rho_{ij})_{m\times m}$ be a correlation matrix, if $C^2 = C \circ C = (\overline{\rho}_{ij})_{m\times m}$, then we call C^2 a composition matrix of C, where $\overline{\rho}_{ij} = \max_k\{\min\{\rho_{ik}, \rho_{kj}\}\}, i, j = 1, 2, \ldots, n$.

Definition 6.23 (Song et al., 2019b). Let $C = (\rho_{ij})_{m\times m}$ be a correlation matrix, if $C^2 \subseteq C$, i.e.,

$$\max_k\{\min\{\rho_{ik},\rho_{kj}\}\} \le \rho_{ij},\quad i,j=1,2,\ldots,n \tag{6.15}$$

then we call C an equivalent correlation matrix.

Definition 6.24 (Song et al., 2019b). Let $C=(\rho_{ij})_{n\times n}$ be an equivalent correlation matrix. The matrix $C_\lambda=\left(\rho_{ij}^\lambda\right)_{m\times m}$ is called the λ-cutting matrix of C, where

$$\rho_{ij}^\lambda=\begin{cases}0 \text{ } if \text{ } \rho_{ij}<\lambda\\ 1 \text{ } if \text{ } \rho_{ij}\ge\lambda\end{cases}\quad i,j=1,2,\ldots,n,$$

and we call $\lambda\in[0,1]$ the confidence level.

As is known to us all, the main goal of cluster analysis is to collect the similar data for classification, so that the objects in one group are much more similar to each other than those in other groups. Many experts have put forward different algorithms for clustering, which can analyze the data from different perspectives.

Suppose that $x=\{x_1,x_2,\ldots,x_m\}$ is a finite set of alternatives and $c=\{c_1,c_2,\ldots,c_m\}$ is a set of criteria. An expert is invited to evaluate the alternatives $x_i(i=1,2,\ldots,m)$ under the criteria $c_j(j=1,2,\ldots,n)$ by a PHFE:

$$h_{ij}(p)=\left\{h_{ij}^{(k)}\left(p_{ij}^{(k)}\right)\middle|k=1,2,\ldots,|h(p)|,\sum_{k=1}^{|h(p)|}p_{ij}^{(k)}=1\right\}$$

where $h_{ij}^{(k)}$ is the kth hesitant fuzzy element of $h_{ij}(p)$ with the corresponding probability $p_{ij}^{(k)}$. Then by collecting the evaluation information, we can build the probabilistic hesitant fuzzy decision matrix R as follows:

$$R=A_i=\left[h_{ij}(p)\right]_{m\times n}=\begin{bmatrix}h_{11}(p) & h_{12}(p) & \ldots & h_{1n}(p)\\ h_{21}(p) & h_{22}(p) & \ldots & h_{2n}(p)\\ \vdots & \vdots & \ddots & \vdots\\ h_{m1}(p) & h_{m2}(p) & \ldots & h_{mn}(p)\end{bmatrix}$$

Applying the new correlation coefficient formula for PHFSs, in the following, we could present a new clustering algorithm for PHFSs by the following steps (Song et al., 2019b):

Algorithm Step 1. Let $\{A_1,A_2,\ldots,A_n\}$ be a set of PHFSs over X. If we have known the weight vector of the criteria, then we can calculate the correlation coefficients of the PHFSs. After that, we construct a correlation matrix $C=(\rho_{ij})_{m\times m}$, where $\rho_{ij}=\rho(A_i,A_j)$:

$$C = \left(\rho_{ij}\right)_{m\times m} = \begin{bmatrix} 1 & \rho_{12} & \cdots & \rho_{1m} \\ \rho_{21} & 1 & \cdots & \rho_{2m} \\ \vdots & \vdots & \ddots & \vdots \\ \rho_{m1} & \rho_{m2} & \cdots & 1 \end{bmatrix}$$

Otherwise, there are many approaches to calculate the weighting vector $w = (w_1, w_2, \ldots, w_n)^T$ of the criteria (Bai et al., 2017b; Yager, 1988;).

Step 2. Make sure that $C = \left(\rho_{ij}\right)_{m\times m}$ is an equivalent correlation matrix. If the correlation matrix C is an equivalent correlation matrix, then it must satisfy $C^2 \subseteq C$, where $C^2 = C \circ C = \left(\overline{\rho}_{ij}\right)_{m\times m}, \overline{\rho}_{ij} = \max\limits_{k}\left\{\min\left\{\rho_{ik}, \rho_{kj}\right\}\right\}, i, j = 1, 2, \ldots, n.$

If not, we should obtain the equivalent correlation matrix through the following method:

$$C \to C^2 \to C^4 \to \cdots \to C^{2k} \to \cdots, \text{ until } C^{2k} = C^{2(k+1)}.$$

Step 3. We construct the λ-cutting matrix $C_\lambda = \left({}_\lambda\rho_{ij}\right)_{m\times m}$ for a confidence level $\lambda \in [0, 1]$ where $\rho_{ij}^{\lambda} = \begin{cases} 0 \text{ } if \text{ } \rho_{ij} < \lambda \\ 1 \text{ } if \text{ } \rho_{ij} \geq \lambda \end{cases}, i, j = 1, 2, \ldots, n.$

Step 4. Classify the PHFSs: We can cluster the PHFSs A_i and A_j into the same group if all the elements of the ith line in C_λ are the same as the corresponding elements of the jth line in C_λ.

The basic step of the above clustering algorithm is to calculate the correlation coefficient between the PHFSs properly. Using our novel correlation coefficient formulas, we can well reduce the loss of information and thus can obtain the relatively reasonable clustering results.

6.4 Application of the Correlation Coefficients Between the PHFSs

In this section, we use a practical example [adapted from (Yang et al., 2016)] to illustrate the application of the correlation coefficients between the PHFSs in cluster analysis. And then, we compare our method with the one of HFSs.

6.4.1 Application of the Correlation Coefficients Between the PHFSs in Cluster Analysis

China has put forward an initiative named "the Silk Road Economic Belt and the Twenty-First Century Maritime Silk Road" in the background of the new era, aiming to build a peaceful and stable neighborly environment. The Belt and Road Initiative mainly relies on the cooperation with the surrounding countries and South Asia, Middle East, Africa and Europe. However, there are many challenges in the construction, as the investment environments are pretty uncertain and some countries are even trapped in ethnic conflicts or political transition. Thus the influencing factors of the environmental risk of "The Belt and Road Initiative" are complicated. What is more, it is difficult to quantify the evaluation results with the certain values. Yang et al. (2016) built the indicator system for human environment risk of The Twenty-First Century Maritime Silk Road shown in Table 6.1, which includes target layer and two indicator layers. Due to the increasing complexity of the practical problems and the uncertainty of the DMs' knowledge, the DMs are invited to evaluate the alternatives by the PHFSs, which can avoid the loss of information and remain the original information to the greatest extent. Then we can construct the evaluation information by the PHFSs shown in Tables 6.2 and 6.3 (Song et al., 2019b).

In the following, we will use the proposed weighted correlation coefficient for the PHFSs and the clustering algorithm above to cluster the ten countries (Song et al., 2019b):

Step 1. According to Yang et al. (2016), we assume that the thirteen corresponding indicators are equally important. Then we can calculate the correlation coefficients between the PHFSs $H_j (j = 1, 2, \ldots, 10)$ and then obtain the correlation matrix as follows:

Table 6.2 Indicator system for human environment risk of The Twenty-First Century Maritime Silk Road

Target layer (A)	First indicator layer (B)	Secondary indicator layer C
Human environment risk of The Twenty-First Century Maritime Silk Road (A1)	Political situation (B1)	State failure instability event (C1)
		State failure internal war event (C2)
		Governance corruption (C3)
		Governance effectiveness (C4)
		Terrorism activity (C5)
	Economic situation (B2)	Poverty population ratio (C6)
		GDP per capita (C7)
		Governance income and expenses (C8)
		Total foreign trade (C9)
		External debt (C10)
	Political alliance (B3)	Alignment with power countries (C11)
		Affiliation with China (C12)
		Trade with China (C13)

Table 6.3 The evaluations of human environment risk of the ten objective countries with the PHFSs (Song et al. 2019a)

	H_1	H_2	H_3	H_4	H_5
C1	{0.1(0.3), 0.5(0.7)}	{0.1(0.3), 0.7(0.7)}	{0.1(0.6), 0.3(0.4)}	{0.1(0.5), 0.5(0.5)}	{0.9(1)}
C2	{0.1(0.2), 0.3(0.8)}	{0.8(0.3), 0.9(0.7)}	{0.1(1)}	{0.3(0.5), 0.5(0.5)}	{0.3(0.8), 0.4(0.2)}
C3	{0.3(0.5), 0.5(0.5)}	{0.5(0.4), 0.7(0.6)}	{0.1(0.5), 0.2(0.5)}	{0.7(0.5), 0.9(0.5)}	{0.4(0.3), 0.5(0.7)}
C4	{0.1(0.3), 0.3(0.7)}	{0.5(0.3), 0.7(0.7)}	{0.1(0.5), 0.3(0.5)}	{0.5(1)}	{0.3(0.8), 0.4(0.2)}
C5	{0.1(1)}	{0.6(0.5), 0.7(0.5)}	{0.1(1)}	{0.8(0.5), 0.9(0.5)}	{0.8(0.3), 0.9(0.7)}
C6	{0.1(0.6), 0.3(0.4)}	{0.5(0.6), 0.7(0.4)}	{0.1(0.2), 0.2(0.8)}	{0.3(0.8), 0.4(0.2)}	{0.2(0.5), 0.3(0.5)}
C7	{0.3(1)}	{0.5(0.5), 0.6(0.5)}	{0.1(0.7), 0.7(0.3)}	{0.5(0.3), 0.7(0.7)}	{0.4(0.2), 0.5(0.8)}
C8	{0.4(0.3), 0.5(0.7)}	{0.5(0.3), 0.9(0.7)}	{0.1(0.5), 0.3(0.5)}	{0.5(0.2), 0.7(0.8)}	{0.7(1)}
C9	{0.3(1)}	{0.4(0.6), 0.5(0.4)}	{0.1(0.8), 0.2(0.2)}	{0.3(0.8), 0.4(0.2)}	{0.1(0.3), 0.3(0.7)}
C10	{0.3(0.3), 0.5(0.7)}	{0.3(1)}	{0.1(1)}	{0.1(0.5), 0.3(0.5)}	{0.3(1)}
C11	{0.6(0.3), 0.7(0.7)}	{0.6(0.5), 0.7(0.5)}	{0.3(0.8), 0.4(0.2)}	{0.7(0.8), 0.8(0.2)}	{0.8(0.5), 0.9(0.5)}
C12	{0.3(0.8), 0.4(0.2)}	{0.4(0.2), 0.5(0.8)}	{0.2(0.5), 0.3(0.5)}	{0.5(1)}	{0.1(0.8), 0.2(0.2)}
C13	{0.3(0.3), 0.4(0.7)}	{0.1(0.3), 0.3(0.7)}	{0.3(1)}	{0.1(0.6), 0.2(0.4)}	{0.1(0.5), 0.2(0.5)}
	H_6	H_7	H_8	H_9	H_{10}
C1	{0.1(0.3), 0.2(0.7)}	{0.6(0.1), 0.7(0.9)}	{0.2(0.5), 0.4(0.5)}	{0.7(0.5), 0.8(0.5)}	{0.9(1)}
C2	{0.1(0.2), 0.2(0.8)}	{0.5(0.3), 0.6(0.7)}	{0.3(1)}	{0.7(0.5), 0.9(0.5)}	{0.5(0.8), 0.6(0.2)}
C3	{0.3(0.8), 0.5(0.2)}	{0.7(0.5), 0.8(0.5)}	{0.8(0.5), 0.9(0.5)}	{0.8(0.2), 0.9(0.8)}	{0.8(0.3), 0.9(0.7)}
C4	{0.3(1)}	{0.5(0.3), 0.7(0.7)}	{0.5(0.4), 0.6(0.6)}	{0.3(1)}	{0.6(0.2), 0.7(0.8)}
C5	{0.1(1)}	{0.2(0.5), 0.3(0.5)}	{0.1(1)}	{0.8(0.5), 0.9(0.5)}	{0.5(0.3), 0.7(0.7)}
C6	{0.1(0.6), 0.2(0.4)}	{0.7(1)}	{0.7(0.5), 0.8(0.5)}	{0.8(0.8), 0.9(0.2)}	{0.8(0.5), 0.9(0.5)}
C7	{0.1(1)}	{0.6(0.5), 0.8(0.5)}	{0.7(0.7), 0.8(0.3)}	{0.8(0.3), 0.9(0.7)}	{0.7(0.2), 0.9(0.8)}

(continued)

Table 6.3 (continued)

	H_1	H_2	H_3	H_4	H_5
C8	{0.1(0.3), 0.2(0.7)}	{0.6(0.3), 0.8(0.7)}	{0.5(0.5), 0.6(0.5)}	{0.5(0.8), 0.6(0.2)}	{0.3(1)}
C9	{0.3(1)}	{0.4(0.4), 0.5(0.6)}	{0.2(0.2), 0.3(0.8)}	{0.3(0.8), 0.4(0.2)}	{0.4(0.3), 0.5(0.7)}
C10	{0.1(0.8), 0.2(0.2)}	{0.9(1)}	{0.3(1)}	{0.6(0.5), 0.8(0.5)}	{0.3(1)}
C11	{0.5(0.4), 0.6(0.6)}	{0.8(0.5), 0.9(0.5)}	{0.1(0.8), 0.2(0.2)}	{0.8(0.2), 0.9(0.8)}	{0.4(0.5), 0.6(0.5)}
C12	{0.3(0.8), 0.4(0.2)}	{0.8(0.2), 0.9(0.8)}	{0.1(0.5), 0.2(0.5)}	{0.5(1)}	{0.3(0.8), 0.4(0.2)}
C13	{0.4(0.3), 0.5(0.7)}	{0.4(0.5), 0.6(0.5)}	{0.1(1)}	{0.3(0.6), 0.4(0.4)}	{0.2(0.5), 0.4(0.5)}

$$
C = \begin{bmatrix}
1 & -0.0875 & 0.5438 & 0.1401 & 0.2558 & 0.5789 & 0.6432 & -0.1409 & 0.0685 & 0.3269 \\
-0.0875 & 1 & -0.204 & 0.6055 & 0.4269 & -0.2016 & -0.0838 & 0.2778 & 0.3814 & 0.2611 \\
0.5438 & -0.204 & 1 & -0.0296 & 0.0017 & 0.7805 & 0.3321 & -0.2549 & -0.2534 & -0.2488 \\
0.1401 & 0.6055 & -0.0296 & 1 & 0.5678 & -0.0953 & -0.0756 & 0.1512 & 0.4668 & 0.2769 \\
0.2558 & 0.4269 & 0.0017 & 0.5678 & 1 & -0.1039 & -0.1209 & -0.0909 & 0.4944 & 0.3321 \\
0.5789 & -0.2016 & 0.7805 & -0.0953 & -0.1039 & 1 & 0.1673 & -0.3334 & -0.3018 & -0.2941 \\
0.6432 & -0.0838 & 0.3321 & -0.0756 & -0.1209 & 0.1673 & 1 & 0.2496 & 0.1612 & -0.112 \\
-0.1409 & 0.2778 & -0.2549 & 0.1512 & -0.0909 & -0.3334 & 0.2496 & 1 & 0.2482 & 0.6066 \\
0.0685 & 0.3814 & -0.2534 & 0.4668 & 0.4944 & -0.3018 & 0.1612 & 0.2482 & 1 & 0.5264 \\
0.3269 & 0.2611 & -0.2488 & 0.2769 & 0.3321 & -0.2941 & -0.113 & 0.6066 & 0.5264 & 1
\end{bmatrix}
$$

Step 2. Construct the equivalent correlation matrix as follows:

$$
C^2 = \begin{bmatrix}
1 & 0.2778 & 0.5789 & 0.2769 & 0.3269 & 0.5789 & 0.6432 & 0.3269 & 0.3269 & 0.3269 \\
0.2778 & 1 & 0.0017 & 0.6055 & 0.5678 & -0.0838 & 0.2496 & 0.2778 & 0.4668 & 0.3814 \\
0.5789 & 0.0017 & 1 & 0.5678 & 0.2558 & 0.7805 & 0.5438 & 0.2496 & 0.1612 & 0.3269 \\
0.2769 & 0.6055 & 0.5678 & 1 & 0.5678 & 0.1401 & 0.1612 & 0.2778 & 0.4944 & 0.4688 \\
0.3269 & 0.5678 & 0.2558 & 0.5678 & 1 & 0.2558 & 0.2558 & 0.3321 & 0.4944 & 0.4944 \\
0.5789 & -0.0838 & 0.7805 & 0.1401 & 0.2558 & 1 & 0.5789 & 0.1673 & 0.1612 & 0.3269 \\
0.6432 & 0.2496 & 0.5438 & 0.1612 & 0.2558 & 0.5789 & 1 & 0.2496 & 0.2482 & 0.3269 \\
0.3269 & 0.2778 & 0.2496 & 0.2778 & 0.3321 & 0.1673 & 0.2496 & 1 & 0.5264 & 0.6066 \\
0.3269 & 0.4668 & 0.1612 & 0.4944 & 0.4944 & 0.1612 & 0.2482 & 0.5264 & 1 & 0.5264 \\
0.3269 & 0.3814 & 0.3269 & 0.4668 & 0.4944 & 0.3269 & 0.3269 & 0.6066 & 0.5264 & 1
\end{bmatrix}
$$

$$
C^4 = \begin{bmatrix}
1 & 0.3269 & 0.5789 & 0.5678 & 0.3269 & 0.5789 & 0.6432 & 0.3269 & 0.3269 & 0.3269 \\
0.3269 & 1 & 0.5678 & 0.6055 & 0.5678 & 0.3269 & 0.3269 & 0.4668 & 0.4944 & 0.4944 \\
0.5789 & 0.5678 & 1 & 0.5678 & 0.5678 & 0.7805 & 0.5789 & 0.3269 & 0.4944 & 0.4668 \\
0.5678 & 0.6055 & 0.5678 & 1 & 0.5678 & 0.5678 & 0.5438 & 0.4944 & 0.4944 & 0.4944 \\
0.3269 & 0.5678 & 0.5678 & 0.5678 & 1 & 0.3269 & 0.3269 & 0.4944 & 0.4944 & 0.4944 \\
0.5789 & 0.3269 & 0.7805 & 0.5678 & 0.3269 & 1 & 0.5789 & 0.3321 & 0.3269 & 0.3269 \\
0.6432 & 0.3269 & 0.5789 & 0.5438 & 0.3269 & 0.5789 & 1 & 0.3269 & 0.3269 & 0.3269 \\
0.3269 & 0.4668 & 0.3269 & 0.4944 & 0.4944 & 0.3321 & 0.3269 & 1 & 0.5264 & 0.6066 \\
0.3269 & 0.4944 & 0.4944 & 0.4944 & 0.4944 & 0.3269 & 0.3269 & 0.5264 & 1 & 0.5264 \\
0.3269 & 0.4944 & 0.4668 & 0.4944 & 0.4944 & 0.3269 & 0.3269 & 0.6066 & 0.5264 & 1
\end{bmatrix}
$$

$$
C^8 = \begin{bmatrix}
1 & 0.5678 & 0.5789 & 0.5678 & 0.5678 & 0.5789 & 0.6432 & 0.4944 & 0.4944 & 0.4944 \\
0.5678 & 1 & 0.5789 & 0.6055 & 0.5678 & 0.5678 & 0.5678 & 0.4944 & 0.4944 & 0.4944 \\
0.5789 & 0.5789 & 1 & 0.5678 & 0.5678 & 0.7805 & 0.5789 & 0.4944 & 0.4944 & 0.4944 \\
0.5678 & 0.6055 & 0.5678 & 1 & 0.5678 & 0.5678 & 0.5678 & 0.4944 & 0.4944 & 0.4944 \\
0.5678 & 0.5678 & 0.5678 & 0.5678 & 1 & 0.5678 & 0.5678 & 0.4944 & 0.4944 & 0.4944 \\
0.5789 & 0.5678 & 0.7805 & 0.5678 & 0.5678 & 1 & 0.5789 & 0.4944 & 0.4944 & 0.4944 \\
0.6432 & 0.5678 & 0.5789 & 0.5678 & 0.5678 & 0.5789 & 1 & 0.4944 & 0.4944 & 0.4944 \\
0.4944 & 0.4944 & 0.4944 & 0.4944 & 0.4944 & 0.4944 & 0.4944 & 1 & 0.5264 & 0.6066 \\
0.4944 & 0.4944 & 0.4944 & 0.4944 & 0.4944 & 0.4944 & 0.4944 & 0.5264 & 1 & 0.5264 \\
0.4944 & 0.4944 & 0.4944 & 0.4944 & 0.4944 & 0.4944 & 0.4944 & 0.6066 & 0.5264 & 1
\end{bmatrix}
$$

$$C^{16}=\begin{bmatrix}
1 & 0.5789 & 0.5789 & 0.5678 & 0.5678 & 0.5789 & 0.6432 & 0.4944 & 0.4944 & 0.4944\\
0.5789 & 1 & 0.5789 & 0.6055 & 0.5678 & 0.5789 & 0.5789 & 0.4944 & 0.4944 & 0.4944\\
0.5789 & 0.5789 & 1 & 0.5789 & 0.5678 & 0.7805 & 0.5789 & 0.4944 & 0.4944 & 0.4944\\
0.5678 & 0.6055 & 0.5789 & 1 & 0.5678 & 0.5678 & 0.5678 & 0.4944 & 0.4944 & 0.4944\\
0.5678 & 0.5678 & 0.5678 & 0.5678 & 1 & 0.5678 & 0.5678 & 0.4944 & 0.4944 & 0.4944\\
0.5789 & 0.5789 & 0.7805 & 0.5678 & 0.5678 & 1 & 0.5789 & 0.4944 & 0.4944 & 0.4944\\
0.6432 & 0.5789 & 0.5789 & 0.5678 & 0.5678 & 0.5789 & 1 & 0.4944 & 0.4944 & 0.4944\\
0.4944 & 0.4944 & 0.4944 & 0.4944 & 0.4944 & 0.4944 & 0.4944 & 1 & 0.5264 & 0.6066\\
0.4944 & 0.4944 & 0.4944 & 0.4944 & 0.4944 & 0.4944 & 0.4944 & 0.5264 & 1 & 0.5264\\
0.4944 & 0.4944 & 0.4944 & 0.4944 & 0.4944 & 0.4944 & 0.4944 & 0.6066 & 0.5264 & 1
\end{bmatrix}$$

$$C^{32}=\begin{bmatrix}
1 & 0.5789 & 0.5789 & 0.5789 & 0.5678 & 0.5789 & 0.6432 & 0.4944 & 0.4944 & 0.4944\\
0.5789 & 1 & 0.5789 & 0.6055 & 0.5678 & 0.5789 & 0.5789 & 0.4944 & 0.4944 & 0.4944\\
0.5789 & 0.5789 & 1 & 0.5789 & 0.5678 & 0.7805 & 0.5789 & 0.4944 & 0.4944 & 0.4944\\
0.5789 & 0.6055 & 0.5789 & 1 & 0.5678 & 0.5789 & 0.5789 & 0.4944 & 0.4944 & 0.4944\\
0.5678 & 0.5678 & 0.5678 & 0.5678 & 1 & 0.5678 & 0.5678 & 0.4944 & 0.4944 & 0.4944\\
0.5789 & 0.5789 & 0.7805 & 0.5789 & 0.5678 & 1 & 0.5789 & 0.4944 & 0.4944 & 0.4944\\
0.6432 & 0.5789 & 0.5789 & 0.5789 & 0.5678 & 0.5789 & 1 & 0.4944 & 0.4944 & 0.4944\\
0.4944 & 0.4944 & 0.4944 & 0.4944 & 0.4944 & 0.4944 & 0.4944 & 1 & 0.5264 & 0.6066\\
0.4944 & 0.4944 & 0.4944 & 0.4944 & 0.4944 & 0.4944 & 0.4944 & 0.5264 & 1 & 0.5264\\
0.4944 & 0.4944 & 0.4944 & 0.4944 & 0.4944 & 0.4944 & 0.4944 & 0.6066 & 0.5264 & 1
\end{bmatrix}$$

$$C^{64}=\begin{bmatrix}
1 & 0.5789 & 0.5789 & 0.5789 & 0.5678 & 0.5789 & 0.6432 & 0.4944 & 0.4944 & 0.4944\\
0.5789 & 1 & 0.5789 & 0.6055 & 0.5678 & 0.5789 & 0.5789 & 0.4944 & 0.4944 & 0.4944\\
0.5789 & 0.5789 & 1 & 0.5789 & 0.5678 & 0.7805 & 0.5789 & 0.4944 & 0.4944 & 0.4944\\
0.5789 & 0.6055 & 0.5789 & 1 & 0.5678 & 0.5789 & 0.5789 & 0.4944 & 0.4944 & 0.4944\\
0.5678 & 0.5678 & 0.5678 & 0.5678 & 1 & 0.5678 & 0.5678 & 0.4944 & 0.4944 & 0.4944\\
0.5789 & 0.5789 & 0.7805 & 0.5789 & 0.5678 & 1 & 0.5789 & 0.4944 & 0.4944 & 0.4944\\
0.6432 & 0.5789 & 0.5789 & 0.5789 & 0.5678 & 0.5789 & 1 & 0.4944 & 0.4944 & 0.4944\\
0.4944 & 0.4944 & 0.4944 & 0.4944 & 0.4944 & 0.4944 & 0.4944 & 1 & 0.5264 & 0.6066\\
0.4944 & 0.4944 & 0.4944 & 0.4944 & 0.4944 & 0.4944 & 0.4944 & 0.5264 & 1 & 0.5264\\
0.4944 & 0.4944 & 0.4944 & 0.4944 & 0.4944 & 0.4944 & 0.4944 & 0.6066 & 0.5264 & 1
\end{bmatrix}\cdots$$

We can see that $C^{64}=C^{32}$, therefore C^{32} is an equivalent correlation matrix.

Step 3. We can construct a λ-cutting matrix $C_\lambda=\left(\rho_{ij}^{\lambda}\right)_{m\times m}$ with a confidence level λ, and get all the possible classifications of $H_j (j=1,2,\ldots,10)$ as follows:

(1) If $0.7805<\lambda\le 1$, then we can classify $H_j (j=1,2,\ldots,10)$ into ten types:

$$\{H_1\},\{H_2\},\{H_3\},\{H_4\},\{H_5\},\{H_6\},\{H_7\},\{H_8\},\{H_9\},\{H_{10}\}.$$

(2) If $0.6432<\lambda\le 0.7805$, then we can classify $H_j (j=1,2,\ldots,10)$ into nine types:

$$\{H_1\},\{H_2\},\{H_3,H_6\},\{H_4\},\{H_5\},\{H_7\},\{H_8\},\{H_9\},\{H_{10}\}.$$

(3) If $0.6066<\lambda\le 0.6432$, then we can classify $H_j (j=1,2,\ldots,10)$ into eight types:

$$\{H_1, H_7\}, \{H_2\}, \{H_3, H_6\}, \{H_4\}, \{H_5\}, \{H_8\}, \{H_9\}, \{H_{10}\}.$$

(4) If $0.6055 < \lambda \leq 0.6066$, then we can classify $H_j (j = 1, 2, \ldots, 10)$ into seven types:

$$\{H_1, H_7\}, \{H_2\}, \{H_3, H_6\}, \{H_4\}, \{H_5\}, \{H_8, H_{10}\}, \{H_9\}.$$

(5) If $0.5789 < \lambda \leq 0.6055$, then we can classify $H_j (j = 1, 2, \ldots, 10)$ into six types:

$$\{H_1, H_7\}, \{H_2, H_4\}, \{H_3, H_6\}, \{H_5\}, \{H_8, H_{10}\}, \{H_9\}.$$

(6) If $0.5678 < \lambda \leq 0.5789$, then we can classify $H_j (j = 1, 2, \ldots, 10)$ into four types:

$$\{H_1, H_2, H_3, H_4, H_6, H_7\}, \{H_5\}, \{H_8, H_{10}\}, \{H_9\}.$$

(7) If $0.5264 < \lambda \leq 0.5678$, then we can classify $H_j (j = 1, 2, \ldots, 10)$ into three types:

$$\{H_1, H_2, H_3, H_4, H_5, H_6, H_7\}, \{H_8, H_{10}\}, \{H_9\}.$$

(8) If $0.4944 < \lambda \leq 0.5264$, then we can classify $H_j (j = 1, 2, \ldots, 10)$ into two types:

$$\{H_1, H_2, H_3, H_4, H_5, H_6, H_7\}, \{H_8, H_9, H_{10}\}.$$

(9) If $0 < \lambda \leq 0.4944$, then we can classify $H_j (j = 1, 2, \ldots, 10)$ into same types:

$$\{H_1, H_2, H_3, H_4, H_5, H_6, H_7, H_8, H_9, H_{10}\}.$$

Based on the classification results, the DMs can formulate different types of policies to deal with the dispute and conflict of different types of countries. When handling the multi-criteria decision-making problems about the human environment risk, it is usually difficult to classify the objects when the experts cannot reach an agreement about an indicator or provide complete evaluations. From the process above, it is obvious that our methods can deal with such kind of uncertain information—the probabilistic fuzzy hesitant information. What is more, our correlation matrix consists of the values ranging from negative values to positive values, which can better reflect the similarities and differences between the clusters.

6.4.2 Comparison with Clustering Algorithm for HFSs

In this subsection, we shall compare our clustering method with the one of the HFSs. Suppose that the DMs are invited to make assessments on the risk level of the above indicators and the preferences of the DMs are expressed by the HFSs. At this time, the evaluations about the human environment risk of the ten objective countries do not contain probabilistic information. The evaluations are given as follows (Table 6.4).

Table 6.4 The evaluations of the human environment risk of the ten objective countries with the HFSs (Song et al. 2019a)

	H_1	H_2	H_3	H_4	H_5
C1	{0.1,0.5}	{0.1,0.7}	{0.1,0.3}	{0.1,0.5}	{0.9}
C2	{0.1,0.3}	{0.8,0.9}	{0.1}	{0.3, 0.5}	{0.3,0.4}
C3	{0.3,0.5}	{0.5,0.6, 0.7}	{0.1,0.2}	{0.7,0.9}	{0.4,0.5}
C4	{0.1,0.3}	{0.5,0.7}	{0.1,0.3}	{0.5}	{0.3,0.4}
C5	{0.1}	{0.6,0.7}	{0.1}	{0.8,0.9}	{0.8,0.9}
C6	{0.1,0.3}	{0.5,0.7}	{0.1,0.2}	{0.3,0.4}	{0.2,0.3}
C7	{0.3}	{0.5,0.6}	{0.1,0.3}	{0.5,0.7}	{0.4,0.5}
C8	{0.4,0.5}	{0.5,0.9}	{0.1,0.3}	{0.5,0.7}	{0.7}
C9	{0.3}	{0.4,0.5}	{0.1,0.2, 0.3}	{0.3,0.4}	{0.1,0.3}
C10	{0.3,0.5}	{0.3}	{0.1}	{0.1,0.3}	{0.3}
C11	{0.6,0.7}	{0.6,0.7}	{0.3,0.4}	{0.7,0.8}	{0.8,0.9}
C12	{0.3,0.4}	{0.4,0.5}	{0.2,0.3}	{0.5}	{0.1,0.2}
C13	{0.3,0.4}	{0.1,0.3}	{0.3}	{0.1,0.2}	{0.1,0.2}
	H_6	H_7	H_8	H_9	H_{10}
C1	{0.1,0.2}	{0.6,0.7}	{0.2,0.4}	{0.7,0.8}	{0.9}
C2	{0.1,0.2}	{0.5,0.6}	{0.3}	{0.7,0.9}	{0.5,0.6}
C3	{0.3,0.5}	{0.7,0.8}	{0.8,0.9}	{0.8,0.9}	{0.8,0.9}
C4	{0.3}	{0.5,0.7}	{0.5,0.6}	{0.3}	{0.6,0.7}
C5	{0.1}	{0.2,0.3}	{0.1}	{0.8,0.9}	{0.5,0.7}
C6	{0.1,0.2}	{0.7}	{0.7,0.8}	{0.8,0.9}	{0.8,0.9}
C7	{0.1}	{0.6,0.8}	{0.7,0.8}	{0.8,0.9}	{0.7,0.9}
C8	{0.1,0.2}	{0.6,0.8}	{0.5,0.6}	{0.5,0.6}	{0.3}
C9	{0.3}	{0.4,0.5}	{0.2,0.3}	{0.3,0.4}	{0.4,0.5}
C10	{0.1,0.2}	{0.9}	{0.3}	{0.6,0.8}	{0.3}
C11	{0.5,0.6}	{0.8,0.9}	{0.1,0.2}	{0.8,0.9}	{0.4,0.6}
C12	{0.3,0.4}	{0.8,0.9}	{0.1,0.2}	{0.5}	{0.3,0.4}
C13	{0.4,0.5}	{0.4,0.6}	{0.1}	{0.3,0.4}	{0.2,0.4}

In the following, we will use the clustering method for the HFSs to cluster the ten countries:

Step 1. Since the HFEs are not of the same length, then we should first extend the shorter HFE by adding the minimum value until they have the same length according to the pessimistic principle. So we can get the revised evaluations expressed by the HFSs for the human environment risk which are given as follows (Table 6.5).

Step 2. We assume that the corresponding thirteen indicators are equally important. Then we can calculate the correlation coefficients between the HFSs $H_j (j = 1, 2, \ldots, 10)$ and then obtain the correlation matrix below:

Table 6.5 The revised evaluations of human environment risk of the ten objective countries with the HFSs (Song et al. 2019a)

	H_1	H_2	H_3	H_4	H_5
C1	{0.1,0.5}	{0.1,0.7}	{0.1,0.3}	{0.1,0.5}	{0.9,0.9}
C2	{0.1,0.3}	{0.8,0.9}	{0.1, 0.1}	{0.3, 0.5}	{0.3,0.4}
C3	{0.3,0.3, 0.5}	{0.5,0.6, 0.7}	{0.1,0.1, 0.2}	{0.7,0.7, 0.9}	{0.4,0.4, 0.5}
C4	{0.1,0.3}	{0.5,0.7}	{0.1,0.3}	{0.5,0.5}	{0.3,0.4}
C5	{0.1,0.1}	{0.6,0.7}	{0.1,0.1}	{0.8,0.9}	{0.8,0.9}
C6	{0.1,0.3}	{0.5,0.7}	{0.1,0.2}	{0.3,0.4}	{0.2,0.3}
C7	{0.3,0.3}	{0.5,0.6}	{0.1,0.3}	{0.5,0.7}	{0.4,0.5}
C8	{0.4,0.5}	{0.5,0.9}	{0.1,0.3}	{0.5,0.7}	{0.7,0.7}
C9	{0.3,0.3, 0.3}	{0.4,0.4, 0.5}	{0.1,0.2, 0.3}	{0.3,0.3, 0.4}	{0.1,0.1, 0.3}
C10	{0.3,0.5}	{0.3,0.3}	{0.1,0.1}	{0.1,0.3}	{0.3,0.3}
C11	{0.6,0.7}	{0.6,0.7}	{0.3,0.4}	{0.7,0.8}	{0.8,0.9}
C12	{0.3,0.4}	{0.4,0.5}	{0.2,0.3}	{0.5,0.5}	{0.1,0.2}
C13	{0.3,0.4}	{0.1,0.3}	{0.3,0.3}	{0.1,0.2}	{0.1,0.2}
	H_6	H_7	H_8	H_9	H_{10}
C1	{0.1,0.2}	{0.6,0.7}	{0.2,0.4}	{0.7,0.8}	{0.9,0.9}
C2	{0.1,0.2}	{0.5,0.6}	{0.3,0.3}	{0.7,0.9}	{0.5,0.6}
C3	{0.3,0.3, 0.5}	{0.7,0.7, 0.8}	{0.8,0.8, 0.9}	{0.8,0.8, 0.9}	{0.8,0.8, 0.9}
C4	{0.3,0.3}	{0.5,0.7}	{0.5,0.6}	{0.3,0.3}	{0.6,0.7}
C5	{0.1,0.1}	{0.2,0.3}	{0.1,0.1}	{0.8,0.9}	{0.5,0.7}
C6	{0.1,0.2}	{0.7,0.7}	{0.7,0.8}	{0.8,0.9}	{0.8,0.9}
C7	{0.1,0.1}	{0.6,0.8}	{0.7,0.8}	{0.8,0.9}	{0.7,0.9}
C8	{0.1,0.2}	{0.6,0.8}	{0.5,0.6}	{0.5,0.6}	{0.3,0.3}
C9	{0.3,0.3, 0.3}	{0.4,0.4, 0.5}	{0.2,0.2, 0.3}	{0.3,0.3, 0.4}	{0.4,0.4, 0.5}
C10	{0.1,0.2}	{0.9,0.9}	{0.3,0.3}	{0.6,0.8}	{0.3,0.3}
C11	{0.5,0.6}	{0.8,0.9}	{0.1,0.2}	{0.8,0.9}	{0.4,0.6}
C12	{0.3,0.4}	{0.8,0.9}	{0.1,0.2}	{0.5,0.5}	{0.3,0.4}
C13	{0.4,0.5}	{0.4,0.6}	{0.1,0.1}	{0.3,0.4}	{0.2,0.4}

$$C = \begin{bmatrix} 1 & 0.8623 & 0.9280 & 0.8560 & 0.8234 & 0.9141 & 0.9392 & 0.7426 & 0.8676 & 0.6399 \\ 0.8623 & 1 & 0.8505 & 0.9457 & 0.8707 & 0.7949 & 0.9034 & 0.8454 & 0.9356 & 0.9062 \\ 0.9280 & 0.8505 & 1 & 0.8344 & 0.7942 & 0.9185 & 0.8993 & 0.7098 & 0.8201 & 0.8109 \\ 0.8560 & 0.9457 & 0.8344 & 1 & 0.9014 & 0.8123 & 0.8670 & 0.8075 & 0.9228 & 0.8841 \\ 0.8234 & 0.8707 & 0.7942 & 0.9014 & 1 & 0.7165 & 0.8260 & 0.7014 & 0.9058 & 0.8668 \\ 0.9141 & 0.7949 & 0.9185 & 0.8123 & 0.7165 & 1 & 0.8671 & 0.6521 & 0.7803 & 0.7619 \\ 0.9392 & 0.9034 & 0.8993 & 0.8670 & 0.8260 & 0.8671 & 1 & 0.8460 & 0.9317 & 0.8941 \\ 0.7426 & 0.8454 & 0.7098 & 0.8075 & 0.7014 & 0.6521 & 0.8460 & 1 & 0.8415 & 0.8953 \\ 0.8676 & 0.9356 & 0.8201 & 0.9228 & 0.9058 & 0.7803 & 0.9317 & 0.8415 & 1 & 0.9451 \\ 0.6399 & 0.9062 & 0.8109 & 0.8841 & 0.8668 & 0.7619 & 0.8941 & 0.8953 & 0.9451 & 1 \end{bmatrix}$$

Step 3. Construct the equivalent correlation matrix as follows:

$$C^2 = \begin{bmatrix} 1 & 0.9032 & 0.9280 & 0.8676 & 0.8676 & 0.9185 & 0.9392 & 0.8460 & 0.9317 & 0.8941 \\ 0.9032 & 1 & 0.8993 & 0.9457 & 0.9058 & 0.8671 & 0.9317 & 0.8953 & 0.9356 & 0.9356 \\ 0.9280 & 0.8993 & 1 & 0.8670 & 0.8505 & 0.9185 & 0.9280 & 0.8460 & 0.8993 & 0.8941 \\ 0.8676 & 0.9457 & 0.8670 & 1 & 0.9058 & 0.8671 & 0.9228 & 0.8841 & 0.9356 & 0.9228 \\ 0.8676 & 0.9058 & 0.8505 & 0.9058 & 1 & 0.8260 & 0.9058 & 0.8668 & 0.9058 & 0.9058 \\ 0.9185 & 0.8671 & 0.9185 & 0.8671 & 0.8260 & 1 & 0.9141 & 0.8460 & 0.9317 & 0.8671 \\ 0.9392 & 0.9317 & 0.9280 & 0.9228 & 0.9058 & 0.9141 & 1 & 0.8941 & 0.9317 & 0.9317 \\ 0.8460 & 0.8953 & 0.8460 & 0.8841 & 0.8668 & 0.8460 & 0.8941 & 1 & 0.8953 & 0.8953 \\ 0.9317 & 0.9356 & 0.8993 & 0.9356 & 0.9058 & 0.9317 & 0.9317 & 0.8953 & 1 & 0.9451 \\ 0.8941 & 0.9356 & 0.8941 & 0.9228 & 0.9058 & 0.8671 & 0.9317 & 0.8953 & 0.9451 & 1 \end{bmatrix}$$

$$C^4 = \begin{bmatrix} 1 & 0.9317 & 0.9280 & 0.9317 & 0.9058 & 0.9317 & 0.9392 & 0.8953 & 0.9317 & 0.9317 \\ 0.9317 & 1 & 09280 & 0.9457 & 0.9058 & 0.9317 & 0.9317 & 0.8953 & 0.9356 & 0.9356 \\ 0.9280 & 0.9280 & 1 & 0.9228 & 0.9058 & 0.9185 & 0.9317 & 0.8953 & 0.9280 & 0.9280 \\ 0.9317 & 0.9457 & 0.9228 & 1 & 0.9058 & 0.9317 & 0.9317 & 0.8953 & 0.9356 & 0.9356 \\ 0.9058 & 0.9058 & 0.9058 & 0.9058 & 1 & 0.9058 & 0.9058 & 0.8953 & 0.9058 & 0.9058 \\ 0.9317 & 0.9317 & 0.9185 & 0.9317 & 0.9058 & 1 & 0.9317 & 0.8953 & 0.9317 & 0.9317 \\ 0.9392 & 0.9317 & 0.9317 & 0.9317 & 0.9058 & 0.9317 & 1 & 0.8953 & 0.9317 & 0.9317 \\ 0.8953 & 0.8953 & 0.8953 & 0.8953 & 0.8953 & 0.8953 & 0.8953 & 1 & 0.8953 & 0.9356 \\ 0.9317 & 0.9356 & 0.9280 & 0.9356 & 0.9058 & 0.9317 & 0.9317 & 0.8953 & 1 & 0.9451 \\ 0.9317 & 0.9356 & 0.9280 & 0.9356 & 0.9058 & 0.9317 & 0.9317 & 0.9356 & 0.9451 & 1 \end{bmatrix}$$

$$C^8 = \begin{bmatrix} 1 & 0.9317 & 0.9317 & 0.9317 & 0.9058 & 0.9317 & 0.9392 & 0.9317 & 0.9317 & 0.9317 \\ 0.9317 & 1 & 0.9317 & 0.9457 & 0.9058 & 0.9317 & 0.9317 & 0.9317 & 0.9356 & 0.9356 \\ 0.9317 & 0.9317 & 1 & 0.9317 & 0.9058 & 0.9317 & 0.9317 & 0.9280 & 0.9317 & 0.9317 \\ 0.9317 & 0.9457 & 0.9317 & 1 & 0.9058 & 0.9317 & 0.9317 & 0.9356 & 0.9356 & 0.9356 \\ 0.9058 & 0.9058 & 0.9058 & 0.9058 & 1 & 0.9058 & 0.9058 & 0.9058 & 0.9058 & 0.9058 \\ 0.9317 & 0.9317 & 0.9317 & 0.9317 & 0.9058 & 1 & 0.9317 & 0.9317 & 0.9317 & 0.9317 \\ 0.9392 & 0.9317 & 0.9317 & 0.9317 & 0.9058 & 0.9317 & 1 & 0.9317 & 0.9317 & 0.9317 \\ 0.9317 & 0.9317 & 0.9280 & 0.9356 & 0.9058 & 0.9317 & 0.9317 & 1 & 0.9356 & 0.9356 \\ 0.9317 & 0.9356 & 0.9317 & 0.9356 & 0.9058 & 0.9317 & 0.9317 & 0.9356 & 1 & 0.9451 \\ 0.9317 & 0.9356 & 0.9317 & 0.9356 & 0.9058 & 0.9317 & 0.9317 & 0.9356 & 0.9451 & 1 \end{bmatrix}$$

$$C^{16} = \begin{bmatrix} 1 & 0.9317 & 0.9317 & 0.9317 & 0.9058 & 0.9317 & 0.9392 & 0.9317 & 0.9317 & 0.9317 \\ 0.9317 & 1 & 0.9317 & 0.9457 & 0.9058 & 0.9317 & 0.9317 & 0.9356 & 0.9356 & 0.9356 \\ 0.9317 & 0.9317 & 1 & 0.9317 & 0.9058 & 0.9317 & 0.9317 & 0.9317 & 0.9317 & 0.9317 \\ 0.9317 & 0.9457 & 0.9317 & 1 & 0.9058 & 0.9317 & 0.9317 & 0.9356 & 0.9356 & 0.9356 \\ 0.9058 & 0.9058 & 0.9058 & 0.9058 & 1 & 0.9058 & 0.9058 & 0.9058 & 0.9058 & 0.9058 \\ 0.9317 & 0.9317 & 0.9317 & 0.9317 & 0.9058 & 1 & 0.9317 & 0.9317 & 0.9317 & 0.9317 \\ 0.9392 & 0.9317 & 0.9317 & 0.9317 & 0.9058 & 0.9317 & 1 & 0.9317 & 0.9317 & 0.9317 \\ 0.9317 & 0.9356 & 0.9317 & 0.9356 & 0.9058 & 0.9317 & 0.9317 & 1 & 0.9356 & 0.9356 \\ 0.9317 & 0.9356 & 0.9317 & 0.9356 & 0.9058 & 0.9317 & 0.9317 & 0.9356 & 1 & 0.9451 \\ 0.9317 & 0.9356 & 0.9317 & 0.9356 & 0.9058 & 0.9317 & 0.9317 & 0.9356 & 0.9451 & 1 \end{bmatrix}$$

$$C^{32} = \begin{bmatrix} 1 & 0.9317 & 0.9317 & 0.9317 & 0.9058 & 0.9317 & 0.9392 & 0.9317 & 0.9317 & 0.9317 \\ 0.9317 & 1 & 0.9317 & 0.9457 & 0.9058 & 0.9317 & 0.9317 & 0.9356 & 0.9356 & 0.9356 \\ 0.9317 & 0.9317 & 1 & 0.9317 & 0.9058 & 0.9317 & 0.9317 & 0.9317 & 0.9317 & 0.9317 \\ 0.9317 & 0.9457 & 0.9317 & 1 & 0.9058 & 0.9317 & 0.9317 & 0.9356 & 0.9356 & 0.9356 \\ 0.9058 & 0.9058 & 0.9058 & 0.9058 & 1 & 0.9058 & 0.9058 & 0.9058 & 0.9058 & 0.9058 \\ 0.9317 & 0.9317 & 0.9317 & 0.9317 & 0.9058 & 1 & 0.9317 & 0.9317 & 0.9317 & 0.9317 \\ 0.9392 & 0.9317 & 0.9317 & 0.9317 & 0.9058 & 0.9317 & 1 & 0.9317 & 0.9317 & 0.9317 \\ 0.9317 & 0.9356 & 0.9317 & 0.9356 & 0.9058 & 0.9317 & 0.9317 & 1 & 0.9356 & 0.9356 \\ 0.9317 & 0.9356 & 0.9317 & 0.9356 & 0.9058 & 0.9317 & 0.9317 & 0.9356 & 1 & 0.9451 \\ 0.9317 & 0.9356 & 0.9317 & 0.9356 & 0.9058 & 0.9317 & 0.9317 & 0.9356 & 0.9451 & 1 \end{bmatrix}$$

We can see that $C^{32} = C^{16}$, therefore C^{16} is an equivalent correlation matrix.

Step 4. We can construct a λ-cutting matrix $C_\lambda = \left(\rho_{ij}^{\lambda}\right)_{m \times m}$ with a confidence level λ, and get all the possible classifications of $H_j (j = 1, 2, \ldots, 10)$ as follows:

(1) If $0.9457 < \lambda \leq 1$, then we can classify $H_j (j = 1, 2, \ldots, 10)$ into ten types:

$$\{H_1\}, \{H_2\}, \{H_3\}, \{H_4\}, \{H_5\}, \{H_6\}, \{H_7\}, \{H_8\}, \{H_9\}, \{H_{10}\}$$

(2) If $0.9451 < \lambda \leq 0.9457$, then we can classify $H_j (j = 1, 2, \ldots, 10)$ into nine types:

$$\{H_1\}, \{H_2, H_4\}, \{H_3\}, \{H_5\}, \{H_6\}, \{H_7\}, \{H_8\}, \{H_9\}, \{H_{10}\}$$

(3) If $0.9392 < \lambda \leq 0.9451$, then we can classify $H_j(j = 1, 2, \ldots, 10)$ into eight types:

$$\{H_1\}, \{H_2, H_4\}, \{H_3\}, \{H_5\}, \{H_6\}, \{H_7\}, \{H_8\}, \{H_9, H_{10}\}$$

(4) If $0.9356 < \lambda \leq 0.9392$, then we can classify $H_j(j = 1, 2, \ldots, 10)$ into seven types:

$$\{H_1, H_7\}, \{H_2, H_4\}, \{H_3\}, \{H_5\}, \{H_6\}, \{H_8\}, \{H_9, H_{10}\}$$

(5) If $0.9317 < \lambda \leq 0.9356$, then we can classify $H_j(j = 1, 2, \ldots, 10)$ into five types:

$$\{H_1, H_7\}, \{H_2, H_4, H_8, H_9, H_{10}\}, \{H_3\}, \{H_5\}, \{H_6\}.$$

(6) If $0.9058 < \lambda \leq 0.9317$, then we can classify $H_j(j = 1, 2, \ldots, 10)$ into two types:

$$\{H_1, H_2, H_3, H_4, H_6, H_7, H_8, H_9, H_{10}\}, \{H_5\}$$

(7) If $0 < \lambda \leq 0.9058$, it is obvious that $H_j(j = 1, 2, \ldots, 10)$ are of the same type:

$$\{H_1, H_2, H_3, H_4, H_5, H_6, H_7, H_8, H_9, H_{10}\}.$$

Analyzing the computing processes of the two methods, we can easily find that our method has several advantages over Chen et al. (2013b)'s. Firstly, it is unrealistic to ensure that all the HFEs have the same length, while Chen et al. (2013b)'s method needs to add some values in the shorter HFEs which will surely change the original information and there may be some defects in the final results. However, our method can deal with the quantitative evaluating information and can retain the original information better. What is more, our method can utilize more probabilistic information, and thus the derived results are much more convincing and reliable. Secondly, the values of the equivalent correlation matrix derived by Chen et al.'s method vary from 0.9058 to 1, whose range is a little narrow so that their method may not distinguish the different clusters convincingly. Yet using the new correlation coefficients for PHFSs we introduced in this section, the values of the equivalent correlation matrix lie between 0.4944 and 1, whose range is five times wider than that of Chen et al.'s method. Thus, our method can better reflect the difference between the samples. Thirdly, in Chen et al.'s correlation matrix, only positive values can be used while our correlation matrix consists of different values varies from negative values to positive values, so our method can reflect the negative relationship between each other and thus can get a more reasonable result.

6.5 Interval-Valued Probabilistic HFS

The PHFS can reserve the information and depict the preferences well not only by quantifying the preference degrees with a few possible values, but also containing probabilistic information, which can overcome the shortcomings of HFS in some respects. However, in some actual risk evaluation issues, there are some difficulties for the experts to quantify their expertise by a crisp number exactly, but they can provide their probabilities of the evaluation information by interval values (Bai et al., 2018; Yue, 2011). Therefore, to depict the interval-valued probabilistic information in the HFS and avoid losing information, we introduce the concept of interval-valued probabilistic hesitant fuzzy set (IVPHFS), which permits the probabilistic information to be interval values. After that, we also discuss its characteristics, comparison approach and some basic operation laws, and then give the definitions of aggregation operators under the interval-valued probabilistic hesitant fuzzy environment.

6.5.1 *Concept of IVPHFS*

Definition 6.25 (Song et al., 2019b). If a HFS H is described as $H = \{\langle x, h_A(x)\rangle | x \in X\}$. Then an IVPHFS is defined as:

$$\widetilde{H} = \{\langle x, h(x)|\widetilde{p}_x\rangle | x \in X\} \tag{6.16}$$

where the HFE $h(x)$ represents the hesitant fuzzy membership, associated with the corresponding interval-valued probability $\widetilde{p}_x$. In order to explain and understand more simply, we name the $\widetilde{h} = \langle h(x)|\widetilde{p}_x\rangle$ as the interval-valued probabilistic hesitant fuzzy element (IVPHFE), which is defined as:

$$h(x)|\widetilde{p}_x = \left\{ r_i(\widetilde{p}_i) \middle| i = 1, 2, \ldots, \#\widetilde{h} \right\} \tag{6.17}$$

where $\widetilde{p}_i = \left[\gamma_i^L, \gamma_i^U\right]$ is the interval probability of the membership degree r_i, with $\gamma_i^L = \inf \widetilde{p}^{(i)}$ and $\gamma_i^U = \sup \widetilde{p}^{(i)}$ representing the lower and upper limits of $\widetilde{p}_i$ respectively, and $\sum_{i=1}^{\#\widetilde{h}} \gamma_i^U = 1$. $r_i(\widetilde{p}_i)$ is called a term of the IVPHFE and the symbol $\#\widetilde{h}$ represents the number of the terms in $h(x)|\widetilde{p}_x$. In order to understand easily, we assume that the values of r_i discussed in this section are ascendingly ordered.

Remark 3 If $\gamma_i^L = \gamma_i^U$ $(i = 1, 2, \ldots, \#\widetilde{h})$, then an IVPHFE reduces to the PHFE; similarly, if all the probability values are equal, then the IVPHFE reduces to the HFE.

Example 4 (Song et al., 2019b). Take the risk assessment and management of popular tourist attraction, the Confucius Temple in Nanjing on the Lantern Festival as an example. Two experts were invited to evaluate the possible risk of crow crushing and trampling accident. If one expert was 50–70% confident in the value 0.6, and felt

20%-30% sure for the value 0.8. And another expert felt 10–20% sure for the value 0.7, and was 80% sure for the value 0.9. Then we can utilize the IVPHFS to present their evaluations, which are denoted by two IVPHFEs:

$$\widetilde{h}_1 = \{0.6[0.5, 0.7], 0.8[0.2, 0.3]\} \text{ and } \widetilde{h}_2 = \{0.7[0.1, 0.2], 0.9(0.8)\}.$$

6.5.2 Normalization of IVPHFS

In actual MCGDM problems, some experts can't provide preferences about every property because they lack certain knowledge related to the domain. Hence, there always exists partial ignorance, which means $\sum_{i=1}^{\#\widetilde{h}} \gamma_i^U \leq 1$. So we put forward the concept of generalized IVPHFS.

Definition 6.26 (Song et al., 2019b). Let $\widetilde{H} = \{\langle x, h(x)|\widetilde{p}_x\rangle | x \in X\}$. If $\#\widetilde{h} \geq 2$, $\sum_{i=1}^{\#\widetilde{h}} \gamma_i^U \leq 1$, where $\#\widetilde{h}$ is the total quantity of the terms in $h(x)|\widetilde{p}_x$. Then we call $\widetilde{H}$ a generalized IVPHFS.

However, how to estimate the ignorance is a major challenge in the normalization of the IVPHFS. There are some useful approaches to normalizing interval values already. Jahanshahloo et al. (2006) introduced a new method which contains the ranges of interval values to normalize interval values as:

$$\dot{\tilde{p}}^{(i)} = \begin{cases} \dot{\gamma}_i^L = \dfrac{\gamma_i^L}{\sqrt{\sum_{i=1}^{\#\widetilde{h}} \left(\gamma_i^U\right)^2 + \left(\gamma_i^L\right)^2}} \\ \dot{\gamma}_i^U = \dfrac{\gamma_i^U}{\sqrt{\sum_{i=1}^{\#\widetilde{h}} \left(\gamma_i^U\right)^2 + \left(\gamma_i^L\right)^2}} \end{cases} \tag{6.18}$$

Hence we are inspired by this method to normalize IVPHFS. Then the normalized form of a generalized IVPHFS is denoted as:

$$\widetilde{H} = \{\langle x, h(x)|\widetilde{p}_x\rangle | x \in X\} \tag{6.19}$$

where $\dot{\tilde{p}}^{(i)} = \left[\dot{\gamma}_i^L, \dot{\gamma}_i^U\right]$ is the interval probability of the membership degree, $\dot{\gamma}_i^L = \inf \dot{\tilde{p}}^{(i)}$ and $\dot{\gamma}_i^U = \sup \dot{\tilde{p}}^{(i)}$ represent the lower and upper limits of $\dot{\tilde{p}}^{(i)}$, respectively. What's more, $\dot{\gamma}_i^L = \frac{\gamma_i^L}{\sqrt{\sum_{i=1}^{\#\widetilde{h}} \left[\left(\gamma_i^U\right)^2 + \left(\gamma_i^L\right)^2\right]}}$ and $\dot{\gamma}_i^U = \frac{\gamma_i^U}{\sqrt{\sum_{i=1}^{\#\widetilde{h}} \left[\left(\gamma_i^U\right)^2 + \left(\gamma_i^L\right)^2\right]}}$.

For the convenience of understanding, it is assumed that all the IVPHFSs discussed in this chapter have been normalized.

6.5.3 Comparison Approach of IVPHEs

In actual MCGDM problems, some experts can't provide preferences about every property because they lack certain knowledge related to the domain. Hence, there always exists partial ignorance, which means $\sum_{i=1}^{\#\widetilde{h}} \gamma_i^U \leq 1$. So we put forward the concept of generalized IVPHFS.

The approach for comparing IVPHFEs is important which can help us select the best alternative. Hence, the definitions of the score function and standard deviation degree for the IVPHFE are provided to rank IVPHFEs. By observing the format of the IVPHFE, we can infer that the form of score function and the standard deviation degree should be both interval values. Hence, we mainly consider how to calculate the upper and lower bounds of the score and standard deviation degree of the IVPHFE.

Definition 6.27 (Song et al., 2019b). Let $h(x)|\widetilde{p}_x = \left\{r_i(\widetilde{p}_i)\middle|i = 1, 2, \ldots, \#\widetilde{h}\right\}$ be an IVPHFE, then the score of the IVPHFE is defined as:

$$s(h(x)|\widetilde{p}_x) = \sum_{i=1}^{\#\widetilde{h}} r_i \cdot \widetilde{p}_i, \tag{6.20}$$

where the symbol $\#\widetilde{h}$ represents the amount of the terms in $h(x)|\widetilde{p}_x$, and $s(h(x)|\widetilde{p}_x)$ is an interval value denoted as s that belongs to [0,1].

Definition 6.28 (Song et al., 2019b). Let $h(x)|\widetilde{p}_x = \left\{r_i(\widetilde{p}_i)\middle|i = 1, 2, \ldots, \#\widetilde{h}\right\}$ be an IVPHFE, then the standard deviation degree of the IVPHFE is defined as:

$$\sigma(h(x)|\widetilde{p}_x) = \frac{1}{\#\widetilde{h}} \sum_{r_i, r_j \in \widetilde{h}} \sqrt{((r_i - r_j))^2} \cdot \widetilde{p}_i \tag{6.21}$$

where the symbol $\#\widetilde{h}$ represents the amount of the terms in $h(x)|\widetilde{p}_x$, and $\sigma(h(x)|\widetilde{p}_x)$ is an interval value denoted as σ that belongs to [0,1].

Since the forms of score and standard deviation degree for the IVPHFE are both interval values, we first review an efficient ranking approach for interval values:

Definition 6.29 (Chen et al., 2013a, 2013b). Let $\widetilde{a} = \left[a^L, a^U\right]$ and $\widetilde{b} = \left[b^L, b^U\right]$, and $l_{\widetilde{a}} = a^U - a^L$, $l_{\widetilde{b}} = b^U - b^L$. Then the possibility degree of $\widetilde{a} \geq \widetilde{b}$ is provided as:

$$p(\widetilde{a} \geq \widetilde{b}) = \max\left\{1 - \max\left(\frac{b^U - a^L}{l_{\widetilde{a}} + l_{\widetilde{b}}}, 0\right), 0\right\} \tag{6.22}$$

According to the possibility formula and due to the scores and standard deviation degrees of the IVPHFEs, we will provide a technique to compare IVPHFEs:

Definition 6.30 (Song et al., 2019b). Let $h_1(x)|\widetilde{p}_1$ and $h_2(x)|\widetilde{p}_2$ be two IVPHFEs.

(1) If $p(s(h_1(x)|\widetilde{p}_1) > s(h_2(x)|\widetilde{p}_2)) > 0.5$, then $h_1(x)|\widetilde{p}_1 >^{p(s(h_1(x)|\widetilde{p}_1)>s(h_2(x)|\widetilde{p}_2))} h_2(x)|\widetilde{p}_2$;
(2) If $p(s(h_2(x)|\widetilde{p}_2) > s(h_1(x)|\widetilde{p}_1)) > 0.5$, then $h_2(x)|\widetilde{p}_2 >^{p(s(h_2(x)|\widetilde{p}_2)>s(h_1(x)|\widetilde{p}_1))} h_1(x)|\widetilde{p}_1$;
(3) If $s(h_1(x)|\widetilde{p}_1) = s(h_2(x)|\widetilde{p}_2)$ and $d(h_1(x)|\widetilde{p}_1) < d(h_2(x)|\widetilde{p}_2)$, then $h_1(x)|\widetilde{p}_1 > h_2(x)|\widetilde{p}_2$;
(4) If $s(h_1(x)|\widetilde{p}_1) = s(h_2(x)|\widetilde{p}_2)$ and $d(h_1(x)|\widetilde{p}_1) > d(h_2(x)|\widetilde{p}_2)$, then $h_1(x)|\widetilde{p}_1 < h_2(x)|\widetilde{p}_2$;
(5) If $s(h_1(x)|\widetilde{p}_1) = s(h_2(x)|\widetilde{p}_2)$ and $d(h_1(x)|\widetilde{p}_1) = d(h_2(x)|\widetilde{p}_2)$, then $h_1(x)|\widetilde{p}_1 \sim h_2(x)|\widetilde{p}_2$.

6.5.4 Basic Operations of the IVPHEs

Similar to the operation laws of HFEs and PHFEs and combining with the probability theory, a few basic operation laws of IVPHFEs are provided as follows:

Definition 6.32 (Song et al., 2019b). Let $h(x)|\widetilde{p}_x$, $h_1(x)|\widetilde{p}_1$ and $h_2(x)|\widetilde{p}_2$ be three IVPHFEs, $\lambda > 0$, then.

(1) $\lambda h(x)|\widetilde{p}_x = \cup_{r_i \in h}\{[1-(1-r_i)^{\lambda}](\widetilde{p}_x)\}$;
(2) $h^{\lambda}(x)|\widetilde{p}_x = \cup_{r_i \in h}\{[r_i^{\lambda}](\widetilde{p}_x)\}$;
(3) $h_1(x)|\widetilde{p}_1 \oplus h_2(x)|\widetilde{p}_2 = \cup_{r_{1_i} \in h_1, r_{2_j} \in h_2}\{[r_{1_i} + r_{2_j} - r_{1_i} \cdot r_{2_j}](\widetilde{p}_{1_i} \cdot \widetilde{p}_{2_j})\}$;
(4) $h_1(x)|\widetilde{p}_1 \otimes h_2(x)|\widetilde{p}_2 = \cup_{r_{1_i} \in h_1, r_{2_j} \in h_2}\{[r_{1_i} \cdot r_{2_j}](\widetilde{p}_{1_i} \cdot \widetilde{p}_{2_j})\}$.

Theorem 2 (Song et al., 2019b). Let $h(x)|\widetilde{p}_x$, $h_1(x)|\widetilde{p}_1$, $h_2(x)|\widetilde{p}_2$ and $h_3(x)|\widetilde{p}_3$ be four IVPHFEs, $\lambda > 0$, $\lambda_1 > 0$, $\lambda_2 > 0$, then

(1) $h_1(x)|\widetilde{p}_1 \oplus h_2(x)|\widetilde{p}_2 = h_2(x)|\widetilde{p}_2 \oplus h_1(x)|\widetilde{p}_1$;
(2) $(h_1(x)|\widetilde{p}_1 \oplus h_2(x)|\widetilde{p}_2) \oplus h_3(x)|\widetilde{p}_3 = h_1(x)|\widetilde{p}_1 \oplus (h_2(x)|\widetilde{p}_2 \oplus h_3(x)|\widetilde{p}_3)$;
(3) $\lambda(h_1(x)|\widetilde{p}_1 \oplus h_2(x)|\widetilde{p}_2) = \lambda h_1(x)|\widetilde{p}_1 \oplus \lambda h_2(x)|\widetilde{p}_2$;
(4) $h_1(x)|\widetilde{p}_1 \otimes h_2(x)|\widetilde{p}_2 = h_2(x)|\widetilde{p}_2 \otimes h_1(x)|\widetilde{p}_1$;
(5) $(h_1(x)|\widetilde{p}_1 \otimes h_2(x)|\widetilde{p}_2) \otimes h_3(x)|\widetilde{p}_3 = h_1(x)|\widetilde{p}_1 \otimes (h_2(x)|\widetilde{p}_2 \otimes h_3(x)|\widetilde{p}_3)$;
(6) $(h_1(x)|\widetilde{p}_1 \otimes h_2(x)|\widetilde{p}_2)^{\lambda} = h_1^{\lambda}(x)|\widetilde{p}_1 \otimes h_2^{\lambda}(x)|\widetilde{p}_2$.

Proof

(1)
$$\begin{aligned} h_1(x)|\widetilde{p}_1 \oplus h_2(x)|\widetilde{p}_2 &= \cup_{r_{1_i} \in h_1, r_{2_j} \in h_2}\{[r_{1_i} + r_{2_j} - r_{1_i} \cdot r_{2_j}](\widetilde{p}_{1_i} \cdot \widetilde{p}_{2_j})\} \\ &= \cup_{r_{2_j} \in h_2, r_{1_i} \in h_1}\{[r_{2_j} + r_{1_i} - r_{2_j} \cdot r_{1_i}](\widetilde{p}_{2_j} \cdot \widetilde{p}_{1_i})\} \\ &= h_2(x)|\widetilde{p}_2 \oplus h_1(x)|\widetilde{p}_1 \end{aligned}$$

.

$$
\begin{aligned}
(2)\ & (h_1(x)|\widetilde{p}_x \oplus h_2(x)|\widetilde{p}_x) \oplus h_3(x)|\widetilde{p}_x \\
&= \bigcup_{r_{1_i}\in h_1, r_{2_j}\in h_2} \left\{\left[r_{1_i} + r_{2_j} - r_{1_i}\cdot r_{2_j}\right]\left(\widetilde{p}_{1_i}\cdot\widetilde{p}_{2_j}\right)\right\} \oplus h_3(x)|\widetilde{p}_3 \\
&= \bigcup_{r_{1_i}\in h_1, r_{2_j}\in h_2, r_{3_k}\in h_3} \left\{\begin{array}{l}\left[\left(r_{1_i} + r_{2_j} - r_{1_i}\cdot r_{2_j} + r_{3_k}\right) - r_{3_k}\left(r_{1_i} + r_{2_j} - r_{1_i}\cdot r_{2_j}\right)\right] \\ \left(\widetilde{p}_{1_i}\cdot\widetilde{p}_{2_j}\cdot\widetilde{p}_{3_k}\right)\end{array}\right\} \\
&= \bigcup_{r_{2_j}\in h_2, r_{3_k}\in h_3, r_{1_i}\in h_1} \left\{\begin{array}{l}\left[\left(r_{2_j} + r_{3_k} - r_{2_j}r_{3_k} + r_{1_i}\right) - r_{1_i}\left(r_{2_j} + r_{3_k} - r_{2_j}r_{3_k}\right)\right] \\ \left(\widetilde{p}_{2_j}\cdot\widetilde{p}_{3_k}\cdot\widetilde{p}_{1_i}\right)\end{array}\right\} \\
&= \bigcup_{r_{2_j}\in h_2, r_{3_k}\in h_3} \left\{\left[r_{2_j} + r_{3_k} - r_{2_j}\cdot r_{3_k}\right]\left(\widetilde{p}_{2_j}\cdot\widetilde{p}_{3_k}\right)\right\} \oplus h_1(x)|\widetilde{p}_1 \\
&= (h_2(x)|\widetilde{p}_2 \oplus h_3(x)|\widetilde{p}_3) \oplus h_1(x)|\widetilde{p}_1 \\
&= h_1(x)|\widetilde{p}_1 \oplus (h_2(x)|\widetilde{p}_2 \oplus h_3(x)|\widetilde{p}_3)
\end{aligned}
$$

.

$$
\begin{aligned}
(3)\ & \lambda(h_1(x)|\widetilde{p}_1 \oplus h_2(x)|\widetilde{p}_2) \\
&= \lambda\left(\bigcup_{r_{1_i}\in h_1, r_{2_j}\in h_2} \left\{\left[r_{1_i} + r_{2_j} - r_{1_i}\cdot r_{2_j}\right]\left(\widetilde{p}_{1_i}\cdot\widetilde{p}_{2_j}\right)\right\}\right) \\
&= \bigcup_{r_{1_i}\in h_1, r_{2_j}\in h_2} \left\{\left[1 - \left(1 - \left(r_{1_i} + r_{2_j} - r_{1_i}\cdot r_{2_j}\right)^{\lambda}\right)\right]\left(\widetilde{p}_{1_i}\cdot\widetilde{p}_{2_j}\right)\right\} \\
&= \bigcup_{r_{1_i}\in h_1, r_{2_j}\in h_2} \left\{\left[1 - \left(1 - \left(1 - r_{1_i}\right)\left(1 - r_{2_j}\right)\right)^{\lambda}\right]\left(\widetilde{p}_{1_i}\cdot\widetilde{p}_{2_j}\right)\right\} \\
&= \bigcup_{r_{1_i}\in h_1, r_{2_j}\in h_2} \left\{\left[1 - \left(1 - r_{1_i}\right)^{\lambda}\left(1 - r_{2_j}\right)^{\lambda}\right]\left(\widetilde{p}_{1_i}\cdot\widetilde{p}_{2_j}\right)\right\} \\
&= \bigcup_{r_{1_i}\in h_1, r_{2_j}\in h_2} \left\{\left[\begin{array}{c} 1 - \left(1 - r_{1_i}\right)^{\lambda} + 1 - \left(1 - r_{2_j}\right)^{\lambda} \\ - \left(1 - \left(1 - r_{1_i}\right)^{\lambda}\right)\left(1 - \left(1 - r_{2_j}\right)^{\lambda}\right)\end{array}\right]\left(\widetilde{p}_{1_i}\cdot\widetilde{p}_{2_j}\right)\right\} \\
&= \lambda h_1(x)|\widetilde{p}_1 \oplus \lambda h_2(x)|\widetilde{p}_2
\end{aligned}
$$

.

$$
\begin{aligned}
(4)\ & h_1(x)|\widetilde{p}_1 \otimes h_2(x)|\widetilde{p}_2 = \bigcup_{r_{1_i}\in h_1, r_{2_j}\in h_2} \left\{\left[r_{1_i}\cdot r_{2_j}\right]\left(\widetilde{p}_{1_i}\cdot\widetilde{p}_{2_j}\right)\right\} \\
&= \bigcup_{r_{2_j}\in h_2, r_{1_i}\in h_1} \left\{\left[r_{2_j}\cdot r_{1_i}\right]\left(\widetilde{p}_{2_j}\cdot\widetilde{p}_{1_i}\right)\right\} = h_2(x)|\widetilde{p}_2 \otimes h_1(x)|\widetilde{p}_1
\end{aligned}
$$

$$
\begin{aligned}
(5)\ & (h_1(x)|\widetilde{p}_1 \otimes h_2(x)|\widetilde{p}_2) \otimes h_3(x)|\widetilde{p}_3 \\
&= \bigcup_{r_{1_i}\in h_1, r_{2_j}\in h_2} \left\{\left[r_{1_i}\cdot r_{2_j}\right]\left(\widetilde{p}_{1_i}\cdot\widetilde{p}_{2_j}\right)\right\} \otimes h_3(x)|\widetilde{p}_3 \\
&= \bigcup_{r_{1_i}\in h_1, r_{2_j}\in h_2, r_{3_k}\in h_3} \left\{\left[r_{1_i}\cdot r_{2_j}\cdot r_{3_k}\right]\left(\widetilde{p}_{1_i}\cdot\widetilde{p}_{2_j}\cdot\widetilde{p}_{3_k}\right)\right\}
\end{aligned}
$$

$$= \bigcup_{r_{2_j}\in h_2, r_{3_k}\in h_3, r_{1_i}\in h_1} \left\{\left[r_{2_j}\cdot r_{3_k}\cdot r_{1_i}\right]\left(\widetilde{p}_{2_j}\cdot\widetilde{p}_{3_k}\cdot\widetilde{p}_{1_i}\right)\right\}$$

$$= \bigcup_{r_{2_j}\in h_2, r_{3_k}\in h_3} \left\{\left[r_{2_j}\cdot r_{3_k}\right]\left(\widetilde{p}_{2_j}\cdot\widetilde{p}_{3_k}\right)\right\} \otimes h_1(x)|\widetilde{p}_1$$

$$= \left(h_2(x)|\widetilde{p}_2 \otimes h_3(x)|\widetilde{p}_3\right) \otimes h_1(x)|\widetilde{p}_1$$

$$= h_1(x)|\widetilde{p}_1 \otimes \left(h_2(x)|\widetilde{p}_2 \otimes h_3(x)|\widetilde{p}_3\right)$$

(6) $$\left(h_1(x)|\widetilde{p}_x \otimes h_2(x)|\widetilde{p}_x\right)^{\lambda} = \bigcup_{r_{1_i}\in h_1, r_{2_j}\in h_2} \left\{\left[r_{1_i}\cdot r_{2_j}\right]^{\lambda}\left(\widetilde{p}_{1_i}\cdot\widetilde{p}_{2_j}\right)\right\}$$

$$= \bigcup_{r_{1_i}\in h_1} \left\{\left[r_{1_i}\right]^{\lambda}\left(\widetilde{p}_{1_i}\right)\right\} \otimes \bigcup_{r_{2_j}\in h_2} \left\{\left[r_{2_j}\right]^{\lambda}\left(\widetilde{p}_{2_j}\right)\right\}$$

$$= h_1^{\lambda}(x)|\widetilde{p}_1 \otimes h_2^{\lambda}(x)|\widetilde{p}_2$$

6.5.5 Some Basic Aggregation Operators for IVPHEs

Two main aggregation operators for the IVPHFEs based on the operations of IVPHFEs which were given are discussed in detail. The aggregation operators are very useful and important in the MCGDM problems with interval-valued probabilistic hesitant fuzzy information.

Definition 6.33 (Song et al., 2019b). Let $h_l(x)|\widetilde{p}_l = \left\{r_{l_i}\left(\widetilde{p}_{l_i}\right)\middle| i = 1, 2, \ldots, \#\widetilde{h_l}\right\}$ $(l = 1, 2, \ldots, n)$ be n IVPHFEs, and the weight vector $w = (w_1, w_2, \ldots, w_n)$ of $h_l(x)|\widetilde{p}_l\ (l = 1, 2, \ldots, n)$ satisfies that $w_l \geq 0,\ l = 1, 2, \ldots, n$ and $\sum_{l=1}^{n} w_l = 1$. Then, the interval-valued probabilistic hesitant fuzzy weighted averaging (IVPHFWA) is defined as follows:

$$IVPHFWA(h_1(x)|\widetilde{p}_1, h_2(x)|\widetilde{p}_2, \ldots, h_n(x)|\widetilde{p}_n) = \bigoplus_{l=1}^{n} w_l h_l(x)|\widetilde{p}_l$$

$$= \bigcup_{r_{1_i}\in h_1, r_{2_i}\in h_2, \ldots, r_{n_i}\in h_n} \left\{\left[1 - \prod_{l=1}^{n}\left(1 - r_{l_i}\right)^{w_l}\right]\left(\prod_{l=1}^{n}\widetilde{p}_{l_i}\right)\right\}$$

Especially, if $ww = (1/n, 1/n, \ldots, 1/n)$, then we can obtain that the IVPHFWA operator is simplified as an interval-valued probabilistic hesitant fuzzy averaging (IVPHFA) operator.

Theorem 3 (Monotonicity) (Song et al., 2019b). Let $h_l(x)|\widetilde{p}_l$ and $h_l^*(x)\left|\widetilde{p}_l^*\right. (l = 1, 2, \ldots, n)$ be two groups of IVPHFSs. If every element in $h_l(x)$ and $h_l^*(x)$ satisfies that $r_{l_i} \leq r_{l_i^*}\left(i = 1, 2, \ldots, \#\widetilde{h_l}\right)$, $\widetilde{p}_{r_{h_{l_i}}} = \widetilde{p}^*_{r_{h^*_{l_i}}}$. Then we have

$$IVPHFWA(h_1(x)|\widetilde{p}_1, h_2(x)|\widetilde{p}_2, \ldots, h_n(x)|\widetilde{p}_n)$$
$$\leq IVPHFWA\left(h_1^*(x)\left|\widetilde{p}_1^*\right., h_2^*(x)\left|\widetilde{p}_2^*\right., \ldots, h_n^*(x)\left|\widetilde{p}_n^*\right.\right)$$

Proof It is obvious that for any $l(l = 1, 2, \ldots, n)$ and $i\left(i = 1, 2, \ldots, \#\widetilde{h}_l\right)$, there is $r_{l_i} \leq r_{l_i^*}$, and according to the aggregated results, we have

$$1 - \prod_{l=1}^{n}\left(1 - r_{l_i}\right)^{w_l} \leq 1 - \prod_{l=1}^{n}\left(1 - r_{l_i^*}\right)^{w_l}$$

Then we get $IVPHFWA(h_1(x)|\widetilde{p}_1, h_2(x)|\widetilde{p}_2, \ldots, h_n(x)|\widetilde{p}_n) \leq IVPHFWA\left(h_1^*(x)|\widetilde{p}_1^*, h_2^*(x)|\widetilde{p}_2^*, \ldots, h_n^*(x)|\widetilde{p}_n^*\right)$ with equality if and only if $r_{l_i} = r_{l_i^*}$.

Theorem 4 (Boundedness) (Song et al., 2019b). Let $h_l(x)|\widetilde{p}_l$, $h_l^-(x)|\widetilde{p}_l^-$ and $h_l^+(x)|\widetilde{p}_l^+$ $(l = 1, 2, \ldots, n)$ be three groups of IVPHFSs. If every element in $h_l(x)$ and $h_l^*(x)$ satisfies $r_{l_i^-} = \min\left(r_{l_i}\right)$ and $r_{l_i^+} = \max\left(r_{l_i}\right)\left(i = 1, 2, \ldots, \#\widetilde{h}_l\right), \widetilde{p}_{r_{h_{l_i}}} = \widetilde{p}^*_{r_{h_{l_i}^*}}$. Then

$$\begin{aligned}&IVPHFWA\left(h_1^-(x)|\widetilde{p}_1^-, h_2^-(x)|\widetilde{p}_2^-, \ldots, h_n^-(x)|\widetilde{p}_n^-\right)\\&\leq IVPHFWA(h_1(x)|\widetilde{p}_1, h_2(x)|\widetilde{p}_2, \ldots, h_n(x)|\widetilde{p}_n)\end{aligned}$$

$$\begin{aligned}&IVPHFWA(h_1(x)|\widetilde{p}_1, h_2(x)|\widetilde{p}_2, \ldots, h_n(x)|\widetilde{p}_n)\\&\leq IVPHFWA\left(h_1^+(x)|\widetilde{p}_1^+, h_2^+(x)|\widetilde{p}_2^+, \ldots, h_n^+(x)|\widetilde{p}_n^+\right).\end{aligned}$$

Proof It is known to us that for any $i\left(i = 1, 2, \ldots, \#\widetilde{h}_l\right)$, $r_{l_i^-} = \min\left(r_{l_i}\right)$ and $r_{l_i^+} = \max\left(r_{l_i}\right)$, then there is $r_{l_i^-} \leq r_{l_i} \leq r_{l_i^+}$. Thus

$$1 - \prod_{l=1}^{n}\left(1 - r_{l_i^-}\right)^{w_l} \leq 1 - \prod_{l=1}^{n}\left(1 - r_{l_i}\right)^{w_l} \leq 1 - \prod_{l=1}^{n}\left(1 - r_{l_i^+}\right)^{w_l}$$

Then we can obtain that:

$$\begin{aligned}&IVPHFWA\left(h_1^-(x)|\widetilde{p}_1^-, h_2^-(x)|\widetilde{p}_2^-, \ldots, h_n^-(x)|\widetilde{p}_n^-\right)\\&\leq IVPHFWA(h_1(x)|\widetilde{p}_1, h_2(x)|\widetilde{p}_2, \ldots, h_n(x)|\widetilde{p}_n)\end{aligned}$$

$$\begin{aligned}&IVPHFWA\left(h_1^-(x)|\widetilde{p}_1^-, h_2^-(x)|\widetilde{p}_2^-, \ldots, h_n^-(x)|\widetilde{p}_n^-\right)\\&\quad\leq IVPHFWA(h_1(x)|\widetilde{p}_1, h_2(x)|\widetilde{p}_2, \ldots, h_n(x)|\widetilde{p}_n)\\&IVPHFWA(h_1(x)|\widetilde{p}_1, h_2(x)|\widetilde{p}_2, \ldots, h_n(x)|\widetilde{p}_n)\\&\quad\leq IVPHFWA\left(h_1^+(x)|\widetilde{p}_1^+, h_2^+(x)|\widetilde{p}_2^+, \ldots, h_n^+(x)|\widetilde{p}_n^+\right)\end{aligned}$$

Definition 6.34 (Song et al., 2019b). Let $h_l(x)|\widetilde{p}_l = \left\{r_{l_i}\left(\widetilde{p}_{l_i}\right)\middle|i = 1, 2, \ldots, \#\widetilde{h}_l\right\}$ $(l = 1, 2, \ldots, n)$ be n IVPHFEs, and the weight vector $w = (w_1, w_2, \ldots, w_n)$ of $h_l(x)|\widetilde{p}_l$ $(l = 1, 2, \ldots, n)$ satisfies that $w_l \geq 0$, $l = 1, 2, \ldots, n$ and $\sum_{l=1}^{n} w_l = 1$. Then, the interval-valued probabilistic hesitant fuzzy weighted geometric

(IVPHFWG) is defined below:

$$IVPHFWA(h_1(x)|\widetilde{p}_1, h_2(x)|\widetilde{p}_2, \ldots, h_n(x)|\widetilde{p}_n) = \bigotimes_{l=1}^{n} h_l^{w_l}(x)|\widetilde{p}_l$$

$$= \bigcup_{r_{1_i} \in h_1, r_{2_i} \in h_2, \ldots, r_{n_i} \in h_n} \left\{ \left[\prod_{l=1}^{n} r_{l_i}^{w_l} \right] \left(\prod_{l=1}^{n} \widetilde{p}_{l_i} \right) \right\}$$

Especially, if $w = (1/n, 1/n, \ldots, 1/n)$, then we can obtain that the IVPHFWG operator is simplified as an interval-valued probabilistic hesitant fuzzy geometric (IVPHFG) operator.

In a similar way, we can easily prove that the interval-valued probabilistic hesitant fuzzy weighted geometric (IVPHFWG) operator also has the above two properties.

6.5.6 MCGDM Based on IVPHFSs

With the ever-increasing complexity of the actual problems and uncertainty of the decision makers' cognitions, the limited knowledge and ability of the experts, it is never easy to achieve optimization with sound accuracy and reliability. The participation of multiple people in decision making analysis named as the multi-criteria group decision making (MCGDM), can avoid extremely individual preferences and has developed into an increasingly significant field of research in the modern decision science research. The theory and method of MCGDM are important tools to solve the decision making problems, which have been widely applied in investment decision making, military evaluation, risk assessment and other fields. Meanwhile, the IVPHFS permits the membership degrees of several possible elements and contains probabilistic information in the format of interval values without loss of information. Hence, in this section, we will develop an approach to solve actual MCGDM problems utilizing the above aggregation operators under the IVPHF environment. The main idea of our approach is to collect the preference information of a single decision maker expressed by hesitant fuzzy information first. After that, we will build an interval-valued possibility degree matrix that contains the full assessment information provided by all the experts, which is also comprehensive and normalized. Then we will aggregate the IVPHFSs after normalizing and fusing all the experts' preferences on each criterion by a proper aggregation operator. Finally, we will evaluate the alternatives and optimize the schemes according to the fusion results of the information. For the sake of understanding it easily, we will provide a detailed description of our approach to illustrate through the following measures:

To a MCGDM problem, suppose that $x = \{x_1, x_2, \ldots, x_m\}$ is a finite set of alternatives, and $c = \{c_1, c_2, \ldots, c_n\}$ is a set of criteria. A group of experts are invited to evaluate some issues or certain alternatives $x = \{x_1, x_2, \ldots, x_m\}$ concerning with the specified set of criteria $c = \{c_1, c_2, \ldots, c_n\}$ by the IVPHFSs.

Step 1. We collect all the normalized evaluated information which is provided by the experts and then build an interval-valued possibility degree matrix R:

$$R = \left[h_{ij}(x)|\widetilde{p}_{ij}\right]_{m\times n} = \begin{bmatrix} h_{11}(x)|\widetilde{p}_{11} & h_{12}(x)|\widetilde{p}_{12} & \dots & h_{1n}(x)|\widetilde{p}_{1n} \\ h_{21}(x)|\widetilde{p}_{21} & h_{22}(x)|\widetilde{p}_{22} & \dots & h_{2n}(x)|\widetilde{p}_{2n} \\ \vdots & \vdots & \ddots & \vdots \\ h_{m1}(x)|\widetilde{p}_{m1} & h_{m2}(x)|\widetilde{p}_{m2} & \dots & h_{mn}(x)|\widetilde{p}_{mn} \end{bmatrix}$$

Step 2. In the interest of obtaining the ranking or clustering consequences, we should use the operators to aggregate the IVPHFEs. The weighting vector $w = (w_1, w_2, \dots, w_n)^T$ satisfies $w_j \geq 0$ and $\sum_{j=1}^{n} w_j = 1$. For example, we use the interval-valued probabilistic hesitant fuzzy weighted averaging (IVPHFWA) operator to fuse the IVPHFEs of $x_i\{i = 1, 2, \dots, m\}$:

$$\begin{aligned} & IVPHFWA(h_{i1}(x)|\widetilde{p}_{i1}, h_{i2}(x)|\widetilde{p}_{i2}, \dots, h_{in}(x)|\widetilde{p}_{in}) \\ & = \mathop{\oplus}_{l=1}^{n} w_l h_l(x)|\widetilde{p}_l \\ & = \bigcup_{r_{1_i}\in h_1, r_{2_i}\in h_2, \dots, r_{n_i}\in h_n} \left\{\left[1 - \prod_{l=1}^{n}(1 - r_{l_i})^{w_l}\right]\left(\prod_{l=1}^{n}\widetilde{p}_{l_i}\right)\right\} \end{aligned}$$

Step 3. For the aggregation results, the final scores of the alternatives $x_i\{i = 1, 2, \dots, m\}$ are depicted as $s(h(x)|\widetilde{p}_x) = \left(s\left(h(x_1)|\widetilde{p}_{x_1}\right), s\left(h(x_2)|\widetilde{p}_{x_2}\right), \dots, s\left(h(x_m)|\widetilde{p}_{x_m}\right)\right)$, which can be obtained by simple calculation.

Step 4. We can build a crisp possibility degree matrix P by comparing $s\left(h(x_i)|\widetilde{p}_{x_i}\right)$ with each other:

$$p\left(\widetilde{s}_i \geq \widetilde{s}_j\right) = \max\left\{1 - \max\left(\frac{\widetilde{s}_j^U - \widetilde{s}_i^L}{l_{\widetilde{s}_i} + l_{\widetilde{s}_j}}, 0\right), 0\right\}, l_{\widetilde{s}_i} = \widetilde{s}_i^U - \widetilde{s}_i^L, l_{\widetilde{s}_j} = \widetilde{s}_j^U - \widetilde{s}_j^L.$$

$$P = p\left(\widetilde{s}_i \geq \widetilde{s}_j\right)_{m\times m} = \begin{bmatrix} 0.5 & p_{12} & \dots & p_{1m} \\ p_{21} & 0.5 & \dots & p_{2m} \\ \vdots & \vdots & 0.5 & \vdots \\ p_{m1} & p_{m2} & \dots & 0.5 \end{bmatrix}.$$

Step 5. By analyzing the above possibility degree matrix P and the equation above, we can obtain the ranking of the scores which are expressed as interval information, and the ranking results are shown as follows:

$$\widetilde{s}_{k_1} \geq^{p\left(\widetilde{s}_{k_1} \geq \widetilde{s}_{k_2}\right)} \widetilde{s}_{k_2} \geq \dots \geq^{p\left(\widetilde{s}_{k_{m-1}} \geq \widetilde{s}_{km}\right)} \geq \widetilde{s}_{k_m}$$

Step 6. Based on the score values and ranking results above, we can deserve the ranking order of the alternatives with the probabilistic information:

$$x_{k_1} \succ^{p\left(\widetilde{s}_{k_1} \geq \widetilde{s}_{k_2}\right)} x_{k_2} \succ \dots \succ^{p\left(\widetilde{s}_{k_{m-1}} \geq \widetilde{s}_{km}\right)} \succ x_{k_m}$$

To depict the interval-valued probabilistic information in the HFS and avoid losing information, we have introduced the concept of interval-valued probabilistic hesitant fuzzy set (IVPHFS), which permits the probabilistic information to be expressed by the interval values. The IVPHFS can deal with the practical issues better when the experts provide their preference values consisting of random variables with interval fuzzy probabilities rather than precise number. In order to deal with the actual MCGDM problems, we have provided a proper approach based on the IVPHF aggregation operators. It can optimize the evaluation results under the interval-valued probabilistic hesitant fuzzy environment and deal with more original information. Moreover, the method will be applied to the geopolitical risk evaluation for the Arctic area in the next section.

6.6 Application and Simulation Experiment of IVPHFSs

In this section, we will implement a geopolitical risk evaluation for the Arctic area taking advantages of the approach proposed above, which also illustrate the effectiveness and reliability of the novel technique. What's more, we present a comparison between our approach and the one from Hao et al. (2017) with probabilistic dual hesitant fuzzy information to test and verify the advantages of our novel approach further.

6.6.1 Application of IVPHFSs to Geopolitical Risk Evaluation Problem of Arctic Area

Due to the rich natural resources of the Arctic and potential new shipping routes connecting Europe and Asia, there are increasingly more nations and social groups showing their interest in Arctic, which brings military or political conflicts that are potential risky for investors (Song et al., 2019b).

In order to manage the hazards and exploit Arctic rationally, we carry out an evaluation experiment for the geopolitical risk in the Arctic region by the proposed approach above. In this section, we mainly consider four principal factor which may lead to risk in resource exploitation: potential military conflicts (MC), diplomatic disputes (DD), dependence on energy imports (EI) and control over marine routes (MR). We take the six countries adjacent to the Arctic for example: Canada, Russia, the USA, Norway, Denmark and China. In some actual risk evaluation problems (Wei et al., 2011; Ye, 2010a, 2010b), there are some difficulties for the experts to depict their expertise by a crisp number exactly, but the probabilistic distribution of their preferences may be expressed by interval values. Accordingly, to convey the interval-valued probabilistic information in the HFS, we suggest that the DMs use the IVPHFSs to express the evaluation information concerning about the four principal factors, which permits the membership to several possible values and the probabilistic information with interval values, and continues to have the primitive information provided by the DMs to the greatest degree (Bai et al., 2017a). At last, three experts were invited to provide their preferences of the given countries over each criterion (Tables 6.6, 6.7 and 6.8), and Hao et al. (2017) assumed that the weight vector of the three experts is $\omega = (0.2, 0.3, 0.5)^T$. Then we can get the normalized group's decision matrix (Table 6.9) through normalizing these three experts' evaluation information and preferences (Yager, 1988). All of them are listed as follows (Song et al., 2019b).

Step 1. According to the procedure, we first fuse the IVPHFSs of the three experts' preferences. For the weight of the four given criteria is given as w = $(0.3, 0.2, 0.3, 0.2)^T$, and we employ the IVPHFWA operator to fuse the normalized information of the six countries $\widetilde{H}_i (i = 1, 2, 3, 4, 5, 6)$ on the four criteria.

Table 6.6 The evaluation matrix M_1 of the six countries by the domain expert G_1

Criteria	MC	DD	EI	MR
USA	{0.5[0.6–0.8], 0.7[0.1–0.2]}	{0.7}	{0.2}	{0.6}
Canada	{0.1}	{0.3}	{0.7}	{0.3}
Russia	{0.6}	{0.56}	{0.1}	{0.2[0.4–0.6], 0.4[0.2–0.4]}
Denmark	{0.05[0.6–0.7], 0.2[0.1–0.3]}	{0.25}	{0.8}	{0.2}
China	{0.15}	{0.5}	{0.6[0.4–0.6], 0.8[0.2–0.4]}	{0.12}
Norway	{0.08}	{0.1[0.5–0.6], 0.3[0.2–0.4]}	{0.3}	{0.5}

Table 6.7 The evaluation matrix M_2 of the six countries by the domain expert G_2

Criteria	MC	DD	EI	MR
USA	{0.5}	{0.2}	{0.4[0.4–0.5], 0.7[0.3–0.4]}	{0.7}
Canada	{0.3[0.4–0.5], 0.5[0.4–0.5]}	{0.1}	{0.3[0.1–0.2], 0.4[0.5–0.8]}	{0.2}
Russia	{0.1[0–0.1], 0.2[0.8–0.9]}	{0.2[0.4–0.5], 0.3[0.3–0.5]}	{0.2}	{0.5}
Denmark	{0.2}	{0.1}	{0.2}	{0.2}
China	{0.2}	{0.45}	{0.6[0–0.1], 0.8[0.8–0.9]}	{0.3}
Norway	{0.4[0.2–0.4], 0.5[0.4–0.5]}	{0.3[0.3–0.4], 0.4[0.5–0.6]}	{0.3}	{0.2}

Table 6.8 The evaluation matrix M_3 of the six countries by the domain expert G_3

Criteria	MC	DD	EI	MR
USA	{0.4}	{0.9}	{0.3}	{0.6}
Canada	{0.75}	{0.4}	{0.2[0.5–0.7], 0.4[0.2–0.3]}	{0.3}
Russia	{0.6[0.5–0.6], 0.8[0.2–0.4]}	{0.5}	{0.1}	{0.2[0.5–0.7], 0.4[0.2–0.3]}
Denmark	{0.2}	{0.5[0.5–0.6], 0.7[0.2–0.4]}	{0.3[0.2–0.3], 0.5[0.5–0.7]}	{0.2}
China	{0.3[0.5–0.7], 0.4[0.2–0.3]}	{0.6}	{0.7}	{0.2}
Norway	{0.1[0.6–0.8], 0.2[0.1–0.2]}	{0.2}	{0.2[0.5–0.8], 0.3[0.1–0.2]}	{0.35}

Table 6.9 The normalized evaluation matrix M_4 of the six countries

Criteria	MC	DD	EI	MR
USA	{0.4(0.5), 0.5[0.42–0.46], 0.7[0.02–0.04]}	{0.2(0.3), 0.7(0.2), 0.9(0.5)}	{0.2(0.2), 0.3(0.5), 0.4[0.12–0.15], 0.7[0.09–0.12]}	{0.6(0.7), 0.7(0.3)}
Canada	{0.1(0.2), 0.3[0.12–0.15], 0.5[0.12–0.15], 0.75(0.5)}	{0.1(0.3), 0.3(0.2), 0.4(0.5)}	{0.2[0.25–0.35], 0.3[0.03–0.06, 0.4[0.25–0.39], 0.7(0.2)}	{0.2(0.3), 0.3(0.7)}
Russia	{0.1[0–0.03], 0.2[0.24–0.27], 0.6[0.45–0.5], 0.8[0.1–0.2]}	{0.2[0.12–0.15], 0.3[0.29–0.35], 0.5(0.5)}	{0.1(0.7), 0.2(0.3)}	{0.2[0.33–0.47], 0.4[0.14–0.23], 0.5(0.3)}
Denmark	{0.05[0.12–0.14], 0.2[0.82–0.86]}	{0.1(0.3), 0.25(0.2), 0.5[0.25–0.3], 0.7[0.1–0.2]}	{0.2(0.3), 0.3[0.1–0.15], 0.5[0.25–0.35], 0.8(0.2)}	{0.2}
China	{0.15(0.2), 0.2(0.3), 0.3[0.25–0.35], 0.4[0.1–0.15]}	{0.45(0.3), 0.5(0.2), 0.6(0.5)}	{0.6[0.08–0.15], 0.7(0.5), 0.8[0.28–0.35]}	{0.12(0.2), 0.2(0.5), 0.3(0.3)}
Norway	{0.08(0.2), 0.1[0.3–0.4], 0.2[0.05–0.1], 0.4[0.06–0.12], 0.5[0.12–0.15]}	{0.1[0.1–0.12], 0.2(0.5), 0.3[0.13–0.2], 0.4[0.15–0.18]}	{0.2[0.25–0.4], 0.3[0.55–0.6]}	{0.2(0.3), 0.35(0.5), 0.5(0.2)}

Then a comprehensive evaluation matrix is available, and in addition, the membership degrees and the relevant interval-valued probabilistic information are listed in Appendix.

$$\widetilde{H}_1 = \left\{ \begin{array}{l} \left\langle h_{1,1}, \{0.4(0.5), 0.5[0.42-0.46], 0.7[0.02-0.04]\} \right\rangle, \left\langle h_{1,2}, \{0.2(0.3), 0.7(0.2), 0.9(0.5)\} \right\rangle, \\ \left\langle h_{1,3}, \{0.2(0.2), 0.3(0.5), 0.4[0.12-0.15], 0.7[0.09-0.12]\} \right\rangle, \left\langle h_{1,4}, \{0.6(0.7), 0.7(0.3)\} \right\rangle \end{array} \right\}$$

$$\widetilde{H}_2 = \left\{ \begin{array}{l} \left\langle h_{2,1}, \{0.1(0.2), 0.3[0.12-0.15], 0.5[0.12-0.15], 0.75(0.5)\} \right\rangle, \left\langle h_{2,2}, \{0.1(0.3), 0.3(0.2), 0.4(0.5)\} \right\rangle, \\ \left\langle h_{1,3}, \{0.2[0.25-0.35], 0.3[0.03-0.06], 0.4[0.25-0.39], 0.7(0.2)\} \right\rangle, \left\langle h_{1,4}, \{0.2(0.3), 0.3(0.7)\} \right\rangle \end{array} \right\}$$

$$\widetilde{H}_3 = \left\{ \begin{array}{l} \left\langle h_{3,1}, \{0.1[0-0.03], 0.2[0.24-0.27], 0.6[0.45-0.5], 0.8[0.1-0.2]\} \right\rangle, \\ \left\langle h_{3,2}, \{0.2[0.12-0.15], 0.3[0.29-0.35], 0.5(0.5)\} \right\rangle, \\ \left\langle h_{3,3}, \{0.1(0.7), 0.2(0.3)\} \right\rangle, \left\langle h_{4,4}, \{0.2[0.33-0.47], 0.4[0.14-0.23], 0.5(0.3)\} \right\rangle \end{array} \right\}$$

$$\widetilde{H}_4 = \left\{ \begin{array}{l} \left\langle h_{4,1}, \{0.05[0.12-0.14], 0.2[0.82-0.86]\} \right\rangle, \\ \left\langle h_{4,2}, \{0.1(0.3), 0.25(0.2), 0.5[0.25-0.3], 0.7[0.1-0.2]\} \right\rangle, \\ \left\langle h_{4,3}, \{0.2(0.3), 0.3[0.1-0.15], 0.5[0.25-0.35], 0.8(0.2)\} \right\rangle, \left\langle h_{4,4}, \{0.2(1)\} \right\rangle \end{array} \right\}$$

$$\widetilde{H}_5 = \left\{ \begin{array}{l} \left\langle h_{5,1}, \{0.15(0.2), 0.2(0.3), 0.3[0.25-0.35], 0.4[0.1-0.15]\} \right\rangle, \left\langle h_{5,2}, \{0.45(0.3), 0.5(0.2), 0.6(0.5)\} \right\rangle, \\ \left\langle h_{5,3}, \{0.6[0.08-0.15], 0.7(0.5), 0.8[0.28-0.35]\} \right\rangle, \left\langle h_{5,4}, \{0.12(0.2), 0.2(0.5), 0.3(0.3)\} \right\rangle \end{array} \right\}$$

$$\widetilde{H}_6 = \left\{ \begin{array}{l} \left\langle h_{6,1}, \{0.08(0.5), 0.1[0.3-0.4], 0.2[0.05-0.1], 0.4[0.06-0.12], 0.5[0.12-0.15]\} \right\rangle, \\ \left\langle h_{6,2}, \{0.1[0.1-0.2], 0.2(0.5), 0.3[0.13-0.2], 0.4[0.15-0.18]\} \right\rangle, \\ \left\langle h_{6,3}, \{0.2[0.25-0.4], 0.3[0.55-0.6]\} \right\rangle, \left\langle h_{6,4}, \{0.2(0.3), 0.35(0.5), 0.5(0.2)\} \right\rangle \end{array} \right\}$$

n**Step 2**. According to the comprehensive matrices of the membership degrees and their corresponding probabilities, we further aggregate the comprehensive information to assess the given six countries. Then we can calculate the scores of the six countries according, and the results are shown as follows (Song et al., 2019b) (Table 6.10).

Step 3. Based on the above scores of the six countries, we can build a crisp possibility degree matrix P by comparing the scores $s\left(h(x_i)\middle|\widetilde{p}_{x_i}\right)$ with each other:

$$P = p\left(\widetilde{s}_{H_i} \geq \widetilde{s}_{H_j}\right)_{6\times 6} = \begin{bmatrix} 1 & 1 & 1 & 1 & 0.853 & 1 \\ 0 & 1 & 0.725 & 0.842 & 0.219 & 1 \\ 0 & 0.275 & 1 & 0.552 & 0.05 & 0.782 \\ 0 & 0.158 & 0.448 & 1 & 0 & 0.786 \\ 0.147 & 0.781 & 0.95 & 1 & 1 & 1 \\ 0 & 0 & 0.218 & 0.214 & 0 & 1 \end{bmatrix}$$

Table 6.10 The scores of the comprehensive interval probabilistic hesitant fuzzy information for the six countries (Song et al. 2019b)

Countries	USA	Canada	Russia	Denmark	China	Norway
Scores	[0.4644,0.5318]	[0.2945,0.4166]	[0.2063,0.3749]	[0.2198,0.3319]	[0.3599,0.494]	[0.134,0.2737]

Step 4. By analyzing the above possibility degree matrix P, we could obtain the ranking of the scores which are expressed as interval information, and the ranking results are shown as follows:

$$\tilde{s}_{H_1} \geq^{0.853} \tilde{s}_{H_5} \geq^{0.781} \tilde{s}_{H_2} \geq^{0.725} \tilde{s}_{H_3} \geq^{0.552} \tilde{s}_{H_4} \geq^{0.782} \tilde{s}_{H_6}$$

Step 5. Based on the score values and ranking results above, we can obtain the ranking order of the potential risk for the six countries:

$$USA \succ^{0.853} China \succ^{0.781} Canada \succ^{0.725} Russia \succ^{0.552} Denmark \succ^{0.782} Norway$$

6.6.2 Comparison with the Traditional Method for PDHFSs

In this subsection, we shall compare the approach with the method with PDHF information. Actually, Hao et al. (2017) constructed an efficient algorithm to produce the Gaussian cloud model of PDHFS, and also introduced a general information fusion process for PDHFSs, which supposes that the experts' preferences are expressed by the PDHFSs on the risk level of the indicators in the application.

For the convenience of understanding, we review some basic concepts of the PDHFS.

Definition 6.35 (Hao et al., 2017). Let X be a reference set and a probabilistic dual hesitant fuzzy set (PDHFS) on X is depicted as $A = \{\langle x, h(x)|p(x), g(x)|q(x)\rangle | x \in X\}$, $\gamma \in h(x)$ and $\eta \in g(x)$, where $h(x)$ and $g(x)$ are two sets of some different values in [0,1], which indicate the possible membership degrees and non-membership degrees of the element $x \in X$ to A. $p(x)$ and $q(x)$ are two sets of probabilities associated with $h(x)$ and $g(x)$, respectively. For convenience and simplicity, the probabilistic dual hesitant fuzzy element (PDHFE) is denoted as $A = \langle h(x)|p(x), g(x)|q(x)\rangle$.

Definition 6.36 (Hao et al., 2017). Let $A = \langle h(x)|p(x), g(x)|q(x)\rangle$ be a PDHFE, the score of the PDHFE is defined as follows:

$$s = \sum_{\gamma \in h} \gamma_i \cdot p_i - \sum_{\eta \in h} \eta_j \cdot q_j \tag{6.23}$$

Then, after aggregating the evaluation information expressed by PDHFEs, Hao et al. (2017) figured out the scores of the six countries. The results are shown as in Table 6.11.

According to the scores of the six countries, it is obvious that the USA has the highest risk, and the detailed risk ranking result is shown as follows:

$$USA \succ Denmark \succ China \succ Canada \succ Russia \succ Norway$$

Table 6.11 The scores of the comprehensive probabilistic dual hesitant fuzzy information for the six countries

Countries	USA	Canada	Russia	Denmark	China	Norway
Scores	0.5289	0.0948	0.0499	0.3269	0.1682	−0.3508

The comparison between the two approaches are shown in Table 6.12 (Song et al., 2019b). It is clear that our method can obtain the same highest risk alternative with that of Hao et al.'s (2017). Nevertheless, it is obvious that our approach is more logical and efficient because in the majority of the cases people cannot be completely sure that one alternative is absolutely superior than another (Yang et al., 2016). And there are some difficulties for the experts to depict their preferences by a crisp number exactly, but the probabilistic distribution of their preferences may be expressed by the interval values in some cases. Actually we can aggregate IVPHFSs without loss of information. Hao et al.'s method for PDHFSs can take into account both affirmative and negative information from the experts, but the aggregation of the PDHFSs may lead to overload information, which not only make the computational process more sophisticated, but also makes the analysis of the aggregating results more difficult. And their ranking method has some deficiencies, because their results are too absolute and cannot deal with interval information. Meanwhile, the approach we proposed can optimize the final evaluation results under interval-valued probabilistic hesitant fuzzy environment and make the calculation simpler. In other words, our approach is more reliable and contains much more probabilistic information, which is relatively more effective at the same time.

6.7 Remarks

In order to deal with the cognitive uncertainty and probabilistic statistical uncertainty information in actual decision making process better, and remain the original decision making information to the greatest extent, this chapter introduce a probabilistic hesitant fuzzy correlation coefficient and clustering algorithm. After that, we further present the concept of interval-valued probabilistic hesitant fuzzy set (IVPHFS), and discuss its properties, ranking and comparison methods, basic operation rules, operators and the corresponding decision making method.

Table 6.12 The ranking results based on the two approaches

	Ranking order	The highest risk alternative
Hao et al. [21]	$USA \succ Denmark \succ China \succ Canada \succ Russia \succ Norway$	USA
Interval approach	$USA \succ^{0.853} China \succ^{0.781} Canada \succ^{0.725} Russia \succ^{0.552} Denmark \succ^{0.782} Norway$	USA

Appendix

This appendix provides the calculation process of the aggregating fuzzy vectors in the form of IVPHFSs based on the comprehensive matrices for the six countries. The subscripts indicate the index of the countries in the text. For example, $\widetilde{h}_1$ represents the final membership degrees of the USA over all the criteria. The membership degrees and their corresponding probabilities are shown as follows (Song et al., 2019b):

$$\widetilde{h}_1 = \left\{ \begin{array}{l} 0.3865, 0.5429, 0.6712, 0.4085, 0.5593, 0.683, 0.4659, 0.6021, \\ 0.7138, 0.4027, 0.555, 0.6799, 0.4241, 0.5709, 0.6914, 0.48, \\ 0.6126, 0.7213, 0.4208, 0.5685, 0.6896, 0.4416, 0.5839, 0.7007, \\ 0.4958, 0.6243, 0.7298, 0.4958, 0.6243, 0.7298, 0.5139, 0.6378, \\ 0.7395, 0.5611, 0.673, 0.7648, 0.4373, 0.5807, 0.6984, 0.4574, \\ 0.5957, 0.7092, 0.5101, 0.635, 0.7375, 0.4521, 0.5918, 0.7064, \\ 0.4717, 0.6064, 0.7169, 0.523, 0.6446, 0.7444, 0.4687, 0.6064, \\ 0.7153, 0.4877, 0.6183, 0.7255, 0.5375, 0.6554, 0.7521, 0.5375, \\ 0.6554, 0.7521, 0.5541, 0.6677, 0.761, 0.5974, 0.7, 0.7842 \end{array} \right\}$$

$$\widetilde{h}_2 = \left\{ \begin{array}{l} 0.1515, 0.2131, 0.2487, 0.1931, 0.2517, 0.2855, 0.2456, 0.3004, \\ 0.332, 0.3432, 0.3909, 0.4185, 0.1738, 0.2338, 0.2685, 0.2143, \\ 0.2714, 0.3043, 0.2655, 0.3188, 0.3496, 0.3605, 0.407, 0.4338, \\ 0.1989, 0.2571, 0.2907, 0.2382, 0.2935, 0.3254, 0.2878, 0.3395, \\ 0.3693, 0.38, 0.425, 0.451, 0.3026, 0.3533, 0.3825, 0.3368, \\ 0.385, 0.4128, 0.38, 0.425, 0.451, 0.4602, 0.4994, 0.522, \\ 0.1848, 0.244, 0.2782, 0.2248, 0.2811, 0.3135, 0.2752, 0.3278, \\ 0.3582, 0.369, 0.4149, 0.4413, 0.2063, 0.2639, 0.2972, 0.2452, \\ 0.3, 0.3316, 0.2943, 0.3456, 0.3751, 0.3857, 0.4303, 0.456, \\ 0.2304, 0.2863, 0.3185, 0.2681, 0.3213, 0.3519, 0.3157, 0.3654, \\ 0.3941, 0.4043, 0.4476, 0.4725, 0.33, 0.3787, 0.4067, 0.3628, \\ 0.4091, 0.4358, 0.4043, 0.4476, 0.4725, 0.4814, 0.5191, 0.5408 \end{array} \right\}$$

$$\widetilde{h}_3 = \left\{ \begin{array}{l} 0.1614, 0.1943, 0.2717, 0.1809, 0.2131, 0.2886, 0.287, 0.315, \\ 0.3807, 0.3793, 0.4036, 0.4609, 0.1809, 0.2131, 0.2886, 0.2, \\ 0.2314, 0.3052, 0.3036, 0.3309, 0.3951, 0.3937, 0.4175, 0.4734, \\ 0.2307, 0.261, 0.3319, 0.2487, 0.2782, 0.3475, 0.3459, 0.3716, \\ 0.4319, 0.4306, 0.4529, 0.5055, 0.2487, 0.2782, 0.3475, 0.2661, \\ 0.295, 0.3627, 0.3611, 0.3862, 0.4452, 0.4438, 0.4657, 0.517, \\ 0.2717, 0.3003, 0.3675, 0.2886, 0.3166, 0.3822, 0.3807, 0.405, \\ 0.4622, 0.4609, 0.4821, 0.5318, 0.2886, 0.3166, 0.3822, 0.3052, \\ 0.3325, 0.3966, 0.3951, 0.4189, 0.4747, 0.4734, 0.4941, 0.5427, \end{array} \right\}$$

$$\widetilde{h}_4 = \left\{ \begin{array}{l} 0.1422, 0.1879, 0.2809, 0.3831, 0.1712, 0.2153, 0.3052, 0.4039, \\ 0.1649, 0.2093, 0.2999, 0.3993, 0.1931, 0.236, 0.3235, 0.4196, \\ 0.2192, 0.2608, 0.3454, 0.4384, 0.2456, 0.2857, 0.3675, 0.4574, \\ 0.3499, 0.3845, 0.455, 0.5325, 0.3719, 0.4053, 0.4734, 0.5483 \end{array} \right\}$$

$$\widetilde{h}_5 = \left\{ \begin{array}{l} 0.3517, 0.37, 0.4108, 0.3596, 0.3776, 0.4179, 0.3764, 0.394, \\ 0.4332, 0.3954, 0.4124, 0.4505, 0.388, 0.4052, 0.4437, 0.3954, \\ 0.4124, 0.4505, 0.4113, 0.4279, 0.4649, 0.4292, 0.4453, 0.4812, \\ 0.4357, 0.4516, 0.4871, 0.4425, 0.4582, 0.4933, 0.4572, 0.4725, \\ 0.5066, 0.4736, 0.4885, 0.5216, 0.37, 0.3878, 0.4274, 0.3776, \\ 0.3951, 0.4343, 0.394, 0.4111, 0.4492, 0.4124, 0.429, 0.4659, \\ 0.4052, 0.422, 0.4594, 0.4124, 0.429, 0.4659, 0.4279, 0.444, \\ 0.48, 0.4453, 0.4609, 0.4958, 0.4516, 0.467, 0.5015, 0.4582, \\ 0.4734, 0.5075, 0.4725, 0.4873, 0.5205, 0.4885, 0.5029, 0.5351, \\ 0.3948, 0.4118, 0.4499, 0.402, 0.4189, 0.4565, 0.4178, 0.4342, \\ 0.4708, 0.4355, 0.4514, 0.4869, 0.4286, 0.4447, 0.4807, 0.4355, \\ 0.4514, 0.4869, 0.4504, 0.4658, 0.5004, 0.467, 0.4821, 0.5156, \\ 0.4731, 0.488, 0.5211, 0.4795, 0.4941, 0.5269, 0.4932, 0.5075, \\ 0.5393, 0.5086, 0.5224, 0.5533, \end{array} \right\}$$

$$\widetilde{h}_6 = \left\{ \begin{array}{l} 0.1477, 0.1773, 0.2096, 0.2453, 0.1515, 0.1809, 0.2131, 0.2487, 0.1712, 0.2, \\ 0.2314, 0.2661, 0.2176, 0.2447, 0.2744, 0.3072, 0.2456, 0.2718, 0.3004, 0.332, \\ 0.1702, 0.199, 0.2305, 0.2652, 0.1738, 0.2025, 0.2338, 0.2685, 0.1931, 0.2211, \\ 0.2517, 0.2855, 0.2382, 0.2646, 0.2935, 0.3254, 0.2655, 0.291, 0.3188, 0.3496, \\ 0.1992, 0.227, 0.2574, 0.2909, 0.2027, 0.2304, 0.2606, 0.294, 0.2213, 0.2483, \\ 0.2778, 0.3105, 0.2648, 0.2903, 0.3182, 0.349, 0.2911, 0.3158, 0.3426, 0.3723, \\ 0.2203, 0.2474, 0.2769, 0.3096, 0.2237, 0.2507, 0.2801, 0.3126, 0.2418, 0.2681, \\ 0.2969, 0.3286, 0.2842, 0.309, 0.3362, 0.3662, 00.3098, 0.3338, 0.3599, 0.3889, \\ 0.2598, 0.2855, 0.3136, 0.3446, 0.2631, 0.2886, 0.3166, 0.3475, 0.2802, 0.3052, \\ 0.3325, 0.3627, 0.3205, 0.3441, 0.3698, 0.3983, 0.3448, 0.3675, 0.3924, 0.4198, \\ 0.2793, 0.3043, 0.3317, 0.3619, 0.2825, 0.3074, 0.3346, 0.3647, 0.2992, 0.3235, \\ 0.3501, 0.3795, 0.3384, 0.3613, 0.3864, 0.4142, 0.3621, 0.3842, 0.4084, 0.4351 \end{array} \right\}$$

$$\widetilde{p}_1 = \left\{ \begin{array}{l} 0.021, 0.014, 0.035, [0.0176 - 0.0193], [0.0118 - 0.0129], [0.0294 - 0.0322], \\ [0.0008 - 0.017], [0.0006 - 0.0011], [0.0014 - 0.0028], 0.0525, 0.035, 0.0875, \\ [0.0441 - 0.0483], [0.0294 - 0.0322], [0.0735 - 0.0805], [0.0021 - 0.0042], \\ [0.0014 - 0.0028], [0.0035 - 0.007], [0.0126 - 0.0158], [0.0084 - 0.0105], \\ [0.021 - 0.0262], [0.0106 - 0.0145], [0.0071 - 0.0097], [0.0176 - 0.0242], \\ [0.0005 - 0.0013], [0.0003 - 0.0008], [0.0008 - 0.0021], [0.0095 - 0.0126], \\ [0.0063 - 0.0084], [0.0158 - 0.021], [0.0079 - 0.0116], [0.0053 - 0.0077], \\ [0.0132 - 0.0193], [0.0004 - 0.001], [0.0003 - 0.0007], [0.0006 - 0.0017], \\ 0.009, 0.006, 0.015, [0.0076 - 0.0083], [0.005 - 0.0055], [0.0126 - 0.0138], \\ [0.0004 - 0.0007], [0.0002 - 0.0005], [0.0006 - 0.0012], 0.0225, 0.015, 0.0375, \\ [0.0189 - 0.0207], [0.0126 - 0.0138], [0.0315 - 0.0345], [0.0009 - 0.0018], \\ [0.0006 - 0.0012], [0.0015 - 0.003], [0.0054 - 0.0067], [0.0036 - 0.0045], \\ [0.009 - 0.0112], [0.0045 - 0.0062], [0.003 - 0.0041], [0.0076 - 0.0103], \\ [0.0002 - 0.0005], [0.0001 - 0.0004], [0.0004 - 0.0009], [0.004 - 0.0054], \\ [0.0027 - 0.0036], [0.0067 - 0.009], [0.0034 - 0.005], [0.0023 - 0.0033], \\ [0.0057 - 0.0083], [0.0002 - 0.0004], [0.0001 - 0.0003], [0.0003 - 0.0007], \end{array} \right\}$$

$$\widetilde{p}_2 = \left\{ \begin{array}{l} [0.0045-0.0063],[0.003-0.0042],[0.0075-0.0105],[0.0027-0.0047], \\ [0.0018-0.0031],[0.0045-0.0079],[0.0027-0.0047],[0.0018-0.0031], \\ [0.0045-0.0079],[0.0112-0.0158],[0.0075-0.0105],[0.0187-0.0262], \\ [0.0005-0.0011],[0.0004-0.0007],[0.0009-0.0018],[0.0003-0.0008], \\ [0.0002-0.0005],[0.0005-0.0013],[0.0003-0.0008],[0.0002-0.0005], \\ [0.0005-0.0013],[0.0013-0.0027],[0.0009-0.0018],[0.0022-0.0045], \\ [0.0045-0.007],[0.003-0.0047],[0.0075-0.0117],[0.0027-0.0053], \\ [0.0018-0.0035],[0.0045-0.0088],[0.0027-0.0053],[0.0018-0.0035], \\ [0.0045-0.0088],[0.0112-0.0175],[0.0075-0.0117],[0.0187-0.0292], \\ 0.0036,0.0024,0.006,[0.0022-0.0027],[0.0014-0.0018],[0.0036-0.0045], \\ [0.0022-0.0027],[0.0014-0.0018],[0.0036-0.0045],0.009,0.006,0.015, \\ [0.0105-0.0147],[0.007-0.0098],[0.0175-0.0245],[0.0063-0.011], \\ [0.0042-0.0073],[0.0105-0.0184],[0.0063-0.011],[0.0042-0.0073], \\ [0.0105-0.0184],[0.0262-0.0367],[0.0175-0.0245],[0.0437-0.0612], \\ [0.0013-0.0025],[0.0008-0.0017],[0.0021-0.0042],[0.0008-0.0019], \\ [0.0005-0.0013],[0.0013-0.0031],[0.0008-0.0019],[0.0005-0.0013], \\ [0.0013-0.0031],[0.0031-0.0063],[0.0021-0.0042],[0.0052-0.0105], \\ [0.0105-0.0164],[0.007-0.0109],[0.0175-0.0273],[0.0063-0.0123], \\ [0.0042-0.0082],[0.0105-0.0205],[0.0063-0.0123],[0.0042-0.0082], \\ [0.0105-0.0205],[0.0262-0.0409],[0.0175-0.0273],[0.0437-0.0682], \\ 0.0084,0.0056,0.014,[0.005-0.0063],[0.0034-0.0042],[0.0084-0.0105], \\ [0.005-0.0063],[0.0034-0.0105],[0.0084-0.0105],0.021,0.014,0.035 \end{array} \right\}$$

$$\widetilde{p}_3 = \left\{ \begin{array}{l} [0-0.0015],[0-0.0035],[0-0.0049],[0.0067-0.0133], \\ [0.0161-0.0311],[0.0277-0.0444],[0.0125-0.0247],[0.0301-0.0576], \\ [0.052-0.0822],[0.0028-0.0099],[0.0067-0.023],[0.0115-0.0329], \\ [0-0.0006],[0-0.0015],[0-0.0021],[0.0029-0.0057], \\ [0.0069-0.0133],[0.0119-0.019],[0.0053-0.0106],[0.0129-0.0247], \\ [0.0223-0.0352],[0.0012-0.0042],[0.0029-0.0099],[0.005-0.0141], \\ [0-0.0007],[0-0.0017],[0-0.0024],[0.0028-0.0065], \\ [0.0068-0.0152],[0.0118-0.0217],[0.0053-0.0121],[0.0128-0.0282], \\ [0.0221-0.0403],[0.0012-0.0048],[0.0028-0.0113],[0.0049-0.0161], \\ [0-0.0003],[0-0.0007],[0-0.001],[0.00012-0.0028], \\ [0.0029-0.0065],[0.005-0.0093],[0.0023-0.0052],[0.0055-0.0121], \\ [0.0095-0.0173],[0.0005-0.0021],[0.0012-0.0048],[0.0021-0.0069], \\ [0-0.0009],[0-0.0022],[0-0.0031],[0.006-0.0085], \\ [0.0146-0.0198],[0.0252-0.0284],[0.0113-0.0158],[0.0274-0.0367], \\ [0.0473-0.0525],[0.0025-0.0063],[0.0061-0.0147],[0.0105-0.021], \\ [0-0.0004],[0-0.0009],[0-0.0013],[0.0026-0.0036], \\ [0.0063-0.0085],[0.0108-0.0121],[0.049-0.0067],[0.0117-0.0158], \\ [0.0203-0.0225],[0.0011-0.0027],[0.0026-0.0063],[0.0045-0.009] \end{array} \right\}$$

$$\widetilde{p}_4 = \left\{\begin{array}{l} [0.0108-0.0126], [0.0072-0.0084], [0.009-0.0126], [0.0036-0.0084], \\ [0.0738-0.0774], [0.0492-0.0516], [0.0615-0.0774], [0.0246-0.0516], \\ [0.0036-0.0063], [0.0024-0.0042], [0.003-0.0063], [0.0012-0.0042], \\ [0.0246-0.0387], [0.0164-0.0258], [0.0205-0.0387], [0.0082-0.0258], \\ [0.009-0.0147], [0.006-0.0098], [0.0075-0.0147], [0.003-0.0098], \\ [0.0615-0.0903], [0.041-0.0602], [0.0512-0.0903], [0.0205-0.0602], \\ [0.0072-0.0084], [0.0048-0.0056], [0.006-0.0084], [0.0024-0.0056], \\ [0.0492-0.0516], [0.0328-0.0344], [0.041-0.0516], [0.0164-0.0344] \end{array}\right\}$$

$$\widetilde{p}_5 = \left\{\begin{array}{l} [0.001-00018], [0.0006-0.0012], [0.0016-0.003], [0.0014-0.0027], \\ [0.001-0.0018], [0.0024-0.0045], [0.0012-0.0032], [0.0008-0.0021], \\ [0.002-0.0053], [0.0005-0.0014], [0.0003-0.0009], [0.0008-0.0022], \\ 0.006, 0.004, 0.01, 0.009, 0.006, 0.015, [0.0075-0.0105], [0.005-0.007], \\ [0.0125-0.0175], [0.003-0.0045], [0.002-0.003], [0.005-0.0075], \\ [0.0034-0.0042], [0.0022-0.0028], [0.0056-0.007], [0.005-0.0063], \\ [0.0034-0.0042], [0.0084-0.0105], [0.0042-0.0073], [0.0028-0.0049], \\ [0.007-0.0122], [0.0017-0.0032], [0.0011-0.0021], [0.0028-0.0053], \\ [0.0024-0.0045], [0.0016-0.003], [0.004-0.0075], [0.0036-0.0067], \\ [0.0024-0.0045], [0.006-0.0112], [0.003-0.0079], [0.002-0.0052], \\ [0.005-0.0131], [0.0012-0.0034], [0.0008-0.0022], [0.002-0.0056], \\ 0.015, 0.01, 0.025, 0.0225, 0.015, 0.0375, [0.0187-0.0262], [0.0125-0.0175], \\ [0.0313-0.0437], [0.0075-0.0112], [0.005-0.0075], [0.0125-0.0187], \\ [0.0084-0.0105], [0.0056-0.007], [0.014-0.0175], [0.0126-0.0158], \\ [0.0084-0.0105], [0.021-0.0262], [0.0105-0.0184], [0.007-0.0122], \\ [0.0175-0.0306], [0.0042-0.0079], [0.0028-0.0052], [0.007-0.0131], \\ [0.0014-0.0027], [0.001-0.0018], [0.0024-0.0045], [0.0022-0.004], \\ [0.0014-0.0027], [0.0036-0.0067], [0.0018-0.0047], [0.0012-0.0031], \\ [0.003-0.0079], [0.0007-0.002], [0.0005-0.0013], [0.0012-0.0034], \\ 0.009, 0.006, 0.015, 0.0135, 0.009, 0.0225, [0.0112-0.0158], [0.0075-0.0105], \\ [0.0187-0.0262], [0.0045-0.0067], [0.003-0.0045], [0.0075-0.0112], \\ [0.005-0.0063], [0.0034-0.0042], [0.0084-0.0105], [0.0076-0.0095], \\ [0.005-0.0063], [0.0126-0.0158], [0.0063-0.011], [0.0042-0.0073], \\ [0.0105-0.0184], [0.0025-0.0047], [0.0017-0.0031], [0.0042-0.0079], \end{array}\right.$$

$$\widetilde{p}_6 = \left\{\begin{array}{l}
[0.0015-0.0048],[0.0075-0.012],[0.002-0.0048],[0.0022-0.0043],\\
[0.0022-0.0096],[0.0112-0.024],[0.0029-0.0096],[0.0034-0.0086],\\
[0.0004-0.0024],[0.0019-0.006],[0.0005-0.0024],[0.0006-0.0022],\\
[0.0004-0.0029],[0.0022-0.0072],[0.0006-0.0029],[0.0007-0.0026],\\
[0.0009-0.0036],[0.0045-0.009],[0.0012-0.0036],[0.0013-0.0032],\\
[0.0033-0.0072],[0.0165-0.018],[0.0043-0.0072],[0.005-0.0065],\\
[0.005-0.0144],[0.0248-0.036],[0.0064-0.0144],[0.0074-0.013],\\
[0.0008-0.0036],[0.0041-0.009],[0.0011-0.0036],[0.0012-0.0032],\\
[0.001-0.0043],[0.005-0.0108],[0.0013-0.0043],[0.0015-0.0039],\\
[0.002-0.0054],[0.0099-0.0135],[0.0026-0.0054],[0.003-0.0049],\\
[0.0025-0.008],[0.0125-0.02],[0.0033-0.008],[0.0037-0.0072],\\
[0.0037-0.016],[0.0187-0.04],[0.0049-0.016],[0.0056-0.0144],\\
[0.0006-0.004],[0.0031-0.01],[0.0008-0.004],[0.0009-0.0036],\\
[0.0008-0.0048],[0.0037-0.012],[0.001-0.0048],[0.0011-0.0043],\\
[0.0015-0.006],[0.0075-0.015],[0.0019-0.006],[0.0022-0.0054],\\
[0.0055-0.012],[0.0275-0.03],[0.0072-0.012],[0.0083-0.0108],\\
[0.0083-0.024],[0.0413-0.06],[0.0107-0.024],[0.0124-0.0216],\\
[0.0014-0.006],[0.0069-0.015],[0.0018-0.006],[0.0021-0.0054],\\
[0.0017-0.0072],[0.0083-0.018],[0.0021-0.0072],[0.0025-0.0065],\\
[0.0033-0.009],[0.0165-0.0225],[0.0043-0.009],[0.005-0.0081],\\
[0.001-0.0032],[0.005-0.008],[0.0013-0.0032],[0.0015-0.0029],\\
[0.0015-0.0064],[0.0075-0.016],[0.002-0.0064],[0.0022-0.0058],\\
[0.0003-0.0016],[0.0013-0.004],[0.0003-0.0016],[0.0004-0.0014],\\
[0.0003-0.0019],[0.0015-0.0048],[0.0004-0.0019],[0.0004-0.0017],\\
[0.0006-0.0024],[0.003-0.006],[0.0008-0.0024],[0.0009-0.0022],\\
[0.0022-0.0048],[0.011-0.012],[0.0029-0.0048],[0.0033-0.0043],\\
[0.0033-0.0096],[0.0165-0.024],[0.0043-0.0096],[0.005-0.0086],\\
[0.0006-0.0024],[0.0028-0.006],[0.0007-0.0024],[0.0008-0.0022],\\
[0.0007-0.0029],[0.0033-0.0072],[0.0009-0.0029],[0.001-0.0026],\\
[0.0013-0.0036],[0.0066-0.009],[0.0017-0.0036],[0.002-0.0032]
\end{array}\right\}$$

References

Bai, C. Z., Zhang, R., Qian, L. X., et al. (2017a). Comparisons of probabilistic linguistic term sets for multi-criteria decision making. *Knowledge Based Systems, 119*, 284–291.

Bai, C. Z., Zhang, R., Shen, S., et al. (2018). Interval-valued probabilistic linguistic term sets in multi-criteria group decision making. *International Journal of Intelligent Systems*, 1–21.

Bai, C. Z., Zhang, R., Song, C. Y., & Wu, Y. N. (2017b). A new ordered weighted averaging operator to obtain the associated weights based on the principle of least mean square errors. *International Journal of Intelligent Systems, 32*, 213–226.

Chen, N., Xu, Z. S., & Xia, M. M. (2013a). Correlation coefficients of hesitant fuzzy sets and their application to clustering analysis. *Applied Mathematical Modelling, 37*, 2197–2211.

Chen, N., Xu, Z. S., & Xia, M. M. (2013b). Interval-valued hesitant preference relations and their applications to group decision making. *Knowledge-Based Systems, 37*, 528–540.

Chiang, D. A., & Lin, N. P. (1999). Correlation of fuzzy sets. *Fuzzy Set and Systems, 102*, 221–226.

Hong, D. H. (2006). Fuzzy measures for a correlation coefficient of fuzzy numbers under T_W-based fuzzy arithmetic operations. *Information Sciences, 176*, 150–160.

Hao, Z. N., Xu, Z. S., Zhao, H., et al. (2017). Probabilistic dual hesitant fuzzy set and its application in risk evaluation. *Knowledge-Based Systems, 127*, 16–28.

Huang, W. L., & Wu, J. W. (2002). Correlation of intuitionistic fuzzy sets by centroid method. *Information Sciences, 144*, 219–225.

Jahanshahloo, G. R., Lotfi, F. H., & Izadikhah, M. (2006). An algorithmic method to extend TOPSIS for decision-making problems with interval data. *Applied Mathematics & Computation, 175*, 1375–1384.

Jiang, F., & Ma, Q. (2017). Multi-attribute group decision making under probabilistic hesitant fuzzy environment with application to evaluate the transformation efficiency. *Applied Intelligence, 1*, 1–13.

Li, J., & Wang, J. Q. (2017). Multi-criteria outranking methods with hesitant probabilistic fuzzy sets. *Cognitive Computation, 9*(5), 611–625.

Liu, S. T., & Kao, C. (2002). Fuzzy measures for correlation coefficient of fuzzy numbers. *Fuzzy Set and Systems, 128*, 267–275.

Liao, H. C., Xu, Z. S., & Zeng, X. J. (2015). Novel correlation coefficients between hesitant fuzzy sets and their application in decision making. *Knowledge-Based Systems, 82*, 115–127.

Park, J. H., Lim, K. M., Park, J. S., & Kwun, Y. C. (2009). Correlation coefficient between intuitionistic fuzzy sets. *Fuzzy Information and Engineering, 2*, 601–610.

Song, C. Y., Xu, Z. S., & Zhao, H. (2019a). New correlation coefficients between probabilistic hesitant fuzzy sets and their applications in cluster analysis. *International Journal of Fuzzy Systems, 21*, 355–368.

Song, C. Y., Zhao, H., Xu, Z. S., et al. (2019b). Interval-valued probabilistic hesitant fuzzy set and its application in the Arctic geopolitical risk evaluation. *International Journal of Intelligent Systems, 34*, 627–651.

Torra, V. (2010). Hesitant fuzzy sets. *International Journal of Intelligent Systems, 25*, 529–539.

Torra, V., Xu, Z. S., & Herrera, F. (2014). Hesitant fuzzy sets: State of the art and future directions. *International Journal of Intelligent Systems, 29*, 495–524.

Wang, L., Ni, M., & Zhu, L. (2013). Correlation measures of dual fuzzy sets. *Journal of Applied Mathematics*, 1–12.

Wei, G., Zhao, X., & Lin, R. (2013). Some hesitant interval-valued fuzzy aggregation operators and their applications to multiple attribute decision making. *Knowledge-Based Systems, 46*, 43–53.

Wei, G. W., Wang, H. J., & Lin, R. (2011). Application of correlation coefficient to interval-valued intuitionistic fuzzy multiple attribute decision-making with incomplete weight information. *Knowledge and Information Systems, 26*, 337–349.

Xu, Z. S., & Da, Q. L. (2002). The uncertain OWA operator. *International Journal of Intelligent Systems, 17*, 569–575.

Xia, M. M., & Xu, Z. S. (2011). Hesitant fuzzy information aggregation in decision making. *International Journal of Approximate Reasoning, 52*, 395–407.

Xu, Z. S., & Xia, M. M. (2011). On distance and correlation measures of hesitant fuzzy information. *International Journal of Intelligent Systems, 26*, 410–425.

Xu, Z. S. (2014). *Hesitant fuzzy sets theory*. Springer.

Xu, Z. S., Chen, J., & Wu, J. J. (2008). Clustering algorithm for intuitionistic fuzzy sets. *Information Sciences, 178*, 3775–4790.

Xu, Z. S., & Zhou, W. (2016). Consensus building with a group of decision makers under the hesitant probabilistic fuzzy environment. *Fuzzy Optimization and Decision Making*, 1–23.

Yang, L. Z., Zhang, R., Hou, T. P., Hao, Z. N., & Liu, J. (2016). Hesitant cloud model and its application in the risk assessment of "The Twenty-First Century Maritime Silk Road." *Mathematical Problems in Engineering, 6*, 1–11.

Yager, R. R. (1988). On ordered weighted averaging aggregation operators in multi-criteria decision making. *IEEE Transactions on Systems, Man, and Cybernetics, 18*, 183–190.

Ye, J. (2010a). Fuzzy decision-making method based on the weighted correlation coefficient under intuitionistic fuzzy environment. *European Journal of Operational Research, 205*, 202–204.

Ye, J. (2010b). Multi-criteria fuzzy decision-making method using entropy weights-based correlation coefficient of interval-valued intuitionistic fuzzy sets. *Applied Mathematical Modelling, 34*, 3864–3870.

Yu, C. H. (1993). Correlation of fuzzy numbers. *Fuzzy Sets and Systems, 55*, 303–307.

Yue, Z. (2011). An extended TOPSIS for determining weights of decision makers with interval numbers. *Knowledge-Based Systems, 24*, 146–153.

Yu, Y., Yang, S., & Liu, X. (2014). Some new dual hesitant fuzzy aggregation operators based on Choquet integral and their applications to multiple attribute decision making. *Journal of Intelligent & Fuzzy Systems, 27*, 2857–2868.

Zhang, Z., & Wu, C. (2014a). A decision support model for group decision making with hesitant multiplicative preference relations. *Information Sciences, 282*, 136–166.

Zhang, Z., & Wu, C. (2014b). Weighted hesitant fuzzy sets and their application to multi-criteria decision making. *British Journal of Mathematics and Computer Science, 4*, 1091–1123.

Zhang, S., Xu, Z. S., & He, Y. (2017). Operations and integrations of probabilistic hesitant fuzzy information in decision making. *Information Fusion, 38*, 1–11.

Zhang, Y. (2015). Research on the computer network security evaluation based on the DHFHCG operator with dual hesitant fuzzy information. *Journal of Intelligent & Fuzzy Systems, 28*, 199–204.

Zhu, B., Xu, Z. S., & Xia, M. M. (2012). Dual hesitant fuzzy sets. *Journal of Applied Mathematics, 22*(1), 100–121.

Zhu, B. (2014). *Decision method for research and application based on preference relation.* Southeast University.

Zhu, B., & Xu, Z. S. (2016). Probability-hesitant fuzzy sets and the representation of preference relations. *Technological & Economic Development of Economy*. https://doi.org/10.3846/tede

Zhu, J. Q., Fu, F., Yin, K. X., et al. (2014). Approaches to multiple attribute decision making with hesitant interval-valued fuzzy information under correlative environment. *Journal of Intelligent & Fuzzy Systems, 27*, 1057–1065.

Printed by Printforce, the Netherlands